RECOGNIZING HERITAGE

RECOGNIZING HERITAGE

The Politics of Multiculturalism in New Mexico

THOMAS H. GUTHRIE

University of Nebraska Press | Lincoln & London

Library of Congress Cataloging-in-Publication Data
Guthrie, Thomas H., 1974–
Recognizing heritage: the politics of multiculturalism
in New Mexico / Thomas H. Guthrie.
pages cm
Includes bibliographical references and index.
ISBN 978-0-8032-4610-2 (cloth: alk. paper) —
ISBN 978-0-8032-4979-0 (pbk.: alk. paper)
1. New Mexico—Ethnic relations. 2. Multicultural-
ism—New Mexico. 3. Cultural pluralism—New
Mexico. 4. New Mexico—Race relations. I. Title.
F805.A1G88 2013
305.8009789—dc23   2013013691

Set in Sabon by Laura Wellington.

For my parents, Vivian Hays Guthrie
and Shirley Caperton Guthrie Jr.

CONTENTS

ILLUSTRATIONS

ACKNOWLEDGMENTS

Many people have helped me along the way since I began this project in 2001, and it is a pleasure to be able to thank them now. In New Mexico, the interim board of the Northern Rio Grande National Heritage Area welcomed me to their meetings, invited me into their homes, and shared their work with me. I have learned so much from them and am grateful for their support. I am especially indebted to Willie Atencio, Kathy Córdova, Sam Delgado, and José Villa. More recently, Glenna Dean and Tom Romero generously gave me their time. A number of National Park Service (NPS) employees also helped me. Chief among these is Ernest Ortega, whose indefatigability, keen intellect, and commitment to his agency and country always impressed me. Ernesto brought me into the NPS as a volunteer, invited me to attend meetings with him, and engaged with me in thoughtful conversations about heritage preservation in New Mexico. Duane Alire, Brenda Barrett, Kathy Billings, Suzanne Copping, Cecilia Matic, Bob Powers, Dick Sellars, and Bob Spude were among the other NPS staff who contributed significantly to my work.

The staff of the Palace of the Governors patiently put up with my unusual questions and lingering presence, providing all the support I needed. I am grateful to Carlotta Boettcher, John McCarthy, Louise Stiver, and especially Fran Levine. Karl Hoerig shared his knowledge of the Palace portal. Tomas Jaehn and Hazel Romero in the Fray Angélico Chávez History Library provided excellent research support. Reference librarians elsewhere in

Santa Fe also deserve credit, especially those who meticulously clipped newspaper articles for vertical files over the years. A number of people helped make my research in Española productive, including Lou Baker, Susan Hazen-Hammond, Richard Lucero, Bernabe Romero, and Clare Villa. I have learned a great deal from Rina Swentzell, one of the wisest people I've ever met. At the University of New Mexico, Chris Wilson and Sylvia Rodríguez shared their deep knowledge of New Mexico, pointed me in the right direction, and provided helpful feedback. Steve Joseph and Beth Preble hired me to house-sit for them in Santa Fe, providing crucial financial support when I was a graduate student, and became good friends. Craig and Trasie Topple, old friends from Georgia, have graciously hosted me during more recent fieldwork. I know that not all these New Mexicans will agree with everything I say, but I hope that my deep respect for each of them will be apparent.

This work began as a dissertation at the University of Chicago, and the Department of Anthropology provided a fine education. I thank the members of my dissertation committee: Ray Fogelson for encouraging me to come to Chicago and supporting me from the beginning, Beth Povinelli for her theoretical insight and interest in the politics of multiculturalism, Joe Masco for his superb advice and careful reading, and Jessica Cattelino for her friendship and professionalism. Michael Silverstein, George Stocking, and Terry Straus also provided crucial support and taught me much. Anne Ch'ien helped me succeed in a long PhD program.

At Guilford College I am grateful to my students, who have allowed me to work out my ideas in class and challenged me to think and write more clearly. Their commitment to social justice has been an inspiration. My colleagues have been supportive and helped me develop my scholarship in a broader, interdisciplinary context. Guilford's commitment to dismantling institutional racism has provided a challenging and rewarding context within which to teach and write.

Matt Bokovoy at the University of Nebraska Press has been an outstanding editor, and I am grateful for his guidance, encouragement, and helpful feedback. Four reviewers also provided constructive criticism. Funding for this research came from a Century Fellowship, Department of Anthropology Leiffer Fellowship, and Mellon Foundation/Social Sciences Division Dissertation-Year Fellowship at the University of Chicago and from the Campbell Fund and several Faculty Research Grants at Guilford College. Parts of chapter 3 appeared in *The International Journal of Heritage Studies* (Guthrie 2010a).

Two of my professors at Davidson College, Grant Jones and Rosemary Lévy Zumwalt, taught me how to think critically as an anthropologist, mentored me, and became friends. Finally, I would like to thank my parents, who first introduced me to New Mexico when I was a child. I still remember walking down the portal at the Palace of the Governors in amazement. The love, support, and encouragement of my mom and dad throughout my life have made all of this possible.

A NOTE ON TERMINOLOGY

The names for the various groups that have settled in New Mexico are notoriously problematic, since none are universally acceptable and most are homogenizing. The terms "Pueblo," "Indian," and "Native American" are all European or Euro-American inventions. Native peoples often prefer to identify themselves more specifically by their particular Pueblo, tribe, nation, language family, or clan. Nevertheless, both indigenous and non-indigenous people in New Mexico today widely use all of these terms. I use all three interchangeably except when a more specific designation is possible. Context should make it clear when I am using "Indian" in the more restricted sense of "Pueblo Indian," but in no case do I mean to imply that all Indians, all Pueblo Indians, or all members of any given Pueblo have the same ideas or experiences, which they do not.

More problematic is the nomenclature for Spanish-speaking people in New Mexico, which reveals a complex history of identity politics. Throughout the Americas, Spanish colonization depended upon a distinction between Spaniards and Indians, but intermixing led to the use of an intricate system of classification, known as the *casta* system, that identified various kinds of *mestizaje*, or racial mixing, corresponding to a social hierarchy (Gutiérrez 1991, 194–206; Nieto-Phillips 2004, 23–37; Wilson 1997, 28–31). New Mexico was part of Mexico when the United States acquired the territory in 1848, but American racism toward Mexicans resulted in a reassertion of "Spanish" identity. To this day some Hispanics in New Mexico identify as Spanish or Spanish American, distinguishing themselves from Mexicans in terms of race, class, national origins, land rights, and citizenship. The rise of Chicano activism in the 1960s further complicated matters by promoting a celebration rather than denial of mestizaje, but many Hispanics in New Mexico continue to insist on pure Spanish heritage. More recent immigrants from Latin America further diversify the population. Today various names for Spanish-speaking New Mexicans circulate in print and everyday conversation, including Spanish, Spanish American, Hispanic, Hispano, Mexicano, Nuevomexicano, Chicano, and Latino (see Lovato 2004, 40). Choice of terms varies widely according to social context and whether people are speaking English or Spanish. Even Spanish speakers themselves are not always sure how best to identify their ethnicity (e.g., deBuys 1985, 213). I use the terms "Hispanic," "Hispano," and "Nuevomexicano" interchangeably, alternatives common in the scholarly literature on New Mexico (see Trujillo 2009, xiv–xvi, 39–43), but fully acknowledge the inadequacy of these terms.

If names for Indians and Hispanics in New Mexico are problematic, so too are those for the people who arrived after American conquest. The term "Anglo" (or "Anglo-American") emerged in the early twentieth century as a correlate of "Spanish American." English speakers who were neither Indian nor Hispanic could no longer simply be called "Americans," since all New Mexicans were now supposedly American. They therefore became *Anglo*-American, regardless of whether they were of English, Canadian, German, Jewish, or some other Euro-American background. Like other New Mexican ethnonyms, then, the term "Anglo" lumps diverse groups together. I use it throughout this book to refer imprecisely, as New Mexicans still do, to non-Indians and non-Hispanics, recognizing, again, its inaccuracy.

The idea that the Southwest is made up of three distinct groups (Indians, Hispanics, and Anglos) further clouds the picture. The rhetoric of triculturalism fails to acknowledge the diversity *within* each group, the intermixing *between* groups, and the presence of people of Asian and African descent who do not fit within this schema at all (cf. Spicer 1972).

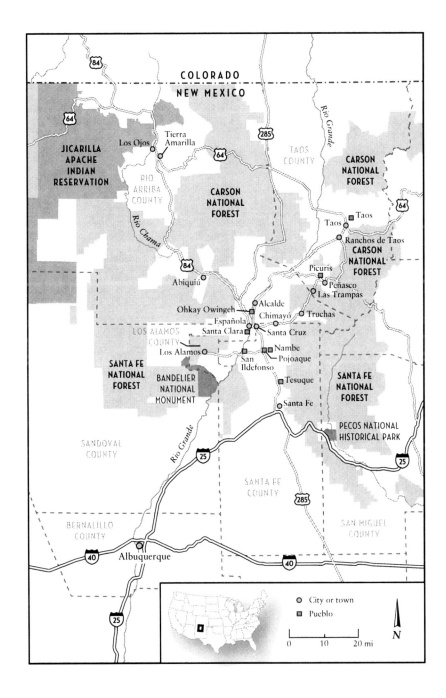

Map of north-central New Mexico. The Northern Rio Grande National
Heritage Area comprises Rio Arriba, Santa Fe, and Taos Counties.

Introduction

On a sunny spring day in 2002 in Santa Fe, New Mexico, U.S. senator Jeff Bingaman announced plans to establish the Northern Rio Grande National Heritage Area. Designated by Congress, national heritage areas are both places and administrative frameworks. They cover nationally significant, living cultural landscapes and provide a way for local communities to partner with the federal government to promote historic preservation, cultural conservation, economic development, education, recreation, and environmental protection. North-central New Mexico ranges from high desert to forested mountains and has a long history of multicultural settlement (see fig. 1). The heritage area would commemorate the four-hundred-year "coexistence" of Spanish and Indian peoples in this region and recognize New Mexico's place within the United States.

Bingaman's announcement took place in the courtyard of the Palace of the Governors, an adobe building on the north side of the Santa Fe plaza. Constructed around 1610, the Palace served as the administrative center of New Mexico for three hundred years. Spaniards, Mexicans, Americans, and Pueblo Indians all occupied the Palace at different times, asserting their authority over the region and its diverse population. In 1909 the territorial legislature converted the building into a museum of history and anthropology, and since then it has become Santa Fe's best-developed historic site. The Palace of the Governors therefore embodies the complex relationship among colonialism, multiculturalism, and heritage preservation in New Mexico.

Fig. 1. The Sangre de Cristo Mountains north of Santa Fe.

Given contentious ethnic relations in this region, suspicion toward the federal government, unsettled land and water rights
claims, and worries about tourism, Bingaman's announcement
raised some concerns. At the senator's side to help explain what
the heritage area designation would mean was Ernest Ortega, the
New Mexico state director of the National Park Service (the agency that oversees the national heritage area program). Bingaman
wore a suit and tie, Ortega his gray-and-green Park Service uniform. Ortega stressed that heritage areas are commemorative designations that bring up to ten million dollars in federal funds over
fifteen years for projects and programs. Unlike national parks,
they involve no new land regulation, a serious concern in the western United States. The federal government already managed almost 60 percent of the land in Santa Fe, Rio Arriba, and Taos
Counties, which make up the heritage area. This included Indian land and former Spanish and Mexican land grants (communal land given to settlers and largely broken up by Americans).
Representatives of several Pueblos, including the governor of San

Juan Pueblo, expressed tentative support for the heritage area and asked why they had not been more involved in the planning process (Tollefson 2002). Bingaman's legislation did specifically protect private property rights and mandate Native American representation (see the appendix).

According to the legislation, the top two reasons for establishing the heritage area were that "northern New Mexico encompasses a mosaic of cultures and history, including 8 Pueblos and the descendants of Spanish ancestors who settled in the area in 1598" and that "the combination of cultures, languages, folk arts, customs, and architecture make northern New Mexico unique."[1] This multicultural affirmation is a far cry from earlier American attitudes toward New Mexico and its residents. After the United States acquired half of Mexico's territory in 1848, at the end of the Mexican-American War, Americans began to dispossess Hispanics and Indians of their land and forcibly assimilate them. New Mexico did not become a state until 1912, largely due to fears that the region was too different to be integrated into the nation, and only after a concerted effort to Americanize New Mexico's economy, culture, and architecture. In 2002 the federal government's recognition of New Mexico not *despite of* but *because of* its cultural distinctiveness illustrated how much attitudes toward cultural difference had changed in the United States. Bingaman's proposal quickly received bipartisan support from New Mexico's entire congressional delegation. In 2006 President Bush signed into law a bill establishing the Northern Rio Grande National Heritage Area and nine other heritage areas in other parts of the country.[2]

Colonialism and Multiculturalism

This book explores the relationship between colonialism and multiculturalism, two seemingly opposite political projects that have long coexisted in New Mexico. Colonizers are usually ethnocentric. When Spaniards began colonizing New Mexico in 1598 they assumed that their religion and way of life were superior to those of the indigenous peoples they encountered. Americans looked down on both Indians and Mexicans. However, colonialism can also involve admiration for cultural difference.

Celebrations of New Mexico's diverse cultures go back almost as far as attempts to wipe them out. At the same time some Anglos were Americanizing New Mexico in hopes of achieving statehood, others worked to preserve its cultural uniqueness. By the early twentieth century an influential group of artists and writers had migrated from the Northeast and Midwest to New Mexico seeking to escape the materialism and alienation of industrial capitalism. These antimodernists idealized Native American and Nuevomexicano communities and worked hard to revive, promote, and shape their artistic traditions. In Santa Fe, civic boosters believed that New Mexico's cultural and architectural heritage could attract tourists and cultivated an exotic image of "the City Different." Yet even the most fervent antimodernists did not oppose the American occupation of New Mexico. Sure of their expertise and good taste, they considered themselves better suited to save the region's cultural heritage than Indians and Hispanos themselves. They also celebrated some aspects of Native American and Hispanic cultures while criticizing others.

As the twentieth century unfolded, the idea that cultural diversity was an asset rather than a problem became dominant in New Mexico.[3] Old-fashioned discrimination has by no means gone away, but it is now less publically acceptable than it once was.[4] Since the 1960s, the national rise of liberal multiculturalism has provided a broader context for the celebration of cultural difference in the Southwest. Multiculturalists value diversity and seek to balance equality and difference. The confluence of regional romanticism and national multiculturalism enabled the establishment of the Northern Rio Grande National Heritage Area. It also makes New Mexico an ideal place to study the politics of multiculturalism.

Nevertheless, the American Southwest remains a colonial region. Native Americans and Nuevomexicanos know this, but many Americans prefer not to think of the United States as a colonial power at all. We mark 1776 as the *end* of our colonial period and the beginning of our independence. But the United States is and always has been a settler colony, where Europeans came, dominated, and never left. This is to say nothing of our overseas colonial exploits (Gómez 2007, 7). If the idea of "postcolonialism" is problematic in countries like India and Jamaica, which formally won their independence in the twentieth century, it is even more so in settler colonies like the United States and Australia, where colonization never ended, regardless of their commitment to multiculturalism (Povinelli 2002).[5] New Mexico is still part of the United States, and Anglo-American political, economic, and cultural systems remain dominant. Indians still have to negotiate their sovereignty with the federal government as "domestic dependent nations," while Nuevomexicanos continue to fight for land rights guaranteed under the 1848 Treaty of Guadalupe Hidalgo. Water rights remain contentious in the Southwest, and their adjudication requires courts to plumb the region's double colonial history to determine prior appropriation. Throughout the Southwest today the myth of "tricultural" harmony belies social, political, and economic hierarchies that remain characteristically (though complexly) colonial.

In this book I argue that dominant forms of multiculturalism challenge colonial hierarchies on the surface but reinforce them at a deeper level. The colonial effects of multiculturalism are more subtle than those of conquest and assimilation but are no less significant. Most of the time they are unintentional. They are not the product of a conspiracy or conscious political strategy but operate "behind the backs" of people who really do value diversity and inclusivity (cf. Ferguson 1994, 17–21, 256). This helps to explain why Native Americans and Hispanics, as well as Anglo-Americans, have invested in multiculturalism. It has become hegemonic in New Mexico, since its ideological premises are now mostly taken for granted and both dominant and subordinate groups reproduce its colonial functions. Multiculturalism has become a *consensual* and often counter-intentional form of domination. It is precisely the subtle and unintentional nature of colonial multiculturalism that makes it powerful and worth studying.

As a social and political ideal, multiculturalism comes up in various contexts and underlies a range of political projects. I focus on one form of multiculturalism—the politics of recognition—and one area where multiculturalism finds expression—heritage interpretation and preservation—that are particularly significant in New Mexico.

Heritage Development in Northern New Mexico

Many New Mexicans, especially the community activists, National Park Service employees, museum professionals, historic preservationists, and civic leaders I worked with, are interested in cultural heritage. Most conceive of heritage as a set of traditions inherited from previous generations. They highlight language, religion, adobe architecture, art, dance and ritual, agricultural practices, and food. Heritage brings together culture, identity, and the past.

People often pay attention to heritage only when they think it is threatened. "I have always had this very strong concern about people in northern New Mexico losing some of their cultural traits," Ernest Ortega (2003) told me, "because some of those . . . traditions are core to a people's being." Concerns about culture and language loss in New Mexico point to the social and economic effects of American colonization. Americans settled the Southwest in increasing numbers after the 1880s. They brought with them unprecedented wealth and a novel set of values, technologies, and laws. Over the course of the twentieth century, assimilation campaigns, land loss, and a shift from subsistence agriculture to an economy based on wage labor, government, and tourism destabilized Native American and Hispanic communities. Today both struggle to overcome poverty and all the social problems associated with it.

Heritage areas provide a framework for addressing these social and economic woes together. They rely on the principle of heritage development: cultivating heritage in order to strengthen community identity and promote economic development. With their inclusion of living communities, focus on both people and nature, integration of conservation and community development, reliance on partnerships, and regional scale, heritage areas exemplify new approaches to conservation (Barrett 2003; Phillips 2003). Heritage tourism is one of the most common ways to integrate conservation and development, but many New Mexicans cringe at the idea of attracting *more* tourists. Although the tourism industry provides a desperately needed source of income, it has resulted in environmental stress and urban gentrification. The Northern Rio Grande National Heritage Area (NRGNHA, or "norgan-ha") promises to help New Mexicans manage tourism, foster cultural understanding, and "tell their own story." It builds upon but attempts to control a long history of cultural representation and commodification in the Southwest — indeed, the *invention* of the Southwest as an American region (Guthrie 2005, 83–103).

The National Park Service (NPS) helped to organize a series of public meetings in 1999 and 2000 to introduce the heritage area concept. The response was positive, and a group of citizens formed the interim board of the Northern Rio Grande National Heritage Area, Inc., a nonprofit organization that became the heritage area's official management entity. Board members represent municipalities and organizations within the heritage area as well as state agencies. Designating legislation requires the management entity to develop a plan outlining short- and long-term goals. The NPS assists the management entity, but the authority to implement the management plan remains local. Congress appropriates funds for heritage areas that must be matched with nonfederal funds. The NRGNHA board has drawn up bylaws, encouraged public involvement, hired an executive director, produced a film, and drafted a management plan. A grant program supports a range of preservation, education, cultural revitalization, arts, and economic development projects through public and private partnerships.[6] The following chapters and "notes from the field" explore the social and political conditions in which this new initiative is emerging.

Recognizing Heritage

Recognition is an important political process in multicultural societies. It can be formal or informal, ranging from the government's acknowledgment of a group's existence and rights to the inclusion of a group's culture and history in school curricula, museum exhibits, or public celebrations. Recognition can affect marginalized groups' economic and political situation as well as their psychological well-being (Taylor 1994). It usually involves negotiating the political status of cultural groups and how much cultural diversity states can accommodate.[7]

National heritage areas have become a vehicle for cultural recognition. According to the National Park Service, heritage areas are "places where natural, cultural, and historic resources combine to form a cohesive, nationally important landscape" (NPS 2012). They "represent distinctive aspects of American heritage worthy of recognition, conservation, interpretation, and continuing use" and reflect "traditions, customs, beliefs, and folk life that are a valuable part of the national story" (NPS 2005). A heritage area designation thus enables the government to affirm that a region is both *culturally distinctive* and *nationally significant*, that it is different and that it belongs. This kind of affirmation exemplifies multicultural nationalism.[8]

A brochure introducing the Northern Rio Grande National Heritage Area called for "a time of recognition." America's strength supposedly lies in its cultural diversity, the brochure stated, but New Mexico's Hispanic and Native American heritage has been underestimated and ignored. As a result it is now endangered. "Our nation's educational system has been conspicuously remiss in teaching, with accuracy and completeness, about New Mexico's influences on countless aspects of our national heritage, in areas such as law, water and land-tenure practices, trade, folklore, ranching, music, food, language, and religion." According to the brochure, academics have contributed to the problem: for 150 years anthropological and historical research has been romanticized or biased. Concerns about inadequate scholarship, misinterpretation, and misrepresentation came up often in conversations I had. The brochure concluded that the "Northern Rio Grande National Heritage Area recognizes and celebrates the rich heritage of the Rio Grande region of northern New Mexico—its culture and traditions, and its countless influences on the development of the United States and the American way of life" (NRGNHA 2007).

The politics of recognition emphasizes accuracy: recognize us for who we really are. This presumes that groups have an *essential* cultural identity that exists independently of their relationship to other groups and the process of recognition itself. But in order for a group to be recognized, it must first make itself visible, differentiate itself from other groups, present itself as more or less cohesive, and, oftentimes, demonstrate "authenticity" and cultural continuity through time. In other words, it must produce—in the sense of both manufacture and offer up for viewing—an identity. As Richard Handler (1988) has shown, national claims are often premised upon a group's "having a culture." The same applies to multicultural regions seeking recognition. Understanding the politics of recognition therefore requires analyzing the social and institutional contexts within which people negotiate identities and produce difference. Heritage development makes cultural difference more recognizable. It brings culture, identity, and the past into consciousness and into view, lifting people, places, and social practices out of everyday existence and holding them up for inspection. This view of heritage as a *process*, which I elaborate in the following chapters, differs from the view of heritage as a collection of objects and traditions I described above.[9]

Notes from the Field

JUNE 20, 2002

Senate Hearing on the Northern Rio Grande National Heritage Area Act, Dirksen Senate Office Building, Washington DC

I moved to New Mexico in early June but happened to be in Washington for a wedding when the Senate Subcommittee on National

Parks held a hearing on three heritage area bills. I never expected to do fieldwork on Capitol Hill in a suit and tie but quite enjoyed it.

Brenda Barrett, the national coordinator of the heritage area program, testified on all the bills and conveyed the National Park Service's support for the NRGNHA. In response to a question from Senator Bingaman, she confirmed that the NRGNHA bill would not preempt the land management authority of any private individuals, local governments, or Pueblos.

Two New Mexicans testified on behalf of the NRGNHA. Kathy Córdova, the chair of the heritage area's interim board, emphasized that this was a grassroots, collaborative initiative. In New Mexico, "American Indians, Hispanics, and other cultures live side by side in scenic beauty," she said. Córdova recounted the history of citizen involvement in the heritage area and presented letters of support from three city governments, three county commissions, the New Mexico state legislature, three Pueblo governors, and the Eight Northern Indian Pueblos Council. She mentioned that she recently ran into the governor of Pojoaque Pueblo at a rosary and that he invited her to come have lunch at their casino to talk about the heritage area. This is how business often gets done in New Mexico.

José Villa, the vice-chair of the board, brought warm greetings from Richard Lucero, the mayor of Española, whose "vision and leadership have guided and inspired us." Villa argued that establishing the NRGNHA would be a way to recognize the contributions of Indians and Hispanics to American history and to educate Americans about New Mexico's place in the United States. He described the importance of family, religion, land, and water in New Mexico. "Our traditions and culture . . . emphasize the American ability to be different while still being American."

Everyone who spoke about the NRGNHA exalted the collaboration between Hispanics and Indians. The hearing was an affirmation of multicultural politics. I found it fitting that the chair of the subcommittee, Senator Daniel Akaka of Hawaii, had both Native Hawaiian and Chinese ancestry.

Multicultural Domination and Multicultural Justice

Attempts to recognize heritage in New Mexico reveal how multiculturalism as a political ideal and practice can subtly reinforce colonial hierarchies. If some liberal theorists equate multicultural justice with the accurate recognition of real identities, an anti-essentialist position requires new theories of power and justice in multicultural settings (e.g., Fish 1997; Markell 2003; Povinelli 2002). Pursuing justice through recognition may have some positive results, but recognition is at best an insufficient and at worst a counterproductive strategy. I identify three characteristics of multiculturalism in northern New Mexico that help to reproduce colonial power relations: the politics of visibility, the politics of authenticity, and the anti-politics of culture.

"Culture" has become a depoliticized and depoliticizing concept. In New Mexico, the rhetoric of triculturalism emphasizes harmonious coexistence and downplays colonial violence, racism, and inequality. While "cultural" celebrations are welcome in public spaces, debates about land and water rights (or anything else that seems "political") are often marginalized. Talking about culture and celebrating cultural survival can be a way of *not* talking about colonial legacies or the need for a redistribution of wealth and resources.[10] This does not mean that culture is any less political (or real) than people's access to land and water. There is nothing apolitical about the anti-politics of culture. Although (or precisely because) cultural projects may appear apolitical, they can have powerful political effects (see chapters 3 and 4).

Dominant groups can ensure their power by making themselves and their authority visible while erasing the presence of the colonized. But the opposite tactic also works (Casper and Moore 2009). Multicultural projects often highlight the cultures, perspectives, and experiences of subaltern (subordinate) groups while leaving dominant groups in the dark and thus immune to criticism. Ensuring the visibility of a group renders it more susceptible to surveillance and discipline (Foucault [1975] 1995; Markell 2003, 145–46). In New Mexico, Hispanics and Pueblo Indians, famous for their "rich" and "colorful" cultures, are often the objects of a controlling colonial and tourist gaze (Rodríguez 1994). They stand out, especially in comparison to Anglo-Americans, who often appear cultureless.[11] While this unequal visibility seems to favor subaltern groups, it allows Anglos to occupy a normative position. If Indians and Nuevomexicanos are *marked* by their difference (which accounts for their high visibility), Anglos are *unmarked*. Marking in this sense represents an assertion of power, because the unmarked category remains the standard or norm (Anglos are just normal, modern) against which others are measured (the others are different, unusual). To the extent that Hispanos and Native Americans are marked by their colorful heritage, they are associated with "tradition" and the past, leaving Anglo-Americans to claim "modernity" and New Mexico's future for themselves (see chapters 1, 3, and 4).

Native American and Hispanic cultures in New Mexico have been scrutinized, studied, curated, and managed more than other cultures. Concerns about their authenticity add an extra burden. Authenticity is an impossible ideal with significant political implications. In New Mexico, the political rights of Native Americans and Nuevomexicanos sometimes depend on their ability to maintain and perform "traditional" cultures. Anglo-Americans have often defined and evaluated the cultural authenticity of these groups, and the ultimate measure of authenticity lies in the (imagined) past. Demands for authenticity therefore constrain Hispanos and Indians, who benefit when they orient their lives to the past rather than the present or future. The successful maintenance of tradition reassures all New Mexicans that American colonization has not been totally destructive. However, New Mexico's double colonial history and highly developed tourism industry fuel anxieties over culture loss, casting doubt on all cultural performances. Subaltern groups bear the political and psychological weight of these anxieties, since they must convince others and themselves of their cultural integrity. The politics of authenticity also excludes people of mixed ancestry, lower- and working-class people, and recent Mexican immigrants from public spaces in New Mexico (e.g., Horton 2010, 163–74) (see chapters 2 and 5).

In order for multicultural projects to dismantle rather than reproduce colonial hierarchies — to nurture equality without requiring homogeneity — they must first foreground political and economic relations. In New Mexico this must involve addressing land and water rights, the social and environmental costs of development, and the unequal benefits of capitalism (Briggs and Van Ness 1987; Ebright 1994; R. Ortiz 1980; Rodríguez 2006). But it is also essential to uncover the politics of *culture* and the relationship between cultural production and material conditions (Kosek 2006; Rodríguez 1994; Wilson 1997). Second, the public interpretation of New Mexican heritage must bring Anglo-Americans, tourists, and capitalists into view, not because they are victims of "reverse discrimination" but because they have had a profound impact on social life in New Mexico. Rejecting a narrow focus on subaltern groups (the usual "targets" of multicultural reforms) may help to reconfigure cultural norms and expose colonial power relations to critique. Finally, I advocate a broad public effort to deconstruct the concept of cultural authenticity. This will require rethinking fundamental concepts such as culture, identity, tradition, modernity, and indigeneity. I discuss all of these recommendations more fully in chapter 5.

Beyond New Mexico

Although this book focuses on a particular place with a distinctive history, it sheds light on a broader set of issues. Multicultural celebrations are ubiquitous in the United States and throughout much of the world. Yet the politics of authenticity, the politics of visibility, and the anti-politics of culture often tether them to colonial orders. Analyzing the unintentional colonial effects of multiculturalism in New Mexico may provide tools for exposing them elsewhere. The politics of recognition deserves special attention. Recognition has become the basis for all kinds of political struggles as indigenous peoples, women, religious and sexual minorities, immigrants, and others assert their identities and rights. Recognition may seem like a clear path toward justice, but I join other scholars in pointing out its pitfalls. New Mexico is also a useful vantage point for analyzing American nationalism, since identity and citizenship have been contentious there for centuries. What does it mean to be American? What is the relationship between cultural identity and political rights in the United States? As I will show, New Mexicans engage with these questions on a daily basis.

Heritage has also become a global concern, expanding in every direction. Writers tend either to treat heritage as an objective reality or to dismiss it as a social construct. I critically analyze heritage projects without writing them off. The people I know in New Mexico take heritage seriously, and so do I. Heritage preservation efforts are a response to the intergenerational stress of rapid social change. They often seek to revive outmoded cultural forms. But my work demonstrates the value of concentrating instead on social, economic, and political context, particularly when colonialism and capitalism have produced structural inequalities. My focus on a national heritage area makes the project unique and timely. Heritage areas represent the cutting edge of conservation practice in the United States, and their popularity is growing. Of the forty-nine national heritage areas established since 1984, forty-three have been created since 1996 and more than half since 2004. Huge regions—including the entire state of Tennessee—have become national heritage areas. What does this mean? Other countries are also integrating environmental protection, cultural conservation, and economic development on a regional scale. This book provides a model for studying similar projects.

Finally, *Recognizing Heritage* illuminates the relationship between heritage projects and anthropology. I discuss the parallel development of anthropology and tourism in the Southwest, identify outdated anthropological concepts in the heritage industry, and suggest that some of the problems with heritage preservation efforts remain entrenched in academic anthropology. Both anthropologists and preservationists can benefit from considering our similarities and differences.

My Research and Writing

I lived in Santa Fe for eighteen months in 2002 and 2003 and have returned to New Mexico almost every year since then for shorter visits. I have attended lectures and panel discussions, taken tours, visited museums, parks, and monuments, shared drinks and meals with people, observed dances and other special events, and generally explored the region. I spent a significant portion of my time investigating and participating in the early development of the Northern Rio Grande National Heritage Area. I attended the heritage area board's monthly meetings and, as a volunteer with the National Park Service in Santa Fe, provided administrative assistance to NPS staff and the board. This gave me an inside view of the bureaucratic dimension of federal heritage projects. I attended several national conferences on heritage areas and heritage development sponsored by the NPS. Finally, I conducted semi-structured interviews with members of the heritage area board, NPS staff, and other preservationists and planners interested in the project. This close involvement in the development of the heritage area gave me insight into how local organizers imagined their region and why they believed New Mexico deserved national recognition.

The following chapters examine four sites within the NRGNHA that illustrate multicultural politics and the social and political conditions under which the heritage area is developing.[12] This collection of sites provides a partial survey not only of the heritage *area* but also of related attempts to recognize New Mexican heritage. My research at these various sites included participant observation, interviews, historical reconstruction, architectural analysis, investigation of legal cases, and analysis of newspaper articles, archival materials, anthropological accounts, memoirs, government reports, and preservation proposals. Site analysis has several advantages (see Dorst 1989, 1999). First, it suits my interest in a region, its construction as a site of cultural difference within the United States, and the various groups that interact there. Second, it lessens the extent to which my work objectifies human beings.

Finally, it makes it easy to combine spatial and historical research, crucial in this study of the Northern Rio Grande National Heritage Area.

Anthropologists sometimes strive to convey "the native's point of view" and often exaggerate their ability to do so (Geertz 1983). I am sympathetic with both Native Americans and Hispanics in New Mexico and am critical of Anglo-American domination. This does not mean, however, that this book privileges Pueblo and Nuevomexicano perspectives. I cannot speak for Hispanics or Indians, who have already spoken for themselves in many diverse voices. I am not a New Mexican (I grew up in Georgia and now live in North Carolina). My status as a newcomer, the brevity of my fieldwork, and my poor command of Spanish and inability to speak any indigenous languages precluded me from gaining full access to Pueblo and Hispano communities. While I am grateful that people have welcomed me to their meetings and into their homes, sat down for interviews, showed me around their communities, and supported my research in countless other ways, I cannot offer a private, insider's view of northern New Mexico. My account sometimes significantly differs, in both content and form, from the self-representations of the people I worked with. I make arguments (e.g., about the social construction of heritage) that they would not make, and I am writing in a language and style that they would not necessarily choose when representing themselves.

However, my status as an "outsider" and my social scientific style of writing should in no way imply objectivity or neutrality. All outsiders are insiders somewhere. My particular identity has hardly been irrelevant in my engagement with New Mexico (see chapter 4). Furthermore, within a larger, national context I am no outsider at all. I acknowledge the specificity of my own position so that readers are better able to evaluate and criticize my interpretations. Disclosing one's position is an important part of confronting the politics of visibility and pursuing multicultural justice. Western culture has long privileged the view from the outside or from above, because such a view supposedly enables rational, disengaged, comprehensive understanding. This "view from no-where" is authoritative and controlling (Gupta 1998, 303). What is more, to stand *nowhere* is to occupy an unmarked, unassailable position. As I argue in the following chapters, this kind of invisibility is an unjust privilege. If anthropologists are to contribute to social justice, we must avoid drawing on and reproducing the very forms of power we are critiquing. I cannot write from someone else's position, and I cannot write from no position. In this book I offer nothing more or less than my own particular perspective on New Mexico, which is both informed and partial.

Notes from the Field

JUNE 27, 2002

Northern Rio Grande National Heritage Area board meeting, the Misión-Convento, Española

I had only been in New Mexico for a few weeks when I attended my first heritage area board meeting. The members of the interim board were all friendly. In addition to Kathy Córdova and José Villa, whom I met a week earlier in Washington after the Senate hearing, seven other board members were present. All were Hispanic professionals at least in their forties. Duane Alire (a National Park Service employee working with the NRGNHA) and a representative from Senator Bingaman's office were also there.

I sat down at the back of the small, plain room, but José told me to come sit next to him at the table. After he introduced me, someone jokingly asked how much I was going to pay to study them. Another anthropologist had studied his town and promised to donate the royalties from her book to their school system, but they never heard back from her. I said I would be happy to do the same but that a book was a long way off.

The board was focused on spreading the word about the heritage area, meeting with city and county government representatives, demonstrating local support for the legislation, and lobbying their congressional delegates. Kathy reported on the Senate hearing and all the politicians they visited in Washington. Pete Domenici, New Mexico's other senator, had expressed concerns about property rights that the board was eager to dispel. Several board members were frustrated that no Pueblo representatives had come to the meeting after they complained to Bingaman about their lack of involvement. José was preparing articles of incorporation for the board, and a discussion about the relationship between the heritage area and the National Park Service ensued.

After the meeting I joined Duane and several board members for a beer at Anthony's at the Delta, a bar just down the street from the Española plaza. José had many suggestions for what I should read and told me about his involvement in the Chicano movement in California. After the drinks and conversation I felt like a real anthropologist.

A Map of the Book

The four central chapters of *Recognizing Heritage* provide a selective tour of the Northern Rio Grande National Heritage Area. In chapter 1, I return to the Palace of the Governors, the site of Senator Bingaman's press conference, to examine the social and political effects of its development as a museum. I argue that the Palace has become a key site for the construction of history and colonial modernity in New Mexico, both of which are subtly racialized. In the early 1900s, museum founders promoted the Palace as a monument to New Mexico's Indian and Hispanic past and American future. Since the 1970s several exhibits have implied that the building's history ended when it became a museum, which leaves the museum establishment to occupy the normative and unmarked space of modernity.

Chapter 2 picks up just outside the front door of the Palace of the Governors, where Indian artists participating in a Museum of New Mexico program sell their work to tourists. The beginning of the chapter explores the semiotics of tourism and the relationship between authenticity and recognition. I then consider the legal and institutional construction of authenticity in the portal market and critiques of "staged authenticity." When critics imply that *true* authenticity lies somewhere *else*, they doubly imperil indigenous people, who are discredited in the public places where they actually are and who cannot possibly inhabit the fantasy spaces where their authentic traditions supposedly exist.

In chapter 3 we leave Santa Fe and head up the road to the town of Española. I examine the production of public cultural identities and the creative use of the past in the Española valley and how both relate to the politics of recognition. The chapter focuses on the development of a tricultural plaza space in Española and a series of attempts in the 1990s to commemorate the Spanish colonization of the Southwest. Both addressed New Mexico's place within the United States, garnered national recognition for the region, and paved the way for the NRGNHA.

The last site I consider is the village of Las Trampas. Chapter 4 marks a shift to rural issues and addresses the decline of New Mexico's agricultural economy. However, its principal concern is how Anglo preservationists have represented and engaged with Las Trampas. They have tended to represent the village as either timeless and traditional or on the verge of collapse. Both discourses have reassured preservationists and helped to perpetuate colonial domination in northern New Mexico. I analyze a proposal in the 1960s to turn the entire village into a living national monument that was a precursor of the national heritage area initiative. I conclude the chapter with a self-reflexive discussion of the politics of ethnography and the relationship between cultural representation and power.

The concluding chapter suggests that the heritage industry relies upon outdated anthropological concepts and principles that impede multicultural justice. One example is a preoccupation with authenticity in discussions of cultural objectification. I elaborate a theory of multicultural justice based on current anthropology and examples from the book.

The epilogue provides an update on the development of the Northern Rio Grande National Heritage Area. I describe an event in 2011 that illustrates the heritage area's social and political potential. The theme of recognition no longer comes up as much in talk about the heritage area. This shift makes it more likely that the NRGNHA may support grassroots efforts that significantly challenge colonial power relations.

CHAPTER ONE

Constructing History at the Palace of the Governors

The Palace of the Governors, a one-story adobe building on the north side of the Santa Fe plaza, has always been Santa Fe's most famous landmark. Its front facade has become a tourist icon (see fig. 2). Under the front portal of the Palace, Indian artists display handcrafted jewelry, pottery, and other goods, and tourists amble along, inspecting the art and enjoying a quintessential New Mexican cultural experience. The Palace is often described as the oldest continuously occupied public building in the United States. Yet how people have thought about and used the Palace has changed significantly over time. Constructed around 1610 when Spanish colonists moved the capital to Santa Fe from San Gabriel (north of Santa Fe on the Rio Grande), the Palace was originally part of a fortified complex of buildings known as the *casas reales*, or royal houses.[1] For three hundred years the Spanish, Mexican, and American governors of New Mexico used the Palace for residential and office space, modifying the building to suit their evolving needs and tastes. A notable exception was the twelve years following the Pueblo Revolt of 1680, when Pueblo Indians occupied the building. Then in 1909, three years before New Mexico became a state, the territorial legislature designated the Palace the home of the newly established Museum of New Mexico and School of American Archaeology. Equally significant a transformation has occurred since then, as the Palace has gone from being a museum mostly about southwestern history, anthropology, and art to being a museum about itself. In 1960 it became a National Histor-

Fig. 2. The Palace of the Governors.

ic Landmark, the highest distinction given to historic sites in the United States.

In this chapter I track how the Palace of the Governors became a sign of history and explore the political effects of that process. Inverting the usual view of the Palace as a history museum inside a historic structure, I show that its construction as a historic site has relied upon its development as a museum. This process has subtly—and perhaps inadvertently—reinforced American power in New Mexico. The Palace illustrates several colonial functions of "history," which I take to be a discursive construct. Many scholars have shown that equating history with Europe and casting all non-Europeans as people without history contributed to the invention of modernity and the establishment of European colonial hegemony. But when modernity is conceived as a transcendent achievement, "history" can serve as its foil. To be modern in this view is to rise above history. The ultimate modernity begins with the *end* of history.

The Palace of the Governors

In New Mexico the notion of "prehistory" persists, despite the fact that Native Americans recorded historical change orally before Spanish colonization. *Histories* of New Mexico usually begin with Spanish exploration and colonization. People take the historicalness of Spaniards, Mexicans, and nineteenth-century Americans for granted. However, the division of New Mexico history into sequential Spanish, Mexican, and American "periods" suggests that Hispanics' time is over and done with. Both Indians and Nuevomexicanos, then, are associated with the past. While the former are excluded from history, the latter are relegated to it. Meanwhile, twentieth-century Anglos often appear beyond history altogether and in control of New Mexico's present and future.

The Palace of the Governors has been a key site in the construction of history and modernity in New Mexico for more than a century now. The first part of this chapter examines the cultural politics surrounding the Museum of New Mexico's establishment in the early 1900s. After a major renovation, museum staff promoted the Palace as a monument to Santa Fe's glorious Spanish past and as a modern scientific institution that exemplified American achievement. These romantic and scientific views of the Palace were complementary, allowing Anglos to assert their dominance as both preservationists and pioneers. Museum administrators envisioned a linear, progressive New Mexican history that led from the Indian and Spanish past to the American future. Far from denigrating or erasing pre-American culture and history in New Mexico, they celebrated them and put them on display. The Palace contained and brought order to the past.

The second part of the chapter examines the more recent development of this process of containment and its visual manifestations. I analyze several areas where the museum has exhibited the Palace of the Governors itself. Self-referential displays developed in the 1970s and 1980s have played a crucial role in the construction of the Palace as a historic site by drawing attention to the building's materiality and antiquity. The exhibits imply that the Palace's history ended when it became a museum, leaving the museum establishment to occupy the unmarked, normative space of modernity. The transparency of the museum apparatus effectively fortifies the museum's authority and the unassailability of a scientific American gaze.

The Palace of the Governors has rendered the pre-American past more visible than twentieth-century American history. More specifically, the gradual withdrawal of museum administrators from their own interpretations of the building illustrates what Sylvia Rodríguez calls the vanishing Anglo. Rodríguez (2001, 195) links Anglos' disappearing act to the transparency of whiteness. "As the unmarked category in the U.S. racial order, whiteness is by definition invisible," she writes. "This invisibility is a product of white privilege, which involves the collective power to name or mark who is 'colored,' 'ethnic,' 'racial,' or nonwhite. It implies that to be white is none of the above and synonymous with what is normal and thus unmarked." Analyzing a number of examples to which the Palace of the Governors could easily be added, Rodríguez notes that "Anglos were previously more visible in New Mexico's public discourses of cultural history than they are today. Their disappearance from the public stage coincides, ironically and significantly, with 'Anglo' (or 'non-Hispanic white') demographic expansion in tourist towns like Santa Fe and Taos." It should come as no surprise that museum administrators have touted their own contributions to the management of New Mexico's cultural heritage less frequently and less boastfully over time, to the point that their scientific curatorial practices no longer attract attention.

Juxtaposing two pivotal moments in the Palace's twentieth-century history helps to reveal the persistence of a colonial power structure that might otherwise be imperceptible. The power I hope to illuminate operates through self-effacement and invisibility. The fact that the museum's power play has been largely unintentional (even counter-intentional) and that it appears "multicultural" on the surface makes it even harder to detect or believe—and thus all the more effective. It is the result of a set of effects, not a conspiracy, and Anglos, Hispanos, and Indians have all contributed to its perpetuation. Museum administrators have consistently emphasized the Palace's Spanish colonial history and deemphasized its twentieth-century history, including Tom Chávez, a Nuevomexicano historian who directed the museum for two decades beginning in the 1980s. The politics of visibility has become hegemonic in New Mexico, which is to say that most people accept the privileging of Native American, Spanish, Mexican, and American territorial heritage in public history. This general consensus notwithstanding, Anglo invisibility remains a cornerstone of American legitimacy in New Mexico. I conclude the chapter by arguing that multicultural justice in cases such as the Palace of the Governors requires not just focusing positive attention on subaltern groups but also making power visible and exposing normativity to critique.

Establishing the Museum of New Mexico

Many Americans who arrived in Santa Fe after the United States took control of it in 1846 disapproved of New Mexico's flat, earthen architecture, which they considered dirty, crude, and uncivilized. In the 1850s the Palace of the Governors was given a simple portico in the Territorial style (a local version of Greek Revival style), and the following decade saw several attempts to make the plaza more park-like. In the 1870s the addition to the Palace of new doors and windows, hard stucco, a plank sidewalk, and elaborate molding around the portal posts, topped with a heavy cornice, inspired public praise and improvements to other downtown buildings (Wilson 1997, 52–63). Progressivist attitudes held sway into the twentieth century as civic boosters campaigning for statehood promoted New Mexico's American achievements, combating suspicions that the region was too Mexican, too Catholic, and too different to be integrated into the United States.

By the 1880s, however, an alternative vision of New Mexico had taken root, inspired by a growing interest among Anglo newcomers in the territory's Spanish and Indian heritage. In 1882 and 1884 the territorial legislature proposed turning the Palace into a museum to house southwestern antiquities, and in 1885 the Historical Society of New Mexico took over several rooms in the eastern part of the building where it exhibited historical artifacts and papers. An 1890 article in the *Santa Fe New Mexican* described the "historic adobe Palace" as an "ancient official edifice, so full of interest to all tourists and sightseers who visit Santa Fe," surpassing "in historical interest and value any other place or object in the United States," "the living center of everything of historical importance in the southwest" ("100 Years Ago" 1990).[2] New capitols were completed in 1886 and 1900, diminishing but not eliminating the Palace's usefulness as an administrative building.

Governor Miguel Otero wrote the secretary of the interior in 1900 that he was afraid the Palace would fall to ruin and believed "this historic old building" should become a branch of the Smithsonian Institution. The following year, the legislature passed a resolution noting that the Palace was "the oldest public building and the most historic edifice in the United States" and suggesting again that it be devoted to a museum of southwestern antiquities. The Palace building should "be preserved in good order, and without material changes in its general structure and appearance forever" (Nusbaum 1978, 67–68; Hobbs 1946b, 176–77). If Governor Otero was concerned about financing the physical upkeep of the building, territorial officials were also beginning to express a preservationist ethic, suggesting that the building should be preserved for its historical significance. Around the turn of the century, then, people began to think of the Palace not just as a building in which to house a museum, historical because of its enduring presence and the events that happened in and around it, but also as a museum and historic building in its *materiality*.

Not coincidentally, the first decade of the twentieth century witnessed an exploding interest in archaeology in the Southwest, with Santa Fe the epicenter of activity. Following on Adolph Bandelier's pioneering work in the 1880s, an enthusiastic group of archaeologists led by Edgar Lee Hewett began excavating and studying Ancestral Puebloan sites on the Pajarito Plateau (northwest of Santa Fe), on Mesa Verde (in southwestern Colorado), and elsewhere in the Southwest. Hewett was a tireless, if controversial, educator, promoter, fund-raiser, and lobbyist. Besides galva-

The Palace of the Governors

nizing New Mexico's emergent anthropological community, he was involved in the development of archaeology internationally and played an important role in the passage of the Antiquities Act of 1906, America's first preservation law. In 1907 the Archaeological Institute of America established the School of American Archaeology (SAA, now School for Advanced Research) and made Hewett its director. That same year a proposal circulated in Santa Fe to designate the Palace of the Governors a national monument in order to preserve it as a historic landmark (Elliott 1991, 2–16; Hobbs 1946a, 1946b, 1946c; Shishkin 1972, 48–49; Wilson 1997, 117–21).

Eager for the SAA to be located in Santa Fe, Hewett lobbied the territorial legislature to offer the Palace to the school for its headquarters. Finally in 1909 the legislature passed a bill establishing the Museum of New Mexico and placing the Palace of the Governors under its control, to serve as the home for the SAA.[3] The legislation provided an annual appropriation of up to three thousand dollars for the physical improvement of the Palace but mandated "that all alterations, extensions and additions to the main Palace building shall be made so as to keep it in external appearance as nearly as possible in harmony with the Spanish architecture of the period of its construction, and preserve it as a monument to the Spanish founders of the civilization of the Southwest" (Nusbaum 1978, 78–79). This mandate makes it clear that by 1909 an exotic tourist image of Santa Fe rivaled a progressive Americanist discourse.

Renovating the Palace of the Governors

Jesse Nusbaum, the Museum of New Mexico's director of architectural reconstruction and photography, oversaw the Palace's renovation and conversion into a museum between 1909 and 1913. Nusbaum had distinguished himself photographing archaeological sites for the School of American Archaeology, and his photographs of New Mexico's Pueblo and Hispano vernacular architecture helped to substantiate Santa Fe's tourist image and civic identity (Wilson 1997, 94–95). As a builder, Nusbaum was attuned to the Palace's materiality, but his "restoration" was also ideological. Nusbaum worked to eliminate "excrescences" from the Palace, since "everywhere inappropriate restorations were in evidence, a hodge-podge of ill-conceived additions conforming to no particular style of architecture" (quoted in Nusbaum 1978, 84–85). He wrote in his journal, "it soon became the consensus and my purpose to preserve in all integrity, in so far as was possible, all surviving archaeological features and traditions that predated the American Military occupation of August 1846, which was progressively responsible for the vast majority of subsequent modifications" (86–87).

Nusbaum reinforced or replaced damaged walls, exposed ceiling beams, removed modern woodwork and wallpaper, demolished interior walls to make larger exhibit rooms, and applied cement stucco meant to look like adobe plaster to the exterior (Nusbaum 1978, 84–87; Wilson 1997, 235). The museum proudly declared that "the rooms thus repaired must represent much of the appearance which they had before the modernizing of the past half century was done" ("Report of the Museum of New Mexico" 1914, 1). This desire to purify New Mexico's cultural record of Anglo-American influences (a tendency also of salvage anthropology) has typified heritage development campaigns in New Mexico.

In preparing the Palace to become a museum, Nusbaum covered part of an adobe wall with glass so that visitors could study its construction. The museum encouraged visitors to notice ceiling beams, historic fireplaces, and the thickness of the Palace's walls. At Hewett's request, Nusbaum cut recessed display cases into the adobe walls, enclosing them with glass. According to his wife, he left the walls behind the cases "visible to visitors and school-children, so that they could . . . view the earliest beginning of this site" (Nusbaum 1978, 90, 92; "Report of the Museum of New Mexico" 1914, 1, 5, 7; "Restoration of the Palace" 1913; "The Museum of New Mexico" 1919, 74, 84). Leaving the walls visible represents a nod to the building's material history, but only after Nusbaum cut away and removed part of the adobe structure in

The Palace of the Governors

order to exhibit the museum's archaeological collections. At this point the museum was primarily a museum about something else (elsewhere) — the material culture of "prehistoric" Pueblo Indians — and only secondarily a museum about itself.

Another important feature of the restoration that directed visitor attention away from the building itself was the installation of murals in three rooms of the building in 1909 and 1910. Nusbaum cut recessed panels into the walls to showcase canvases commissioned by Hewett and his patron Frank Springer and painted by Carl Lotave. Three paintings in the museum's entryway depicted Santa Fe's tricultural history, illustrating "the three epochs which this ancient monument has looked upon": a sunrise scene of a lone Indian crouching by the Santa Fe River, a noonday depiction of de Vargas and his entourage peacefully reclaiming Santa Fe in front of the Palace of the Governors in 1692, and a sunset portrayal of an American wagon train arriving over the Santa Fe Trail ("Links Historic Past with Living Present" 1913, 6; Nusbaum 1978, 89; Wilson 1997, 128; Museum of New Mexico 1912, 10–11). The focus of these murals was clearly not the Palace itself but the people and events surrounding it.

Lotave also painted scenes for two of the three rooms in the museum dedicated to displaying artifacts from the School of American Archaeology's excavations: the Puye Room and the Rito de los Frijoles Room. Panoramic murals of landscapes and ruins on all four walls gave visitors an idea of what the Puye cliff dwellings and Frijoles Canyon looked like. Working with Lotave, Nusbaum was careful that the murals accurately depicted the ruins' environment, oriented to the four cardinal directions (Nusbaum 1978, 87–89). Historian Chris Wilson (1997, 128) observes that rather than re-creating these villages "at their peak, Lotave portrays them abandoned, with only an occasional person gazing forlornly across a twilight landscape. Lotave's panels . . . comforted the children of Manifest Destiny with the fiction that the Indians were passing quietly from the scene." These murals literally covered up the Palace of the Governors and imported into the Palace a spatially and temporally distant atmosphere. "The whole environment and culture of these ancient towns is thus brought before one in realistic manner" ("Report of the Museum of New Mexico" 1914, 2, 6). The murals also transported visitors away from the Palace. One reviewer mused, "the Old Palace rooms seemed mellow with the romance of past ages. The pictures of the ancient cliffs of the Puye and in the delightful Rito were lit up by shaded electric bulbs, and visitors were transported in fancy, back to the days of the ancient civilization" (Nusbaum 1978, 94; see also "Good Work Well Done" 1913, 2; Museum of New Mexico 1912, 10).

The Santa Fe–Style Palace

Nusbaum's transformation of the Palace's exterior was more public than his work inside. To create a facade more representative of the Palace's Spanish history, Nusbaum replaced the square columns and classical balustrade added in the 1870s with tree-trunk posts. He added a high parapet with projecting vigas and room projections at either end of the portal. In the Spanish buildings the museum was imitating these rooms would have been enclosed, but Nusbaum made them open-ended to accommodate pedestrian traffic along the front of the building. The museum described the Palace restoration, completed in 1913, as "historically true," but the resulting facade, a product of contemporary tastes and styles, is "best understood as a speculative or interpretive recreation" (Wilson 1997, 125–27, 235).

The renovation of the Palace of the Governors, which Anglos began to call "el palacio," was part of a larger architectural movement that transformed the city's appearance (Tobias and Woodhouse 2001, 73–78). According to Nusbaum, "The threat to the future preservation of the traditional Spanish-Colonial atmosphere of Santa Fe became a matter of increasing concern to a limited and far-seeing segment of Santa Fe's residents, and of vigorous public protest" (quoted in Nusbaum 1978, 91). Ironically, the newly arrived Anglo-Americans Nusbaum portrayed as the saviors of traditional Spanish and Mexican Santa Fe were in part responsible for the city's transformation. But the most important word here is "atmosphere," since Nusbaum and his allies were concerned not just with individual buildings but with the ambiance they produced as an ensemble. Wilson (1997, 236) notes that "the restoration of the Palace of the Governors and its conversion into a museum paralleled eastern house museums. But Santa Fe's civic leaders also sought the recreation of an entire historic environment—to make the city itself into a tourist attraction."

Museum of New Mexico staff played an important role in reversing several decades of Americanization and promoting what today we might call heritage tourism. In 1912 Santa Fe mayor Arthur Seligman appointed Edgar Lee Hewett and Sylvanus Morley, a Museum of New Mexico archaeologist, to the City Planning Board, which he charged with creating a plan for Santa Fe's economic revitalization. The board drew inspiration from the City Beautiful planning and civic improvement movement but rejected the Beaux Arts classicism typical of City Beautiful architecture in favor of a distinctive local style. The result of their work was the Plan of 1912, which included the first systematic attempt to define "Santa Fe–style" architecture, an inventive combination of Spanish and Indian building traditions. "Soon the chamber of commerce was promoting Santa Fe not as another 'City Beautiful,' but as the 'City Different,'" a label that endures to this day (Wilson 1997, 121–22).[4] In order to promote the board's proposals, the city, the chamber of commerce, and the School of American Archaeology sponsored the "New-Old Santa Fe" exhibit at the Palace of the Governors. The exhibit included drawings and photographs of typical Pueblo-style buildings, a map of proposed streets and parks, and models of historic structures around Santa Fe (123–25). Nusbaum created a ten-foot scaled model of the Palace for the exhibit showing his proposed renovation of the front facade, which won the support of the museum board. The architectural transformation of downtown Santa Fe between the 1910s and 1960s was "profoundly antihistorical," concealing railroad-era architecture beneath an adobe veneer (101; see also Wilson and Polyzoides 2011, 106). It exemplifies Anglos' decreasing visibility in public culture and history.

The Museum of New Mexico worked in other areas as well to cultivate Santa Fe's exotic Indian and Spanish tourist image. It promoted the production and sale of Indian art and revived the Santa Fe fiesta, a commemoration of Diego de Vargas's 1692 reconquest of New Mexico. The museum's fiesta celebrated not only Indian and Nuevomexicano heritage but also the triumph of Anglo-American civilization, a theme echoed in its interpretation of the Palace.[5]

Spanish Past, American Future

After Nusbaum's restoration, the Museum of New Mexico began promoting the Palace as a monument to New Mexico's Spanish past. It explained that the "restoration of the Palace did not mean renovation, for every care was taken to adhere to the old architectural lines, to replace modern accretions with the simpler and more dignified architecture of the past, so well adapted to the environment and reflecting the very traditions and history of New Mexico." Such careful restoration protected the Palace's historicity: "The Palace of the Governors is the most noteworthy historical building in the United States. It is now in such condition, that it can be preserved for centuries to come, a monument to the Spanish Conquistadores, the devoted Franciscans and the pioneers that came over the Santa Fe Trail. It is the noblest specimen of early Spanish architecture on American soil" ("Report of the Museum of New Mexico" 1914, 1–2; cf. Museum of New Mexico 1912, 6–7). Note how this interpretation bypasses New Mexico's Mexican history, incorporates the Spanish past into the history of the United States, and appropriates the Palace as a site of *American* heritage. Chris Wilson interprets Nusbaum's renovation differently: "The facade of the Palace of the Governors stands not as an example of Spanish architecture, but as a key monument in the development and popularization of a regional revival" (Wilson 1997, 127; see also Weber 1974, 39). Certainly historical monuments tell us at least as much about the period in which they were created as they do about the period they claim to represent (Loewen 1999).

The Palace of the Governors

But even in the 1910s the Palace symbolized not just the Spanish past but also modern science and rationality.[6] The archaeological exhibits inside the museum, for instance, exemplified the most recent scientific practices: "The Museum, by exploration and through excavations, is securing material from the ancient pueblo and cliff ruins, that is being displayed in the beautiful Museum rooms, not as a vast conglomeration of meaningless material, unauthenticated and unclassified, but as typical of various cultures and in a way that is educational" ("Report of the Museum of New Mexico" 1914, 2; see also "Good Work Well Done" 1913, 2). The Puye Room illustrated "ideally the modern museum method of grouping exhibits geographically in proper sequence as distinguished from the old method of crowding rooms with bewildering masses of objects. . . . The modern museum is not a curio shop but a well arranged educational institution" ("The Museum of New Mexico" 1919, 77).

Archaeology has multiple colonial functions here. First, it produces material evidence (in the form of artifacts and ruins) of New Mexico's Indian and Hispanic *past*. This contrasts sharply with the modernity of its Anglo practitioners. Second, just as Nusbaum implied that newly arrived Anglos were saving Santa Fe's cultural heritage, salvage archaeology allowed museum officials to assume the patronizing role of rescuers. The museum declared that it was "preserving for the people the archaeological and historical reminders of a glorious past. But for the work that is now being done, these remains and relics would soon have been hopelessly scattered, irretrievably lost" ("Report of the Museum of New Mexico" 1914, 2). Third, "the task of gathering, studying, correlating, classifying, displaying and preserving the mementos of the past" (2), far from being objective or neutral, entailed imposing order and discipline on an unruly Other (and an improvement over pre-scientific display practices). Emboldened by an optimistic faith in science, the museum confidently claimed the authority to interpret New Mexico's pre-American past (and present). Pueblo and Hispanic people had already been exiled from the present, so there was no chance that curators might solicit *their* opinions. In fact, the museum went so far as to teach Pueblo artists more "authentic" ways of making Pueblo art based on archaeological artifacts.

The Palace of the Governors thus brought together old and new, linking "the historic past with the living present. . . . Today, bereft of the accretions of the days of transition, restored to its former simplicity of strength, it houses the spirit of modern culture and art, a spirit reverend in the presence of achievements of the past, and yet ever striving to be in advance of the present, to lead to greater heights and to mightier achievements" ("Links Historic Past with Living Present" 1913, 1). The museum boasted that within two years it had told approximately fifteen thousand visitors "of the reverence for the past, of the pride in the deeds of the Spanish ancestors, [and] of the culture, art, [and] science ideals, which animate the present day commonwealth" ("Report of the Museum of New Mexico" 1914, 2).[7] Sometimes a colonial teleology was more explicit. The museum described the Palace as a monument "to and for a proud people who are patiently, hopefully, triumphantly rearing a great commonwealth on soil hallowed by the blood of martyrs and glorified by the deeds of Conquistadores who conquered in the name of the Crucified One, planting the standards of Christian culture beyond the then farthest bounds of civilization" ("Links Historic Past with Living Present" 1913, 6; see also Nusbaum 1978, 92).

The Museum of New Mexico's celebration of both the ancient past and scientific modernity suggests that it brought together two competing visions of New Mexico: one romantic and exoticizing, the other progressivist and Americanizing. But this rapprochement was hierarchical, since the museum (a modern, American establishment) provided a frame within which to contain and display the pre-American past, glorious but over. Its scientific aspirations are crucial here, since science (and particularly the new science of archaeology) provided a privileged position from which to study, collect, and interpret Indian and Hispanic culture. The scientific objectification and containment of history represents a powerful assertion of authority and control and an implicit expression of dominance.[8]

With the creation of the Museum of New Mexico and the re-invention of a "new-old" Palace of the Governors, Santa Fe and the Palace had fully begun their "second life as heritage" (Kirshenblatt-Gimblett 1998, 129). Yet the development of this historic site had just begun. Jumping ahead several decades, we will see just how far the Palace has come as an exhibit of itself.

Notes from the Field

JULY 25, 2002

Northern Rio Grande National Heritage Area board meeting, the Bond House, Española

I just made it to the meeting on time after driving back from a National Park Service conference in Denver on western heritage areas. The conference brought together NPS and heritage area veterans from across the country, including Ernest Ortega, the state director of the NPS in New Mexico. Ernest was the chief advocate of the NRGNHA in the Park Service, and over time we developed a close working relationship. He made an effort to include me in the conversation at the Bond House, suggesting that I help to organize the NRGNHA archives, which turned out to be mutually beneficial.

The board was beginning to network regionally and nationally. Various board members reported on the contacts they had made with nonprofit organizations, municipal governments, and Pueblos. Julianne Fletcher, the executive director of the New Mexico Heritage Preservation Alliance, was at the meeting, and everyone agreed that the two groups should collaborate. Ernest encouraged the board to contact the Museum of Spanish Colonial Art in Santa Fe. The board decided to invite one of the two Hispanic members of the museum board to a meeting. Three board members reported positively on their participation in a conference in Atlanta organized by the National Parks Conservation Association on the relationship between the NPS and communities of color. Kathy Córdova, a well-connected Republican, planned to host a barbeque for Senator Domenici in Taos in August. Several people suggested asking Richard Lucero, the mayor of Española and a close ally of Domenici, to persuade the senator to express his support for the heritage area at that event and to offer financial assistance. Willie Atencio agreed to make a presentation about the NRGNHA at a conference on "Heritage Tourism and the Federal Government" organized by the Advisory Council on Historic Preservation, an independent federal agency. The event (which I attended) was held in August in the Misión in Española and attracted a large and diverse audience including state, federal, and Pueblo officials.

Exhibiting the Palace

In 1909 the Palace of the Governors was the only unit of the state-run Museum of New Mexico, but four other museums in Santa Fe opened later: the Museum of Fine Arts (in 1917), Museum of International Folk Art (1953), Museum of Indian Arts and Culture (1987), and New Mexico History Museum (2009).[9] The sixty years following the opening of the Palace museum represented a period of relative stability in terms of the building's function and social meaning. Its exterior continued to serve as an iconic backdrop for the plaza as the city focused on promoting its romantic image. Museum administrators occasionally discussed exhibiting the building's historic structure, but the changing exhibits inside the museum mostly presented New Mexican history, ethnology, archaeology, art, and material culture, not the building itself.[10] This began to change in the 1970s with the development of new kinds of exhibits in the Palace and a renewed interest in the structure itself.

The remainder of this chapter presents a critical reading of the exhibits that have drawn attention to the Palace itself and rendered it self-reflexive in different ways: two period rooms, the Evolution of the Palace of the Governors exhibit, and the Jesse Nusbaum Memorial Room.[11] The Nusbaum Room was replaced in 2003, but the other areas remain on display today. Together these long-lived exhibits have played a major role in the construction of the Palace as a historic site. Their visual and narrative logic entrenched the political effects I outlined in the previous section. By highlighting the Palace's history up to the point it became a museum, they effectively rendered the museum establishment invisible, beyond culture and history. These exhibits therefore illustrated, quite literally, a framing technique that contrasts "history" with "modernity" and perpetuates the power relations inherent in that contrast. This political effect is subtle, implicit, and probably unintentional, but powerful nonetheless.

Most of these exhibit areas were installed in the 1970s when Michael Weber was director of the museum. Weber refocused attention on the Palace itself and sought to integrate its functions as historic building and history museum. In an article on "the problems of preservation," Weber (1974, 39) lamented that "the major thrust of consideration of the Palace has been as a museum rather than as a historic structure." Its museum function must "be combined with the preservation of historic architecture in order to be true to the history of the building." But this posed a problem: "How does one have a successful and modern museum that interprets the history and anthropology of New Mexico and at the same time creates an environment which makes the visitor aware of the great historic nature of the structure itself?"[12] Weber's response was to develop exhibits that emphasized the Palace's historicity.

One of the techniques Weber employed was the installation of two period rooms, a standard feature of house museums. The Mexican Governor's Office and Prince Reception Room depict the Mexican and American territorial phases of the building's history (see fig. 3).[13] Interpretive panels and railings that prevent visitors from fully entering the rooms make it clear that the rooms function as exhibits (see Weber 1974, 42–44).

The Evolution of the Palace Exhibit

The Evolution of the Palace exhibit, which interprets the building's architectural history, has done the most to highlight the Palace's antiquity. In 1974 the Museum of New Mexico excavat-

Fig. 3. Mexican Governor's Office, as seen from the doorway.

ed two rooms in the Palace, digging beneath the floors to reveal new information about the structure's history. Most notably, archaeologists exposed artifacts and features dating from the period following the Pueblo Revolt when Indians occupied the Palace (Snow 1974).[14] Between 1975 and 1984 Conron and Lent Architects worked with the museum "to carry out significant changes to the Palace's exhibit space and begin substantial renovations to the building itself" (Conron and Woods Architects 2004, 146). John Conron considered this work a "restoration" and contrasted it to Hewett and Nusbaum's "so-called 'restoration,'" which produced "an illusion of their interpretation of history" (197).[15] George Ewing, the director of the Museum of New Mexico, declared that "the public will see a fantastic change in the rooms. . . . Our work has been to establish the Palace as a historical structure" (quoted in Gins 1975). The excavation and renovation substantiated the Palace's historicity by producing both physical evidence and knowledge. They provided the basis for the Evolution of the Palace exhibit. The exhibit takes up one room in the museum but spills into other parts of the building. Three introductory panels and a display case with text, drawings, photographs, and artifacts present the history of the Palace through the Spanish, Mexican, and territorial periods. "Since its construction 369 years ago, the Palace has undergone continuous architectural change," the first panel states. "This room is intended to show how the Palace of the Governors has evolved during its long history."

The museum exposed, displayed, and interpreted the building's actual material structure in several places. It covered an adobe fireplace in hard clear plastic and mounted a sign on the wall next to it: "post 1850 fireplace cut into the adobe wall" (see fig. 4). Curators dissected the wall that divides the main Evolution room from the entryway. Two doorways in the wall (see fig. 5) have been covered with Plexiglas and railings and labeled:

EIGHTEENTH CENTURY SPANISH COLONIAL DOORWAY. Doorways during the Colonial Period were small by modern standards. This helped to conserve heat and also served a defensive purpose. Before the ad-

Fig. 4. An exposed fireplace in the Evolution of the Palace exhibit.

Fig. 5. A wall on display in the Evolution of the Palace exhibit showing the eighteenth-century doorway (*left*), the territorial doorway (*right*), and layers of plaster and calcimine, with an interpretive panel and several architectural artifacts.

vent of the sawmill, lintels were hand-adzed. Raised sills were also common, although some interior doorways lacked sills and were covered with animal hides to keep heat in and cold out.

TERRITORIAL DOORWAY (circa 1890). Door construction changed significantly after American occupation and as new construction methods, better tools and milled lumber became available. Eastern styles of architecture, especially Greek Revival, were incorporated into the local architecture and the result was a new style called Territorial.

The plastic coverings and railings make it clear that these are not doorways but exhibits of doorways. A sign next to the Spanish colonial doorway describes four different layers of plaster visible in the doorjamb. On the other side of the wall, back in the Evolution room, a waist-level panel includes a diagram of the wall. Besides the two doorways, it points out and interprets the different kinds of plaster on the wall and the wood floor.

The exhibit status of other architectural features is less clear. Two other doorways that merit interpretation still serve their original function as doorways. A sign just inside the museum's main entrance door discusses the architectural features of this "nineteenth century entrance door." And a doorway leading between the Evolution room and the Frontier Experience exhibit is not just any doorway but another "eighteenth century Spanish colonial doorway." Once one becomes aware of them, these small, plain signs seem to pop up everywhere; I have counted fifteen in three rooms of the Palace. These signs rescue the building's material features from obscurity by naming them and bringing them into existence as museological objects: "WALL," "WINDOWS," "SPANISH COLONIAL CEILING." Scattered throughout the building, these signs suggest a dissemination and decentering of the Evolution of the Palace exhibit, which begins to lose any bounded meaning as "an exhibit" contained in one room. It is an exhibit leaking exhibitness, as the entire building becomes part of the exhibit—an exhibit of itself.

A Historic Building in a History Museum

The Evolution of the Palace exhibit is based upon the assumption, explicitly articulated by Michael Weber, that the Palace of the Governors functions in two modes: as a historic structure and as a history museum. The exhibit signs highlight these two modes. On the one hand, they draw attention to the building's material features (made of adobe, wood, glass, plaster) and suggest that these are historic because they are old. On the other hand, the text panels provide an interpretation of the building, representing its history as a story or narrative. The exhibit then encourages visitors to recognize a *relationship* between these two modes of being and these two historical registers, a relationship signified by the placement of interpretive signs directly on (or next to) the architectural features to which they refer.

According to the logic of the Evolution exhibit, however, the Palace's material structure is meaningful in and of itself. The premise of the exhibit is that modifications to the building over time reveal (or signify) changing uses, needs, technologies, and social values. We can thus read the building, as a record of human activity, like a text. This understanding suggests that the building's architectural features are already representations. Taking the idea of the exhibit to its logical conclusion, then, the interpretive signs affixed to the building become redundant, signs of signs. The information they contain is already encoded in the building itself. They simply publicize this information for those of us not skilled or knowledgeable enough to read it directly from the building, imparting curatorial expertise to museum visitors. In other words, they imply that the Palace would be museum-like even without any museum apparatus.

Transferring the Palace's museum function to the building itself has two related effects. First, it naturalizes the Palace's status as a historic structure, making its historicalness seem obvious. The museum has pressed its historical narrative into the building itself. We take it for granted that the Palace is historic, that its historical meaning is fixed and given, even concrete. Second, it renders the museum apparatus and the act of interpretation transparent: this is a self-effacing exhibit. I realized the Evolution exhibit's effectiveness when I asked twenty-five museum visitors in 2003, "What is the Palace of the Governors?"[16] Twenty-one answered that it was a government building of some sort, six knew it was the oldest something, but only four mentioned that it was a museum. Yet when I then asked the same visitors whether they found the Palace most interesting as a historic building, a history museum, or both, only two answered historic building while five answered history museum and seventeen said both. These visitors seemed to look through the museum to the "historic" structure that houses it.

There is nothing natural about the Palace's status as a historic site. I do not dispute that parts of the Palace of the Governors are in fact *old*, and that the building was already old when the Museum of New Mexico inherited it. Yet "historic" implies something more, a certain meaningfulness or significance. We do not consider everything that was built in the past—in other words, the totality of the built environment around us—to be historic. A building's historicity is therefore the result of a social, not a natural, process. As Barbara Kirshenblatt-Gimblett (1998, 149) suggests, "heritage is a new mode of cultural production in the present that has recourse to the past." It relies upon discursive practices, technologies of display (such as exhibition), and marking techniques that bring certain parts of culture, identity, and the past into consciousness and into view.[17]

With the Palace of the Governors, we can trace this process back to the nineteenth century, when people first began to talk about the building's historical significance. The establishment of the Museum of New Mexico, and particularly Nusbaum's renovation, strengthened this understanding of the building's historicity. But the Evolution of the Palace exhibit has done the most to direct visitors' attention to the antiquity of the building and to make its historicity seem natural. Far from being superfluous or redundant, the museum apparatus is absolutely essential to the meaning of the Palace, since it points out, names, and interprets the building's material features, bringing them into existence as museological objects and christening the Palace as a historic site. After all, if not for the signs hanging on the walls, we might actually miss noticing the walls themselves (and their age), the *"nineteenth century* entrance door," the *"Spanish colonial* ceiling." The signs make the building into an attraction by contributing to what Dean Mac-Cannell ([1976] 1999, 43–45) calls sight sacralization. In short, the Palace's *meaning* as a historic structure is largely the product of its effectiveness as a museum, not vice versa.

The Palace of the Governors is not unique, of course, in representing its own history. The real effect of the Evolution exhibit is therefore not to transform the Palace but to transform the visitor. Leaving the Palace of the Governors, visitors may thus be better equipped to experience the city of Santa Fe as an exhibit of itself, as if through one of the sheets of Plexiglas that now cover some of the building's architectural features. The world-as-exhibit effect relies not so much on the extension of the museum apparatus itself but on casting museum visitors as amateur anthropologists or

Fig. 6. An exposed section of wall under the portal at the Palace of the Governors.

architectural historians and awakening them to the signification all around them.[18]

Framing the Palace's Historicity

What is important here is not simply that the Museum of New Mexico has played a role in constructing the Palace as a historic site but that its particular interpretation of the Palace has subtly reinforced certain power relations. In order to return to a more political argument, let me step just outside the building. In 1985, workers discovered a nineteenth-century plaster finish beneath the hard stucco on the building's front facade. The museum decided to leave two sections of this wall exposed, framed them,

The Palace of the Governors   45

and covered them with Plexiglas (see fig. 6).[19] Signs affixed to the peeled-away wall sections read: "CUT STONE FACADE. A Territorial period embellishment, ca. 1870, this simulated stone facade is actually plaster with a rectangular pattern to make it appear that the Palace was constructed of cut stone. In fact, all exterior and interior walls of the Palace are built of sun-dried mud bricks called adobe." One of the wall sections reveals multiple layers of plaster as well as some of the original adobe.

The exposure and interpretation of this simulated stone facade reveal evolving attitudes toward the Palace with moral undertones. Americans arriving in Santa Fe in the nineteenth century found adobe buildings repugnant and covered them with hard plaster, which they sometimes stenciled to resemble stone, a more "civilized" building material. With the creation of the Museum of New Mexico, amid a romantic revival, Nusbaum reversed this understanding and covered the Palace with a hard stucco meant to look like mud plaster (on these flip-flopping aesthetics and their preservation in Santa Fe, see Wilson 1997, 99). Then in the 1980s a more self-reflexive museum establishment came along. Leaving in place most of the hard stucco (a faux-historic finish that by then could be considered historic in its own right), the museum exposed and interpreted this material history. Peeling away veneers to interpret people's past predilections, the museum then applied its own veneer: hard clear plastic.

The museum's historical interpretation under the portal was carefully contained, though. The signs mention neither the hard stucco that frames the exposed wall sections nor the act of exposure itself. These two displays thus represent a literal manifestation of a more general framing effect that characterizes the museum's historical interpretation. In the 1970s Michael Weber (1974, 41) acknowledged that in a building as old as the Palace, sometimes "the restoration or display of one feature will mean the removal or covering of another." The museum worked from the assumption that the prime historic significance of the Palace was as a governmental structure, not a museum, and that pre-1909 architectural features should therefore be considered more impor-

The Palace of the Governors

tant than post-1909 features.[20] Although Tom Chávez, the director of the museum when the two sections of wall were exposed, explained that the stucco itself was "historic" (Sandoval 1985), the museum *interpreted* only the underlying surface.

The museum has focused critical attention on the past by regimenting visual experience. The excised plaster, clear coverings, and interpretive signs all direct our gaze toward an artifact of the nineteenth century. And from the enlightened, scientific perspective that the museum recruits visitors to adopt, those early American settlers seem somewhat quaint, if not silly. However, if we ignore the museum's visual cues and focus our gaze instead on the *frame* and what lies outside of it, a different interpretation of this exhibit becomes possible. We begin to see that the museum, by directing our attention to the past, simultaneously *deflects* attention from the present (in this case the entire history of the institution since Nusbaum's time), which becomes normative and unassailable. "Unassailable" is not even the right word here, because there is no reason we would even *think* to question the museum or its interpretation. What museum? All we have before us are nineteenth-century Americans embarrassed by adobe.

This interpretive pattern is characteristic of the Evolution exhibit. In the main room of the exhibit an interpretive panel discusses Nusbaum's renovation of the Palace, and a few small signs point out architectural features dating to that period. But the exhibit focuses attention on the Palace's history before it became a museum, and all interpretation ends in 1913, as if the Palace's *history* ended in 1913. Most published accounts of the Palace's history similarly stop with the creation of the Museum of New Mexico in 1909. J. K. Shishkin (1972, 52) concluded her account: "Now that building, in which has lived so much of history, as a part of the Museum of New Mexico, serves to recreate its history for future generations." Thirty-five years later, Emily Abbink (2007, 99) reproduced this sentiment in her book on the Palace: "The building where so much history had happened would no longer stage that history but would showcase it for future generations."[21]

Consider also the museum's treatment of the 1974 excavation and subsequent renovation that led up to the Evolution exhibit. The excavation and renovation involved tearing up floors, stripping off layers of wall, blocking doorways, replacing architectural features, and more, significantly changing the Palace's interior. They were the most significant modifications to the building since Nusbaum's restoration (Conron and Wood Architects 2004, 147–50, 197–213). Yet the text panels in the main Evolution room mention the excavation only as a source of knowledge and do not mention the renovation at all. There is never any suggestion that these modifications to the building's structure were equivalent to previous modifications, all of which are associated with culturally and historically specific social values and ideologies. In other words, the archaeological excavation and renovation stand outside of the architectural history the exhibit interprets. The implication is that the excavation, conducted in the name of science, transcended both history and ideology. The museum establishment itself, apparently above the social history it appropriated as its object of study, is left to occupy the transcendent space of modernity.

The problem with this treatment of "history" at the Palace is not simply that it is incomplete. To understand its full significance, we must recall that when the Museum of New Mexico was established in the early twentieth century, it was a colonial institution. Its founders—all recently arrived Anglos—claimed the authority to interpret and represent the cultures and histories of Native Americans and Hispanics (who were still being directly subjugated at the time). Although the museum celebrated these cultures, it consistently affirmed their association with the past. Excavating, collecting, studying, and displaying Indian artifacts presupposed and demonstrated American ascendancy in the Southwest, even if archaeologists did not think of their work that way. And recall that when the museum occupied the Palace of the Governors (which had been the seat of colonial government in New Mexico for three hundred years), it presented the building as a monument both to Santa Fe's Spanish past and to modern science (the "culture" of Anglo-Americans in the tricultural Southwest). Given this colonial history, the fact that the museum in the 1970s and 1980s interpreted the past from the vantage point of normative, transcendent science takes on added significance. This was the same perspective, after all, that museum founders associated with Santa Fe's Anglo-American present and juxtaposed to its Spanish past.

To be sure, a number of changes occurred in the intervening years, and the work of the museum in the 1970s and 1980s was less obviously colonial. Gone were the explicit exaltations of science and the narratives about Anglos rescuing Santa Fe's cultural heritage. Curators since the 1970s have avoided romanticism and boosterism, adopting a more objective interpretive voice. Yet these changes suggest more, not less, of a commitment to science. No longer self-consciously ideological, science has become hegemonic — implicit and taken for granted. Another difference concerns the treatment of New Mexico's territorial period. With the Evolution of the Palace exhibit the museum historicized nineteenth-century *Anglos* too, confirming their pastness and subjecting them to critical examination. This suggests a departure from a racist colonial logic. Yet as early Anglo settlers became incorporated into history, Indians and Hispanos receded further into the past. And what is more, this expanded historical interpretation actually strengthened the museum's claim to modernity, implying that even those early settlers were not as enlightened as twentieth-century Anglos.[22]

I do not believe that the museum staff in the 1970s and 1980s *intended* to reproduce colonial power relations in any way. My aim is not to expose a conspiracy (racist archaeologists and curators attempting to perpetuate colonial rule) but to analyze a set of effects. To conclude this analysis, I would like to pay closer attention to the rolling limit of historical interpretation I noted above. How are the limits of critique managed when the (slightly) more recent past is held up for inspection? For there was one exhibit in the Palace of the Governors that did explicitly acknowledge and foreground museum practice.

The Jesse Nusbaum Memorial Room

The Nusbaum Room was also a product of the 1970s. It was dismantled in December 2003 as part of a reorganization of the museum. At first blush this exhibit, which occupied one small room, seemed like a straightforward archaeological exhibit filled with Pueblo pottery. But a text panel hanging on the wall stated: "This exhibition is a re-creation of a display originally installed in this room in 1910 by Jesse L. Nusbaum." It "serves a dual purpose: to acknowledge Nusbaum's tireless efforts to bring the Museum of New Mexico into physical existence and also to serve as an example of early 20th century museum practices and intellectual pursuits." The sign went on to explain that the artifacts on display in the room came from School of American Archaeology excavations. "Although the design of the very first exhibition is no longer in step with modern museum exhibit technology," it illustrates archaeological interests and achievements in the early 1900s.

The Nusbaum Room was *partly* a re-creation of the Puye Room (one of the three archaeological exhibits Nusbaum developed). Three cases built into the wall and two free-standing cases displayed Pueblo pottery and other artifacts with almost no interpretation. A fourth built-in display case contained a few pots, six photographs of and by Nusbaum, and three more text panels about the exhibit and Nusbaum's contributions to the museum. Carl Lotave's panoramic murals of the Puye area (near Santa Clara Pueblo) once again graced the walls, although instead of providing a backdrop to artifacts and a substitute (exterior) environment within the Palace walls, they had become part of the room display itself.

Although the text panels in the Nusbaum Room equated "this exhibit" now on display with Nusbaum's original exhibit, the two exhibits were not identical. First of all, none of the material that referred to Nusbaum and his work was part of the original. The original exhibit was called the "Puye Room" and was about the Puye area before Spanish colonization. The reinstalled exhibit was called the "Jesse Nusbaum Memorial Room" and was about Nusbaum and the history of the Museum of New Mexico. The artifacts on display were not exactly the same, either. One of the exhibit signs noted that "because some [artifacts] were deemed 'sensitive objects' by tribal and Museum officials, they have been returned to their respective cultural groups." The substitution of new artifacts demonstrated changing conditions in museum anthropology, most notably the practice of repatriation. Nevertheless, the new exhibit mostly looked like an old-fashioned exhibit of Indian pottery.

The Nusbaum Room was a period room that depicted what the Palace looked like when it first became a museum.[23] More specifically, it was an exhibit of an exhibit, a meta-exhibit. Unlike the other period rooms in the Palace, visitors could fully enter and interact with the Nusbaum Room. They could reinhabit the space of the past and reenact the experiences of earlier museum visitors, identifying with or distinguishing themselves from their earlier counterparts.[24]

Metatourism and the Limits of Critique

As a meta-exhibit, the Nusbaum Room exemplifies a larger phenomenon I call metatourism: tourism about tourism, or tourism that needs no object other than itself for display. This is a form of tourism that I suspect tends to emerge in places such as New Mexico that have long histories of tourism development. Metatourists are tourists primarily interested in other (usually earlier) forms of tourism and in the history and social dimensions of the tourism industry. Their attitude may be nostalgic or ironic, but in general metatourism casts tourists as critics; their relationship to earlier (but not necessarily current) forms of tourism is a critical one. Jonathan Culler (1981, 130–31) has shown that tourists inevitably dislike other tourists and delight in finding "someone more touristy than themselves to sneer at." Elaborating Dean MacCannell's point, he suggests that this denigration is not a basis for differentiating "travelers" from "tourists" (a distinction Daniel Boorstin made) but an integral feature of tourism itself. Anyone who has ever traveled knows that watching other tourists can be as entertaining as taking in the tourist attraction itself. Metatourism institutionalizes and formalizes this dynamic, making explicit what is an implicit structure in all tourism.

Metatourists can be self-reflexive to varying degrees. Most of the metatouristic sites I have encountered in New Mexico are un-self-critical, and in this way they help to manage social critique. Unself-reflexive metatourism leads to a critique of earlier forms of tourism as social practice but renders the metatouristic frame (i.e., current touristic practice) even more invisible, strengthening the (meta)tourist's position of power and the unassailability of the tourist gaze. The Nusbaum Room, when it succeeded as a meta-exhibit, thus left visitors thinking about the 1910s (the era of the Puye Room), not the 1970s (when the re-created exhibit was installed), their own time, or their own status as tourists. In deflecting attention from current museum and touristic practice, the exhibit insulated these from critique. This deflection may have been an unintended effect or the result of an optimistic faith in science and progress: "look how far we've come" was implied but not stated.

So long as metatourism remains unself-critical, its effects will be the same no matter how recent the practices being inspected. Indeed, the more critical people become of the past—even the recent past—the more self-assured they can feel in the present.[25] Metatourism can thus function as a sort of safety valve, limiting critical self-awareness and deflecting critique from powerful institutions. Metatouristic frames contain critique and keep sites of self-reflexivity from completely turning in on themselves and destabilizing institutional authority. The critical understanding of the Palace promoted by curators thus stopped short of the present, which became an unquestioned and untheorized vantage point for critiquing the past.

The limits of critique are also managed semiotically, as an example not directly related to the Palace of the Governors illustrates. Route 66 has become a focus of metatourism in New Mexico (and elsewhere).[26] That celebrated highway, opened in 1926, played an important role in bringing automobile tourism to the Southwest and cultivating the region's romantic tourist image. Today tourists come to the Southwest to rediscover Route 66 ro-

The Palace of the Governors

mance (the motels with their neon signs, the gas stations, the kitschy roadside businesses), retracing the paths of earlier tourists nostalgically, ironically, or both.[27]

Commemorative brown road signs now mark the original Route 66 from Illinois to California, which has mostly been replaced with bigger, faster highways. These signs are actually signs of signs: the words "historic route" now frame the old "U.S. 66" (see fig. 7). There is a second frame here, however, that would probably go unnoticed were I not to draw attention to it myself: my *photograph* of the sign. And the photograph is likewise embedded in an even larger semiotic frame: the text you are now reading. Each of these frames recasts the meaning of the first sign ("U.S. 66") and any embedded frames, but my point is that the outermost frames remain mostly invisible. The more semiotic distraction going on (a photograph of a sign of a sign), the more powerfully entrenched are the limits of critique. For it is precisely transparency that guarantees power here. In using this photograph to make an argument, I have trumped the signifying importance and meaning of both the original (referenced) Route 66 sign and its metatouristic frame.

This example helps us better understand the power effect I associated with the two framed sections of wall under the Palace portal. First, we begin to see why the force of this visual arrangement is so compelling. The frame regiments our visual experience such that it becomes difficult to see anything but what lies within the frame; everything else escapes notice and thus becomes unquestionable. Even more significantly, the very act of framing becomes invisible, such that we seem to encounter an *object* rather than a *social process*. Instead of seeing a selective representation reproduced in the service of a particular argument, we see a road sign. The "historic route" sign appears even more objective (is it not actually a metal road sign?). But in what way is this route historic? Who said so? Who decided to post this sign in downtown Santa Fe, and why? Our attention is so focused on the 66 at the center of the sign that none of these questions come to mind. Under the portal, all we see is stenciled plaster. We are unlikely to think about

Fig. 7. Historic Route 66 sign in downtown Santa Fe.

the process of exposure or its relationship to the construction of the Palace as a very particular kind of historic site. Because frames are usually self-effacing, directing our attention to what appears to be a picture-object, critique becomes virtually unthinkable.

The second lesson we can take from this discussion has to do with intentionality. The decision to frame something always involves a simultaneous decision *not* to frame something else. Marked and unmarked fields are thus interdependent and mutually constitutive. Yet the maintenance of an unmarked surround does not necessarily require deliberate acts of concealment or denial. I did not try to hide the fact that the Route 66 illustration was a photograph taken under particular circumstances. I did not have to: I trusted that since this is not a book about photography, readers would look "through" the photograph to focus on its content. Likewise, the Museum of New Mexico left clear evidence of its dissection of the wall under the Palace portal. It was not *trying* to become invisible or to make the exposed sections of wall look natural.

Although the effects of visual framing may be unintentional, they are still powerful. Indeed, the fact that framing is not intended to be an assertion of power and does not appear as such may actually *increase* its effectiveness. No one is to blame here, it seems, since even the most powerful players really do look innocent. For if the process of enframing appears neutral, even the power I am associating with it seems natural and intrinsic (having to do with visual experience, not the schemes of interested actors). Yet even accidental assertions of power can contribute to injustice, a point I elaborate at the end of this chapter.

Notes from the Field
SEPTEMBER 19, 2002
Northern Rio Grande National Heritage Area board meeting, the Bond House, Española

I became an official National Park Service volunteer in order to provide administrative support to the heritage area board. They were helping me with my research, and I was eager to reciprocate. "I felt more confident than ever going to this meeting," I wrote in my journal, because I had typed the agenda and was beginning to feel like a participant. Concerned about overcommitting, I passed out a memo outlining the limited role I expected to play. Loretta Vigil, a board member from Española, pointed out that they were all volunteers too. I was also conscious that I was an outsider. I took minutes at the meeting but afterwards became uneasy about producing the official record of what had been said. Self-representation was an important goal of the heritage area. Apparently, though, the board was happy for me to assume this responsibility, and I served as note taker at future meetings.

The board wanted to expand its membership. Ernest Ortega reported that the director of the Palace of the Governors was interested in becoming involved. The Palace could become an interpretive center for the heritage area after designation. When someone suggested asking the archdiocese to appoint a representative, others pointed out the need to avoid church-state conflicts.

José Villa and Ernest got into a discussion about the relationship between the heritage area and the National Park Service. José insisted that this was a grassroots organization and wanted to keep the federal government at bay. The board continuously negotiated this relationship, seeking NPS support while simultaneously asserting its autonomy.

A New History Museum

Both the director and the curator of the Palace of the Governors told me that the Nusbaum Room "didn't work" because of bad lighting, inadequate interpretation, and the substitution of artifacts that made the Nusbaum Room an inaccurate re-creation of the Puye Room. They were not sorry to dismantle it in 2003 as the Museum of New Mexico began a major new project, the construction of a new state history museum directly behind the Palace.[28] The New Mexico History Museum opened in 2009,

The Palace of the Governors

a significant addition to the state system that provides greatly enhanced and expanded exhibit and storage space. Its core exhibition, "Telling New Mexico: Stories from Then and Now," includes a much more substantial and critical interpretation of American colonization and recent history than the Palace of the Governors provided. As a straightforward history museum in a new building, though, the museum is conceptually less complicated than the Palace.

Museum administrators say that the new museum will allow them to improve the Palace of the Governors through an architectural division of labor. Fran Levine (2003), the director of both museums, explained to me that the Palace has been neither a fully developed historic site nor a fully developed history museum. The new museum will relieve the Palace of the burden and responsibility of being both. As a press release put it, "Freed of the demands to be all things historical, the Palace can now focus on telling its own story, as the History Museum's largest artifact" (Museum of New Mexico n.d., 2). Tom Chávez, who preceded Levine as director and guided the Palace for twenty years, affirmed that with the new museum, "we get to use the Palace as the Palace. . . . It gets to be itself" (quoted in Lopez 1999; see also Levine 2008, 121).

Building a new history museum and restoring the Palace as a historic structure parallel the establishment of the Museum of New Mexico and the conversion of the Palace into a museum in 1909.[29] But one hundred years later, these new projects reveal how much more self-aware and precise the museum establishment has become. The new museum was built directly behind the Palace, and a major archaeological excavation of the site preceded its construction (Abbink 2007, 111–14; Post 2003, 2006). The architectural firm that designed the new museum prepared a historic structure report on the Palace of the Governors as it "evolves again, this time from exhibition and office space to restored historic site" (Darko 2003). The two-volume report documents the building's uses, material history, and current conditions and makes suggestions for future restoration and preservation (Conron and Woods Architects 2004). It includes extensive historical, archaeological, and architectural documentation and hundreds of photographs, illustrations, and drawings. Its coverage of the Palace's history as a museum is thorough, ending in 2006. However, the authors reiterate the museum's position that the Palace's prime historical era was when it was a seat of government. Therefore, the museum should preserve and exhibit pre-1909 features whenever possible (213).

In 2009, as part of Santa Fe's four hundredth anniversary, an exhibit on precolonial and colonial New Mexico opened in the west wing of the Palace. The exhibit focused both on what archaeologists have learned and on the history of archaeology in New Mexico itself (including Cordelia Snow's excavation of the Palace in 1974). Visitors could see what lies beneath the building's floor through five well-lit hatches (a product of the 1974 excavation) (see fig. 8). In one of the rooms of the exhibit, an interactive computer simulation titled "The Virtual Palace: 17th Century Santa Fe Through the Eyes of History, Archaeology, and Digital Technology" featured three-dimensional digital representations of the Palace of the Governors in its early days.[30] Excavations, reports, exhibitions, and virtual reconstructions all advance a process that began in the 1880s: the construction of the Palace of the Governors as a historical artifact and site of history.

The Palace will probably continue to feature period rooms, exhibits on the building's history and architecture, and exhibits not related to the building itself (see Palace of the Governors 2006). Fran Levine told me that she does not foresee the installation of any exhibits on the Palace's history as a museum. This more recent history is both intriguing and significant, since the Museum of New Mexico played an important role in the development of Santa Fe, American archaeology, and modern museum practice, not to mention the American colonization of New Mexico. If curators stick to the position that the Palace's greatest historical significance is as an administrative building, not a museum, the Palace may continue to reproduce both a critical view of "history" and a normative understanding of "modernity."

Fig. 8. A floor hatch revealing the seventeenth-century foundation.

Normativity and the Politics of Visibility

Whatever historical narrative the reconfigured museum conveys, my analysis in this chapter suggests not only that "historic" sites are socially constructed but that *how* they are constructed inevitably represents an assertion of power. I have argued that the promotion of the Palace of the Governors as a monument both to Santa Fe's Spanish past and to science represented a subtle expression of American dominance in New Mexico. This expression was never explicit. Quite the contrary, Americans reveled in Spanish glory and acknowledged their own presence in New Mexico (and their own interventions in the Palace's material history) only in limited terms.[31] Yet the objectification of history often entails containment: at the Palace of the Governors we see pre-American New Mexico bound up and relegated to the past. Furthermore, when the semiotic operations involved in the production of history remain transparent, as they have at the Palace of the Governors, their institutional locus remains unassailable.

The Palace exemplifies a late-modern relationship between history making and power. Colonizers sometimes erase the colonized from history and exaggerate their own historical position. But affirming the historical position of the colonized while stepping out of history to occupy the unquestioned space of modernity can have similar effects. Of course, these tactics often overlap in complex ways. Self-effacing institutions like the Palace of the Governors may not appear colonialist at all. It would, in fact, be accurate to describe the Palace today as a "postcolonial" or "multicultural" institution, so long as we do not oppose these terms to colonialism (see S. Hall 1996). In New Mexico, multiculturalist ideologies date to the emergence of a romantic movement in the late 1800s that led, among other things, to the creation of the Museum of New Mexico and Nusbaum's "restoration" of the Palace. The early history of these institutions provides clear evidence that romanticism and colonialism are often complementary. Indeed, throughout New Mexico's modern history the discourse of "tricultural" harmony has coexisted with (and partially justified) blatantly colonial policies and programs.

One important way in which multiculturalist practices can perpetuate colonial power relations is through the reproduction of normativity. Any group able to identify with a norm occupies a position of privilege and power, no matter how much respect it pays to groups marked as "different." Multicultural justice, then, requires not just recognizing cultural Others but also exposing normativity to critique. This may well involve a reversal of the usual logic of multiculturalism, which leads culture workers and public historians to focus less attention on powerful white people and more attention on subaltern groups. My point is not that marginalized groups should disappear from public interpretation but that dominant groups and powerful institutions must no longer remain invisible. This holds for social scientists too: we must disclose our own particular position as actors, interpreters, and writers if we hope to affect the politics of visibility.

In New Mexico, scientific modernity has long been symbolically associated with Anglo-Americans. Because it seems normal, it no longer requires explanation. A more just public history at the Palace must therefore do away with the notion of a modern institution existing outside of history. It will be important, but not sufficient, to interpret the Palace's museum history, since "history," no matter how recent, always has the potential to deflect critical attention from the present. The museum must also open its *current* practices to critique, inviting visitors to question its institutional authority, its interpretations, its place in New Mexico's (post)colonial history, and the Palace's historicity. These steps might prove unpopular, especially among groups invested in the historical narrative that has been told about the Palace for more than a century now (including some Nuevomexicanos). Yet they might enable the construction of a more inclusive New Mexican modernity that is less impervious to social and political critique.

CHAPTER TWO

Authenticity under the Palace Portal

Perhaps the most important, and certainly the most popular, part of the Palace of the Governors today is the portal market. Almost every day of the year, through the heat of summer and cold of winter, Indian artists sit with their backs against the front wall of the Palace under Nusbaum's restored portal (see fig. 9). In front of them they neatly display handmade jewelry, pottery, and other works of art on fabric spread on the ground. Walking the length of the portal and checking out these artists and their work is de rigueur for tourists, whether or not they are actually interested in buying something.[1] Although the portal market has an informal appearance, it is actually a program of the Museum of New Mexico (the Native American Artisans Program).

If the Museum of New Mexico is a colonial institution, as I argued in the last chapter, it is not colonial in any straightforward sense. Its history demonstrates the overlap between colonialism and multiculturalism. The portal program complicates the picture even further. It is more than a colonial exhibition of indigenous bodies (although it is related to such displays), and the Museum of New Mexico has not simply imposed its will on the artists (although it has significantly influenced the production and sale of Native American art). True, living Native Americans have had a more significant presence *outside* the Palace of the Governors than inside, but one of the most remarkable features of the portal program is the degree to which the artists regulate themselves, in cooperation with museum administrators. Despite occasional dis-

Fig. 9. Portal market, Palace of the Governors.

agreements over regulations, both groups have gotten along fairly well over the years, uniting in the face of outside threats.

The Native American artists in front of the Palace of the Governors are highly visible to tourists, and more than their artwork is on display. This chapter, though, focuses not on the visibility of the portal market but on its authenticity, which has been managed and contested over time. I explore the social construction and deconstruction of authenticity under the portal and the political significance of these processes. After a discussion of the semiotics of tourism, the first part of the chapter considers what the artists and the museum have done since the 1970s to construct and defend the "traditional" nature of the portal market. The stakes of this cooperative effort have been high, since the market's authenticity became a legal justification for the museum's exclusion of non-Indian artists from the portal. The second part of the chapter takes a step back to focus on critiques of the portal program. I argue that critics who challenge the "staged" authenticity of the market often imply that *truly* authentic Native American traditions exist somewhere else. Deconstructing authenticity halfway is not only theoretically problematic but also politically dangerous, since it delegitimizes indigenous peoples where they actually are while perpetuating the fantasy of *real* Indians where they are not. I advocate neither defending nor deconstructing Native American authenticity but rather displacing the concept of authenticity altogether as a measure of indigenous legitimacy. Although anthropologists have been critiquing the concept of authenticity for decades now (Crick 1989, 336), it is so deeply embedded in Western culture that its influence remains powerful. My analysis in this chapter is fairly theoretical. For an excellent ethnography of the portal program, see Karl Hoerig's (2003) *Under the Palace Portal*.

The Semiotics of Tourism

Scholars who have written about the semiotics of tourism can help us understand the significance of authenticity under the Palace portal and its relationship to the politics of recognition. Dean MacCannell ([1976] 1999, 110) maintains that tourist attractions—people, places, or things—consist of the relationship among tourists, sights, and markers. Markers provide information about sights and can take many forms: plaques, guidebooks, souvenirs, stories. "The information given by a sight marker often amounts to no more than the name of a sight, or its picture, or a plan or map of it."[2] Jonathan Culler (1981, 127–28) elaborates MacCannell's theory by showing that a sight can also serve as its own marker. "The tourist is interested in everything as a sign of itself, an instance of a cultural practice: a Frenchman is an example of a Frenchman, a restaurant on the Left Bank is an example of a Left-Bank-Restaurant: it signifies 'Left-Bank-Restaurantness.'" All over the world, tourists constitute an unsung army of semioticians, "fanning out in search of . . . exemplary Oriental scenes, typical American thruways, traditional English pubs." Ignoring functional explanations of these sights (pubs are places to have a drink), they regard them as cultural signs, "reading cities, landscapes, and cultures as sign systems."

Though they may be attuned to signifiers of typicality, some tourists quest for unmediated encounters with sights. The basic model of sightseeing, which MacCannell ([1976] 1999, 121–23) calls first contact recognition, involves the tourist arriving at a sight with a marker in her hand or head. Recognition involves measuring the sight against its marker: imagine a tourist comparing the sight of the actual Louvre with a picture of the Louvre in her guidebook. This comparison sometimes has the effect of making the actual sight appear as if it were an image of itself, requiring the sightseer to do a "double take." Eventually, though, "information about the object gives way to the object itself" and the tourist *recognizes* the site. Yet recognition by no means suggests unmediated perception. "Tourists have been criticized for failing, somehow, to *see* the sights they visit, exchanging *perception* for mere *recognition*."

For example, Walker Percy ([1954] 1975, 47) doubted that tourists could ever actually see the Grand Canyon directly, since "the Grand Canyon, the thing as it is, has been appropriated by the symbolic complex which has already been formed in the sightseer's mind." Postcards, brochures, stories, and other representations of the canyon all contribute to this complex. It is impossible to escape measuring a sight like the Grand Canyon against its markers or seeing it as a component of a sign relationship. "The sightseer measures his satisfaction *by the degree to which the canyon conforms to the preformed complex.* . . . The highest point, the term of the sightseer's satisfaction, is not the sovereign discovery of the thing before him; it is rather the measuring up of the thing to the criterion of the preformed symbolic complex."[3]

Sightseers seriously committed to authenticity may attempt to escape the semiosis of tourism altogether. They try to get off the beaten track in order "to see life as it is really lived, even to get in with the natives" (MacCannell [1976] 1999, 94).[4] Tourist sites are often set up to accommodate this quest for authenticity. Drawing on Erving Goffman, MacCannell contrasts front regions, where locals entertain tourists, and back regions, accessible only to the locals themselves. The locals "perform" in front regions and drop their act backstage. MacCannell associates back regions with intimacy, authenticity, and reality and front regions with superficiality, inauthenticity, and artificiality.[5] In between these two poles are front regions staged to look like back regions (a seafood restaurant decorated like a fishing shack) and back regions cleaned up for outsiders (a home or factory open for tours). All of these illustrate "staged authenticity," or the illusion of backstage reality created specifically for tourists (92–102).

Intrepid tourists unsatisfied with staged authenticity go farther and farther to find life as it is really lived. But the ultimate impediment to authentic experience is semiotic, not spatial. Recall that for a sightseer to appreciate a sight *as* a sight, to understand and enjoy it, it must be marked and authenticated. In response to Daniel Boorstin's claim that American tourists in Japan prefer the Japanesey to the Japanese, Culler (1981, 133) notes: "In fact, this is scarcely surprising, for to be Japanesey is to signify 'Japaneseness,' to be marked by various sorts of representations as typically, interestingly Japanese." Boorstin assumed that "tourists pay to see tourist traps while the real thing is free as air. But the 'real thing' must be marked as real, as sight-worthy." Contrasting this realization with Percy's Grand Canyon lament, we see that "the paradox, the dilemma of authenticity, is that to be experienced as authentic it must be marked as authentic, but when it is marked as authentic it is mediated, a sign of itself, and hence not authentic in the sense of the unspoiled" (Culler 1981, 137).[6] John Frow (1991, 130) has shown that serious interpretive problems arise from this paradox: "how can I come to terms with that which is Other without reducing it to the terms of my own understanding? In semiotic terms, this is a problem of the constitutive role of representation for the object." The object is inseparable "from its semiotic status—that is, . . . any valued object is, minimally, a sign of itself, and hence . . . *resembles itself.*"

The semiotics of recognition that MacCannell and Culler have described with respect to tourism is typical of other modes of cultural recognition as well. Both tourists and government agencies recognize cultural difference with reference to some preestablished idea about what is characteristic of the place, group, or practice under question. A wide range of textual, visual, and discursive representations—what MacCannell calls markers—contribute to this preconception. The very act of *recognition*—which involves an uncanny sense of familiarity, a reassuring experience of déjà vu—depends upon the priorness of these markers: we are able to recognize something precisely because we think we have encountered it (or at least representations of it) before.

These semiotic theories of authenticity and recognition will help us understand the perspectives of museum administrators, lawyers, artists, anthropologists, and critics who have conceptualized the portal market. They are less useful in explaining the experience of tourists themselves, because they tend to project a *scholarly* concern with authenticity onto tourists (Bruner 2005, 162–63, 205–9). Many tourists have little interest in culture or authenticity. Among those who do, some are content to experience marked authenticity that is openly staged. For those turned off by "touristy" settings, more subtle stagings are always available. If the theme park does not satisfy, a local restaurant might.

Only those seeking *unmarked* authenticity, a smaller subset than MacCannell and Culler suggest, will have serious trouble. The art market under the Palace portal is set up to appeal to all kinds of tourists. The Museum of New Mexico has authenticated its traditionalness, but for most tourists the museum's presence is invisible, which gives the market an informal appearance. I turn now to consider the portal as a museum program and site of staged authenticity. In the second part of the chapter I examine critiques of this staged authenticity that compare the portal market to an imaginary *unmarked* authenticity that exists vaguely elsewhere.

Constructing Authenticity under the Palace Portal

Indian artists have so long been a fixture of the Palace that it is almost as if they were part of its architecture, "a world-famous landmark" in and of themselves ("Bakke and Portal" 1978). However, their presence under the portal today is the result of a long history in which they have carefully negotiated their status. The Santa Fe plaza has been a center of commerce since the Spanish colonial period, with different groups of people trading a wide assortment of goods in front of the Palace of the Governors at various times. Indian artists began selling their work to tourists in the 1880s in Pueblos and railroad depots but did not have a sustained presence under the Palace portal until after the establishment of the Museum of New Mexico.

Edgar Lee Hewett and his colleagues enthusiastically supported Indian art and culture, which they feared were in danger of dying out. They encouraged Indian artists, especially potters, to study archaeological artifacts and imitate precolonial (or at least pre–curio trade) designs, which they believed were relics of the most authentic and pure form of Indian culture. The museum provided space for artists to work, promoted artistic production as a means of economic development, and incorporated exemplary artists into the museum's educational programming. The portal market has roots in Santa Fe's early fiestas and Indian fairs of the 1910s and 1920s, but it did not begin to look something like it does today until after World War II, when non-Indians generally ceased using the portal as a marketplace. By the 1970s the marketplace had become so popular that both the vendors and the Museum of New Mexico began to regulate it. In 1974 the artists organized and formed a committee to set rules to ensure order under the portal (Hoerig 2003, 21–67; Evans-Pritchard 1987, 288).

Today a ten-member administrative committee made up of program participants works in partnership with the Palace of the Governors to direct the daily operation of the market, allocate spaces along the porch, enforce regulations, and settle disputes. On any given day, up to sixty-eight artists court the attention of prospective buyers under the Palace portal (the numbers are usually greatest during the summer and holidays when there are a large number of tourists in Santa Fe). Altogether, the Native American Artisans Program has about one thousand regular participants and over four thousand certified participants, who represent a range of backgrounds and experiences. A third come from Kewa Pueblo (formerly called Santo Domingo), another third from the Navajo Nation, and the remaining third from New Mexico's other Pueblos and tribes (Hoerig 2003, 7–9). Hoerig (2003) describes the portal market's multiple, overlapping meanings: as a community of Native American artists, as a workplace, and as a museum program. I want to focus narrowly on the latter.

The Portal as a Living Exhibit

In 1972 the Museum of New Mexico made a policy (already established as custom) that only Indians could sell their work on museum property, and in 1976 it confirmed the policy's legality. Not surprisingly, when the museum began removing Anglo and Hispanic vendors from the portal, these artists were not happy about losing access to such a lucrative, high-profile spot, and tensions mounted (Hoerig 2003, 67–69; *Livingston v. Ewing* 1978, 1111–12; *Livingston v. Ewing* 1979, 828). A series of lawsuits followed, the most important of which was filed in 1977 by Paul and Sara Livingston, eastern Anglos who made Indian-style jewelry. With the support of the American Civil Liberties Union, the Livingstons filed a reverse-discrimination suit against Museum of New Mexico director George Ewing, the museum board of regents, and the mayor, police chief, and city council of Santa Fe, claiming that their equal protection under the law, guaranteed by the Fourteenth Amendment, had been violated. Debate raged locally about the racial and cultural politics surrounding the museum policy. The local press carried daily reports on tensions under the portal and the impending lawsuits, and the Livingston case garnered national press coverage as well. The Livingstons eventually lost the case in the U.S. District Court for New Mexico, appealed to the Tenth Circuit Court of Appeals, and lost again.

In the course of the trials the two courts articulated several principles. Indians have a unique legal position in the United States. The state has an interest in supporting Native American political, cultural, and economic independence and self-determination. The museum has an interest in promoting authentic Indian crafts, and the traditional Indians-only portal market is an important tourist attraction and component of the museum's educational program. Finally, the portal policy is based on cultural, not racial, discrimination (Evans-Pritchard 1987, 289). While the appellate court agreed with the trial court's findings, it ruled on the narrower issue of whether employers could give preference to Indians living near reservations.[7]

The finding "that the Museum's policy excludes certain vendors on a cultural, not a racial, basis" as part of its educational, curatorial, and preservation mission is particularly significant (*Livingston v. Ewing* 1978, 830–31). Deirdre Evans-Pritchard (1987, 289), who analyzed these legal proceedings in her doctoral dissertation, argues "that while the Livingston case, on the surface, was entered on the issue of racial discrimination and exited on the issue of protecting the Indians economically, it implicitly revolved around the issue of authenticity." The authenticity and traditionality of the art, the artists, and the portal market itself were in question. Who is an Indian? What is Indian art? In what way is the portal market traditional?

The Palace Portal

In the midst of these legal challenges, a wide range of people—in letters to the editor and official statements—declared that the portal was traditionally a place where Indians came to trade (Hoerig 2003, 205; Myers 1978; Palace of the Governors 1997).[8] More importantly, the museum claimed that the portal was not an open market but an educational program or living exhibit. According to former acting director David Phillips, the museum realized in the 1970s "just how important that program was to the museum as well as to the vendors. It essentially is the most popular exhibit the museum has" (quoted in Hoerig 2003, 86). Presenting the portal as an exhibit or educational program allowed the museum to justify its curatorial control over the portal, to continue its exclusive support of Native American artists, and to recast the alleged racial discrimination as cultural selectivity. To put it another way, treating the portal not as a market but as a representation of a market allowed the museum to apply its own rules to the space and to ignore laws guaranteeing equal rights.

The district court found that "the portal program is authentic in that it presents what remains of a traditional market" (*Livingston v. Ewing* 1978, 829). It agreed that the museum "must, by its very nature, be culturally selective" and that the Indians-only policy was "based upon cultural considerations." According to the ruling, the museum "seeks to foster native Indian arts, give impetus to the communities from which these arts arise, educate the public, and protect a unique tradition from assimilation so as to maintain, as best they can, its purity." This is why the museum promotes "traditional Indian arts and crafts." The court went on to say that "to maintain its own standards of authenticity and historical relevancy, the Museum could not allow for the sale of imitation crafts by non-indigenous craftsmen."[9] It agreed with the museum's preference for exhibits that focus on a single ethnic group, since "co-mingling the cultures is less instructive because this fails to clarify the lines of historical development within each culture." Furthermore, "the Indians are the only remaining, relatively unchanged craftsmen of the original group who sold their wares under the portal" (*Livingston v. Ewing* 1978, 829, 831).

The idea that Native Americans and their art were pure and unchanged was absurd, but it proved essential to the authenticity argument.

Bodies on Display

Karl Hoerig (2003, 153–57) shows that the portal program stems from a long history of putting indigenous bodies on display in museums, world's fairs, Wild West shows, and folklife festivals. He and Sarah Laughlin interviewed artists in order to explore the social meaning of the portal.[10] The interviews reveal diverse perspectives on the portal's status as a "living exhibit." For example, Mary Eustace (Zuni and Cochiti) observes: "You know we're actually listed as living exhibits? I tell people that. I say 'See? But I'm not on the wall. You know, I'm not hung on a wall, but we are living exhibits.' . . . I feel like a monkey in a zoo. (Laughs) Because they take pictures of you, and they want to take pictures of the most authentic, traditional-looking one." This makes artists mad. "And I can understand that because it's like, 'Wow, there's a real live Indian, let me take a picture.' One person even said that he sat there and pulled out a camera and took a picture of the tourist. (Laughs)" (158). Pueblo Indians have a long history of imitating, imaging, and parodying tourists (e.g., Evans-Pritchard 1989; Hoerig 2003, 81; Sweet 1989). This reversal of the tourist gaze under the Palace portal represents one way in which Indians actively negotiate their status as objects on display.

Some artists take pride in being associated with the museum or being called a "living exhibit." Glenn Paquin (Laguna and Zuni) calls the portal market "a modern, changing, dynamic museum that is there every day." James Faks (Blackfoot, Onondaga-Oneida, Maya, Apache) adds: "We're the living museum, as far as I'm concerned. We are the indigenous ones, so this is a living museum, living art, visual art. I think that's basically what we contribute. . . . I mean it's not a zoo." He wants tourists "to know that we do still exist and yeah, we are museum pieces. I mean I see some of my grandmas out there, you know like S. and a lot of the old ladies, they look like they need to be in a museum, as far as I'm concerned, just the way they dress and carry themselves, it's the old way" (Hoerig 2003, 158–59).

Some portal artists are only vaguely aware of the program's educational focus, but others enjoy making the portal an educational experience. Sarah Martinez (Santo Domingo) understands the "living exhibit" as an opportunity for tourists to talk to artists and learn about their lives. "I try to educate the tourists when they do come in. And if they don't buy anything from me I feel good that I helped them to understand a little about Pueblo or Indian culture." The museum enables artists "to meet with other people and know where other people come from and know that, I think that we're all in the same boat, we all have the same problems, it's that we deal with them differently, and we educate each other" (Hoerig 2003, 159–60). Glenn Paquin also takes pleasure in talking to visitors about the Pueblos. "We're like ambassadors for our people," he says (160).

Living Exhibit, Educational Program, or Market?

The Museum of New Mexico has always been ambivalent about treating the portal market as an exhibit. On the one hand, the legal challenges of the 1970s led the museum to emphasize its curatorial control of the market. On the other hand, it seemed to prefer a hands-off approach to the portal, encouraging the artists to run it themselves. Hoerig (2003, 157) notes a shift over time in how the museum has conceptualized the portal. In the 1970s the portal could no longer "be considered merely a market. The museum had to affirm that the program had an educational content and was not simply a commercial venture." This is when the language of "living exhibit" came into use. "As the relationship between the program and the museum has become better defined, it has come to be called an "educational program" in an effort to move away from the blatant objectification of indigenous people inherent in the language of living exhibits." To its credit, even under increased scrutiny, the museum continued to affirm that the artists themselves were the best qualified to run the program. The formal organizational structure of the portal continued to develop, and the museum and artists have struck a working balance in terms of institutional responsibility and cultural flexibility (Hoerig 2003, 72, 152).[11]

One important feature of the portal program, at least since its formalization in the early 1970s, is that the museum exerts no pressure on vendors to dress in traditional costumes or conform to idealized images of American Indians (contra Evans-Pritchard 1987, 292). Instead, they wear the kind of clothes they wear at home and are often indistinguishable, at least in dress, from tourists. Hoerig (2003, 80) praises this decision among the artists "to represent themselves as they are: contemporary Native American people."

Although it has left the appearance of the artists alone, the museum has, since the 1970s, worked with the artists to develop a set of regulations regarding what is sold under the portal and how (see Hoerig 2003, 205–20). Sections eight through fifteen of the rules specify what kind of materials and techniques artists may use (what kind of silver may be used in jewelry, how pots may be fired, how artwork must carry a maker's mark, etc.). These rules emphasize the local, traditional, and handmade. Other sections provide detailed guidelines regarding the orderly operation of the portal market (rules of conduct, how space under the portal is allocated, how disputes are resolved, etc.). Consider rule 2c: "The use by Portal Program participants of televisions, radios, tape recorders and players, binoculars, cellular phones, cameras, credit card machines and other modern appliances or equipment not essential to participation in the Portal Program shall not be permitted" (Hoerig 2003, 207). The main justification for this regulation was that such devices would be distracting and improper (80–81). Rule 2b prohibits the use of tables or elevated stands to display crafts. Artists display their wares on fabric laid on the ground, which requires tourists to bend down to inspect the art. Whether or not these rules grew out of practical concerns, they clearly give the portal a more rustic, picturesque, and exotic appearance, which adds considerably to its tourist appeal. Program participants have voted to uphold these restrictions and regulations on several occasions.

Tourists generally like the portal market, but they are not always sure what to make of it. Less than half of the twenty-five visitors I surveyed in 2003 knew that the artists were participants in an institutionalized program. Almost all recognized the portal as a marketplace where one could buy Indian art, but two-thirds also associated the portal with having a cultural experience and interacting with Indians. Most of the visitors downplayed the portal's educational qualities, although they may have learned more than they realized. Encountering living Indians not wearing war paint or feathered war bonnets may be an educational experience in and of itself for some tourists. No written information about the artists, artwork, or market is readily available to tourists under the portal itself, so many tourists do not even realize that there is a connection between the Indian artists and the Palace of the Governors.

Fran Levine (2003), the director of the Palace, was not happy with this lack of information. The portal is "an opportunity that we have to really talk about tourism, to talk about issues, but we don't," she told me. "Many people don't understand that it's an educational program . . . of the Palace. I even have people come up, 'oh, I didn't realize that there was even a museum behind that, I thought that was just like a wall.'" Levine prefers to think of the portal as an educational program rather than a living exhibit. "I don't necessarily want to turn it into an exhibit," she said when I asked, "'cause I want the portal vendors to be able to do what they do." She and Carlotta Boettcher (2003), the portal program coordinator, envision developing an exhibit inside the Palace on the history and operation of the portal market, acquiring work by portal artists for the museum's collection, including the portal in docent tours of the museum, taking visitors on tours of artists' studios, using the portal as a place to educate visitors about Indian art and culture, and sponsoring more special events related to the portal program.

One step Levine took to inform visitors about the relationship between the portal program and the Palace of the Governors was to rehang an interpretive panel on the wall inside the Palace's entryway. She found the sign sitting in a closet in the museum when she became director of the Palace in 2002. The sign, titled "The Portal: A Cultural Exhibit," describes the Palace as a historic marketplace. After 1913, "the pueblo-style portal became an area where Indians gathered to barter their handmade crafts. The spectacle rapidly grew in popularity under the Museum of New Mexico's sanction." Under the portal, tourists "can partake in a living Native American cultural experience. For almost eighty years the Palace of Governors Portal has maintained Native American integrity. It is one of the few places remaining where a visitor may receive a handmade, Indian artifact from an Indian who is more than likely the artisan." A 1985 room-by-room museum guide for docents encouraged tour guides to point out this sign to visitors: "Explanation of portal as cultural exhibit is especially important. (Explain to visitors that people sitting under portal are not just there to make money, but as an expression of a cultural tradition etc. etc.)" ("For Our Beloved Docents" 1985). Levine told me that there are a few problems with the sign but that it is better than nothing. The main thrust of the text is to present the portal market as "traditional," as something that has gone on in front of the Palace for a long time. The sign also suggests that tourists can participate in a living "cultural experience" under the portal, but it does not explicitly acknowledge that the portal is also a place to shop. It includes only one reference to people actually selling something, noting instead that in the past the portal provided a place for Indians to "barter" their crafts and that today tourists "receive" works of art there.

The Uncommercial Market

The status of the portal as a commercial marketplace has been deeply problematic for the museum, which faces contradictory legal, economic, moral, and cultural demands. During the legal attacks of the 1970s, the museum was at pains to protect the portal from becoming "merely commercial." Despite the fact that the portal market is actually a commercial venture, the director of the museum stressed that "we are running a museum, not a market" (quoted in Evans-Pritchard 1987, 290). Again and again the museum, its lawyers, and the court emphasized that the portal was a "living exhibit" and not an "open market," a distinction that justified the exclusion of non-Indians. Non-Indian plaintiffs disagreed with this categorization. When five Hispano artists challenged the museum in 1979, for instance, their lawyer "contended that the portal was an 'open market' in which the state exercised 'regulatory powers that run afoul of the Human Rights Act.'" The assistant attorney general, counsel for the museum, countered that the portal was a museum exhibit, not an open market. "The museum is seeking only the preservation of tradition, it's not in business to operate a market" (Stingley 1979; see also Schuchart 1978, 38).

Yet, as Paul Livingston's lawyer pointed out, in practice the museum had always taken a hands-off approach in operating the portal market, treating it more like a market than a museum exhibit. In fact, one of the main reasons for the market was to provide Indians with an opportunity for economic development. The fact that the artists were selling art for money was crucial both to the museum and to the artists. One museum employee affirmed the museum's commitment to providing Indians a place to sell their work in one breath and in another stated, "Another reason not to open the portal for everybody is that this place is determined not to become a big commercial market. It is not supposed to become as professional as the shops of the town" (quoted in Schuchart 1978, 42).

The aversion to commercialism, widespread among non-artists, had moral underpinnings. Local Santa Feans defending the portal program praised its uncommercial character. One suggested that "*even though* the Indians of the portal are profit making individuals, they are every bit as much a historical monument in Santa Fe as the Palace of the Governors" (McDonald 1978; emphasis added). Another imagined that if the courts forced the portal market to change, he would "miss the colorful yet dignified, and delightfully uncommercial way the pueblo craftspeople have conducted their business there for all these years." The alternative was unappealing: "people selling anything from tooled belts to quilted pillows, with the accompanying trappings we all inject into our commercial lives; trademarks, 'sale' signs, huge price tags, markdowns, Mastercharge [sic] machines etc." (Field 1978).

So although the portal is a site of market capitalism (where people exchange money for art) and late consumer capitalism (where tourists consume cultural experiences), some observers seemingly prefer to think of it as a site of precapitalist trade.[12] This aversion to making the portal's underlying capitalist structure too apparent relates to the popular image of Native Americans either hunting and gathering or living in poverty. Indians and money, in other words, do not mix. It also reflects a widespread belief that money corrupts art and tradition (Evans-Pritchard 1990, 120; Hoerig 2003, 170–72). The oxymoronic notion of an uncommercial market thus evokes a reassuring sense of morality and authenticity in a corrupt capitalist world.

The museum's ambivalence about regulating the market also reveals competing notions of authenticity under the portal. On the one hand, the museum's involvement *authenticates* the market and ensures curatorial standards. On the other hand, heavy-handed regulation implies constructed or staged authenticity. A market in which the artists are simply "able to do what they do," as Fran Levine put it, might convey an *unmarked* authenticity. In this sense, acknowledging the commercial nature of the market might make it seem more real, since real markets (unlike exhibits of markets) *are* commercial.[13] It is to these conflicting notions of authenticity that I now turn.

Notes from the Field

OCTOBER 17, 2002

Northern Rio Grande National Heritage Area board meeting, the Lucero Center, Española

I arrived at the Bond House only to discover that José Villa, who had the key, couldn't make the meeting, so we had to relocate to a civic center named after Española's longtime mayor Richard Lucero. I was a little embarrassed the meeting began thirty minutes late, because it was the first time representatives appointed by the Eight Northern Indian Pueblos Council attended. Cameron Martinez worked for the Bureau of Indian Affairs at San Juan Pueblo, and Donovan Gomez (whom Kathy Córdova had taught at Taos High School) worked for Eight Northern, also at San Juan. Both were from Taos Pueblo. The board had been trying to get Pueblo representatives to participate for months, so it was exciting that they came. I realized that "representation" was becoming complicated. Were Cameron and Donovan representing Taos Pueblo, all eight northern pueblos, or the organizations for which they worked? It wasn't always clear whether board members were representing their communities or employers. Rivalries between cities, between counties, and between Pueblos further complicated this issue of representation.

The board discussed a letter from Paul Tosa, the governor of Jemez Pueblo, to U.S. representative Tom Udall requesting that Jemez be included in the heritage area. The board agreed that Jemez's history was worthy of recognition but that enlarging the NRGNHA would make it unmanageable. Communities in southern Colorado and eastern New Mexico were also interested in heritage area designation. Ernest Ortega noted that heritage areas in the Northeast are a stone's throw from one another. In 2009 Congress established the Sangre de Cristo National Heritage Area in southern Colorado, adjacent to the NRGNHA.

The Authentic Elsewhere

Among those tourists interested in authenticity, some seek that which has been *authenticated*, or marked as authentic. Others consider anything represented as authentic to be a sham — staged specifically for tourists, fabricated, self-conscious. These skeptics tend to associate tourism with artificiality. They attempt to dissociate themselves from other tourists and look for *true* authenticity (the really real) beyond the realm of tourism itself. Their ideal is to be the first outsiders to come upon a scene, to be the first ones to authenticate it. Their ability to do this depends upon their knowledge and expertise. The "natives" they discover are unselfconscious and uninfluenced by tourism. There is plenty of room between these two views of authenticity, and most tourists interested in authenticity rely on both. They may, for example, avoid shops that look "touristy" but seek out the authentication of an art dealer.

The portal market is set up to attract both kind of tourists. The Museum of New Mexico stands behind the market, but its imprimatur is not immediately visible. Rules regarding what kind of art can be sold under the portal, how, and by whom represent a sort of curatorial standard. The formal regulation of the portal since the 1970s thus ensures the technical authenticity of the art and the artists (tourists can rest assured that the art is handmade by Native Americans). Given this regulation, Deirdre Evans-Pritchard (1987, 294) argues that "the Portal market is now much more 'authentic'—as the museum and general public see it—than it ever was traditionally." Some vendors actually display permits and newspaper clippings authenticating their work. "At the same time, however, everyone is at pains to maintain the informal atmosphere of a traditional Indian market; and so the portal market does not *appear* to have any quality control" (Evans-Pritchard 1990, 142).

Tourists are not the only ones concerned about authenticity. So too are many anthropologists, folklorists, and other cultural specialists, who long considered tourist sites and anything marked as "traditional" before their arrival on the scene to be inauthentic. The remainder of this chapter examines critiques of the portal market as a site of staged authenticity. I show that critics who argue that staged authenticity is not real frequently state or imply that true authenticity exists somewhere else or in the past, "a variant of the myth of the vanishing primitive" (Bruner 2005, 218; see also 163). This authentic elsewhere is doubly marginal in their texts: it exists outside of an institutional site (such as the Palace of the Governors portal program) and it exists outside of their critical narrative. Part of its allure comes from its marginality and the fact that it is not significantly scrutinized or written about. This contrast between staged authenticity and the really real is already evident in Evans-Pritchard's assessment of the portal market above: note how she puts the word "authentic" in quotation marks (indicating that she does not think the market is *really* authentic) and compares the regulated market to the way it was "traditionally" (no quotation marks). In her comparison traditional implies truly authentic.

In the following sections I will lay out the contrast between real and fake authenticity, suggest that there is no reason to consider sites of staged authenticity unreal, maintain that unmarked authenticity does not exist (although it is a powerful and productive fantasy), and argue that the quest for authenticity not only is doomed to fail but also perpetuates injustice. Indigenous peoples, including the artists selling their work under the Palace portal, are unfairly enmeshed in the politics of authenticity, which scholars should work to dismantle or displace, not reproduce. In this part of the chapter I am less interested in understanding or representing the portal itself than in analyzing what people have said about it and what they imagine existing beyond it. My analysis of authenticity is purely metacritical: I am only interested in others' use of the concept and never attempt to distinguish between the authentic and inauthentic myself. I agree with Edward Bruner (2005, 5) "that authenticity is a red herring, to be examined only when the tourists, the locals, or the producers themselves use the term." To this list I would add one more: the critics.

Inauthenticity Framed

Arguments about authenticity under the Palace portal since the 1970s typically compare what is going on there to what Native American artists are doing (or, more generally, to Native American communities) elsewhere. They therefore rely upon a distinction between inside and outside, and the boundary between the two is an institutional and spatial frame. Both critics and defenders of the portal tend to assume that the measure of authenticity lies elsewhere, beyond an institutional context. This is a departure from the days when New Mexico's tourism industry was still fledgling and museum administrators, anthropologists, and art patrons assumed that *they* were the arbiters of authenticity. Commentators disagree only about whether the frame is permeable (in which case the art and artists on the inside are like those on the outside and are therefore authentic) or impermeable (in which case there is a significant contrast between inside and outside and the portal is artificial and fossilized). Both sides of the argument seem to share the view that traditions that are regulated and self-conscious are inauthentic. This assumption helps to explain the Museum of New Mexico's relatively light touch under the portal.

Defenders of the portal market emphasize its connection to surrounding Native American communities, whose authenticity they do not question. In the Livingston trial the district court found that "most of the Indians who sell their arts and crafts under the portal live within the Pueblos of New Mexico, maintain their own native culture and remain unassimilated into the predominant American culture. They primarily speak their native languages and maintain strong ties with the traditional religious and social customs of their people" (*Livingston v. Ewing* 1978, 828). Twenty-two years later, the museum made the same claim in its portal program brochure, which it recently republished. The brochure states that the majority of the artists participating in the program "live in the pueblos or on the reservations and are deeply conservative people with many traditional obligations—both civic and ceremonial—at home. . . . The portal as a workplace provides vendors with the scheduling flexibility to fulfill these obligations without jeopardizing their livelihoods" (Palace of the Governors 1997). These statements confirm the authenticity of the (culturally pure and "deeply conservative") artists. But they also confirm the authenticity of the market by describing the free flow of tradition between Indian communities and the portal.

Critics of the portal, on the other hand, describe a much less permeable frame around the market, one that inhibits the flow of real tradition (cf. Handler 1988, 150–51). For example, in

1987 the Museum of New Mexico introduced several new reg-ulations aimed at making the growing portal market more man-ageable. One stated that portal vendors could only sell work made by members of their own household, despite the fact that Indian artists often work together within extended families that occu-py more than one household. The rule effectively degraded and prohibited trading, a well-established practice among southwest-ern Indians. According to Evans-Pritchard (1990, 93), "it was be-coming abundantly clear that what many Indians had thought of as their traditional market [was] in fact a Museum of New Mexi-co program." One vendor remarked, "I think if the museum peo-ple are talking about tradition then they better go back and check what tradition was. A lot of old people used to sell up here at the porch. They were traders. They bartered whatever they could trade, whatever they could find" (quoted in Evans-Pritchard 1990, 93).[14] The household rule thus conflicted with tradition elsewhere and in the past.

Brian Joyce, another Anglo vendor who challenged the Muse-um of New Mexico's Indians-only policy in the 1970s, was also critical of the cultural and institutional barrier the museum erect-ed. Although his main argument was that the museum's policy was racially discriminatory and violated his human rights, Joyce was also skeptical about the museum's cultural conservation mis-sion: "Despite its alleged expertise in anthropology and history, the Museum of New Mexico has yet to learn that cultures are not protectable. Cultures cannot be enclosed or encased from the so-cial, political or economic environment. To attempt to do so, is to encumber and perhaps embalm a culture." Joyce went on to make an argument about "cultural ecology," contrasting the govern-ment's support of Native Americans and "a free [unregulated?] society" in which cultures either adapt or dissolve ("Artisan Dis-putes Ruling" 1978).

Dierdre Evans-Pritchard (1987, 292) notes how various factors have restricted the production of art under the Palace portal. She critiques strict museum regulations and the New Mexico Indian Arts and Crafts Sales Act of 1978, which promote the production of "traditional" Indian art but seem to cut the portal off from dynamic cultural processes. She also notes that tourist expectations significantly shape the production of "traditional" Indian art in Santa Fe, where artists are "aware that they must project a particular image for their work to be evaluated as true Indian craft and for them to be able to sell it." One therefore "rarely sees an Indian selling expressionist paintings or sculpture—although the Portal policy would not prevent this."[15] She concludes that "touristic stereotypes and marketplace economics tend to freeze overall stylistic development, while the strengthened regulations freeze technological innovation. One potter complained to me that she now could not use a pottery wheel without her pots losing their status as authentic" (Evans-Pritchard 1987, 294; see also Hoerig 2003, 171, 176, 185–88). Here again the contrast between practices under the portal and elsewhere (or in the past) diminishes the portal's authenticity.

Portal Regulations Reconsidered

Critics not only challenge the specific content of the rules and regulations that govern the portal market (suggesting that they violate custom) but also seem suspicious of regulation in general. Yet in both cases, to interpret the rules as indicators of artificiality is to simplify their social meaning and function. The portal may be regulated to a greater extent than other places in the Southwest where Indian art is sold more informally, but Hoerig (2003, 92–94) recounts how the portal program has gradually become more structured over time. "The program rules have grown out of practices that had become customary over the decades," he writes. And "even today much of the smooth daily operation of the program relies on participants' following practices that are not explicitly laid out in the rules." Rules are codified or changed, usually by program participants themselves, based on changing conditions under the portal. They thus "provide a flexible framework for the maintenance of the Portal as a community. The continuing development of the program rules is a reflection of community building."

Carlotta Boettcher (2003), the coordinator of the portal program, explained to me that the rules are commonsensical and ensure that vendors will be treated fairly and equally. She also emphasized their fluidity and flexibility: "It's sort of an innocent set of rules because it's grown out of the day-to-day use of the porch, and when an issue comes up and people aren't happy and there's a disagreement on how to deal with it, that's when a new rule comes into play. So it's an evolving set of rules and it's not really imposed." Even from the beginning, Boettcher noted, program participants created and approved the rules, and they discuss and vote on new rules at annual meetings.[16]

The idea that the portal rules evolved from "custom" or "use" evokes the Museum of New Mexico's invocation of custom in justifying its Indians-only policy and should be regarded critically, especially since it naturalizes institutional practices. However, there is no denying that the operation of the portal market is mostly the responsibility of the Indians who sell there and that program participants work together and with the museum to ensure a mutually satisfactory social environment.

Finally, lest we forget, all human groups rely on rules at all times to make social interactions meaningful and productive. Many of these rules are informal, even unconscious, yet some of the most informal rules are also the most inflexible. Many societies, including the United States, also have a formal set of written rules—called laws—to govern their members. In addition to rules regarding social interactions, all societies also recognize standards for what kind of artistic productions are valued and acceptable. The image of artists working without any external constraints is idealized (Hoerig 2003, 185). There is nothing intrinsically artificial or inauthentic about rules and regulations, or the social groups that rely upon them.[17]

Real-Life Tourist Market

Nor is there any reason to assume that "invented" traditions or sites of staged authenticity are insignificant to participants. Richard Handler and Jocelyn Linnekin (1984, 286) maintain that recently developed cultural practices can be as meaningful as ancient ones. "The scholar may object that such customs are not genuinely traditional, but they have as much force and as much meaning for their modern practitioners as other cultural artifacts that can be traced directly to the past. The origin of cultural practices is largely irrelevant to the experience of tradition; authenticity is always defined in the present." Tourist sites provide important opportunities for cultural production, representation, and negotiation, which may be meaningful for local populations (Bender 2002, 9–10).

In his analysis of the Palace portal, Hoerig notes that theorists "have criticized the concept of staged authenticity, arguing that in varying ways all cultures are 'staged' and that the supposed inauthenticity of the tourist setting is fundamentally no different from the constructed authenticity of all cultures." Hoerig warns against conflating the experiences of tourists and locals. There is no reason to assume that what tourists perceive as unreal also reflects indigenous views. "Not only do cultural performances in touristic settings have meaning and authenticity for those who perform them, but engaging in the business of tourism is also real and authentic experience for indigenous people. . . . What might be constructed authenticity for tourists is also a part of the authentic lives of the people who are the subjects of ethnic tourism." If "Santa Fe is a quintessential example of staged or constructed authenticity . . . , the fact of the matter is that living in Santa Fe is real life for those who do it. One of the points of this work is to demonstrate that the Portal Program is an important, vital part of Native American artists' economic, social, and cultural lives" (Hoerig 2003, 16).[18] Tourism makes Santa Fe no less real. If "tourism is Balinese culture" (Bruner 2005, 210), the same could easily be said of New Mexico (see also MacCannell ([1976] 1999, 106).

The idea of a social frame, within which some cultural practices are staged for tourist consumption and outside of which (in some periphery or elsewhere) real traditions exist, is primarily a preoccupation of tourists and anthropologists. It is itself a social production. Hoerig's ethnography documents the meaningful sense of community that exists among Indian artists under the portal and the multiple connections between the portal and the surrounding Pueblos, reservations, cities, and towns where the artists live. This fluidity substantiates claims that what goes on under the portal is rooted in communities elsewhere, but without the essentializing, racialized rhetoric of tradition.

Halfway Deconstruction and the Search for the Really Real

If considering the reality and meaningfulness of the portal market is worthwhile, critically examining the idea of an authentic elsewhere may be even more important. Studies of staged authenticity often focus too exclusively on "front regions," leaving "back regions" untheorized. For example, Evans-Pritchard's analysis of the restricted scope of Indian art under the portal is astute but distracts from an examination of similar forces *beyond* it. She observes: "Public opinion, the media, the law, the museums, and the consumer are joining *internal Indian processes* in dictating the shape of Indian craft traditions. Where in the past *the persuasive force of tradition* may have limited the range of invention available to an Indian jeweler, now that limitation is imposed by the pervasive force of the marketplace and external conservationism. Most newly made Indian jewelry is recognizably similar not simply because of *common heritage* but because these are the things that sell well, because of the expectations of tourists, and because of the strictures of the law" (Evans-Pritchard 1987, 294; emphasis added). Evans-Pritchard has very little to say about the social processes that take place *elsewhere*, when Indians leave the portal: the "internal Indian processes," "persuasive force of tradition," and "common heritage" that otherwise, or used to, shape Indian art. Yet these processes are an essential (though implicit) part of her argument, since they represent the background against which she contrasts the artificiality of the portal.

Analyzing the relationship between the portal and its larger social context might have revealed that these "internal" and "external" processes are interrelated and functionally equivalent.[19]

In her critique of staged authenticity, Evans-Pritchard therefore exaggerates the difference between what goes on under the portal and in Indian communities elsewhere. Highlighting degrees of regulation may have been more helpful. After all, market forces and the efforts of Anglo anthropologists, curators, and patrons have significantly shaped Indian art *throughout the Southwest* since the nineteenth century (Mullin 2001), and state and federal legislation defining "authentic" Native American art is far-reaching. Moreover, Native American artistic traditions in the Southwest were cross-pollinating even before the Spanish arrived, making it difficult to distinguish internal from external forces.

I agree with defenders of the portal that the frame that separates Indian life under the portal from Indian life elsewhere is permeable. Yet while the museum imagines the uninhibited flow of Indian tradition from Pueblo to portal, I believe that social conditions under the portal provide a particularly clear model of social conditions elsewhere in that they reveal the self-conscious constructedness of "tradition." Critiquing staged authenticity at a site like the portal market is useful only to the extent that it helps us deconstruct authenticity everywhere.

The problem with Evans-Pritchard's analysis is not simply that it is incomplete but that it reinscribes the concept of tradition in the process of deconstructing it.[20] Evans-Pritchard contrasts fake tradition (the product of "external" interventions under the portal) and real tradition (the result of "internal" processes beyond the portal). Deconstructing tradition and authenticity only halfway makes little sense and is, as I will suggest, politically dangerous.

In an article titled "Tradition, Genuine or Spurious," Richard Handler and Jocelyn Linnekin (1984) finish the job. They suggest that in a world increasingly suspicious of "invented traditions" (Hobsbawm and Ranger 1983), genuine traditions are thought to be those practices passed down from one generation to the next unself-consciously, habits that remain to be discovered by outside scholars such as anthropologists or folklorists. The idea that it is anthropologists who discover real traditions helps to distance anthropologists from tourists and to explain why Evans-Pritchard (1990, 88, 95) refers to the world beyond the portal as "the ethnographic context" and "ethnographic reality." Spurious traditions, on the other hand, have been deliberately and self-consciously shaped under various political and economic circumstances. But Handler and Linnekin (1984, 287) argue that traditions do not exist naturally and objectively in the world waiting to be found. Rather, to recognize a social practice as traditional is "a process of interpretation, attributing meaning in the present though making reference to the past." All traditions are self-conscious, then, and "to do something because it is traditional is already to reinterpret, and hence change it" (281). Citing two ethnographic examples, Quebec and Hawaii, they dispel the myth of the unconscious upon which the concept of tradition relies, showing that people have always been self-conscious about tradition and identity, even referencing anthropological accounts as they make claims about their own authenticity. The authors conclude that "it is doubtful that Quebec ever existed as a folk society in which traditions were unreflectively handed down in unchanging form" and "it is unlikely that Keanae villagers were ever pristine and unselfconscious, that is, that they ever failed to interpret their identity in terms of a wider social context" (281, 285).

The quest for unconscious traditions is structurally equivalent to the tourist's quest for authentic otherness and reveals the same paradox: for a practice to be recognized as traditional it must be marked as such, but once it is marked it can no longer be considered genuine. The tourist's—and critic's—desire to escape the world of semiosis and representation into the real always ends in disappointment. Timothy Mitchell (1988, 7, 10, 13) makes a similar point when he argues that nineteenth-century world expositions led visitors to encounter the external world as if it were an exhibit of itself. This experience produces a sense of continuously deferred reality: recognizing the artificiality of the exhibit (and of the world around it) leads one on an unending quest for a reality somewhere beyond that is not a representation. Yet "the real world, like the world outside of the exhibition, despite everything the exhibition promises, turns out to consist only of further representations of this reality."

Self-Regulation and Private Authenticity

One of the most remarkable features of the portal program is the extent to which the artists (and, more specifically, their elected governing committee) regulate themselves. If the regulations restrict what artists can sell under the portal and how they sell it, cutting the portal off from true tradition, as critics suggest, how can we account for the artists' willingness to uphold them?[21] Among the historical, institutional, and personal explanations for the cooperative relationship between the Native American artists and the Museum of New Mexico, one of the simplest and most convincing is that the artists acquiesce to these restrictions because it is in their best economic interest. They profit from giving tourists what they are looking for, in terms of both the art and the ambience of the market. It follows, then, that the artists might behave differently and produce different kinds of art in private. While this is true to a certain extent, it would be misleading to overemphasize the distinction between public and private.

Sylvia Rodríguez (1994, 117–18) makes this public/private distinction in a provocative essay on the tourist gaze and the commodification of subjectivity in Taos.[22] In Taos, Native Americans (and to a lesser extent Nuevomexicanos) realized that they were the object of a romantic gaze and struggled to control idealized images of themselves produced by Anglo artists.[23] Just as the colonized come to see themselves through the eyes of the colonizer as debased, they can also internalize tourist perceptions. "But this is a much more complex psychological 'moment' than the prerequisite colonizing instance, because it combines contradictory elements of empowerment with yet a new form of subjugation." One strategy for manipulating this romantic gaze is the creation of "a split . . . between the self offered up to or hunted down by the tourist gaze and the self who tries to live where the gaze cannot penetrate." Both Indians and Hispanics have experienced a kind of double ethnicity, recognizing "a distinction between cul-

The Palace Portal

tural practice for themselves and cultural practice exposed to the all-consuming tourist gaze." The emergence of "professional ethnicity," which in Taos began with natives modeling for artists, is one result of this experience. "The point," Rodríguez concludes, "is not that natives sold out to tourism but that individuals as well as groups respond to its inescapable advance in different, complex, and often contradictory ways. Today, a few resist it outright while others quite consciously pair outward compliance with private grumbling or small acts of sabotage" (118). In a later essay, Rodríguez (2001, 207) describes the internalization of the tourist gaze as "a process in which the ethnic objects of the tourist gaze come, as ethnic subjects, to believe in and perform according to the idealized image projected onto them by" romantic yearners. "This can result in a kind of split consciousness, between the scripted, performed self and the 'backstage,' 'real' self."

A significant contradiction runs through Rodríguez's analysis. On the one hand, she identifies a split or distinction between outside and inside, public and private subjectivity. Borrowing Goffman's and MacCannell's theatrical metaphor, she suggests that subjects perform while on stage but drop their act, becoming their true selves, once backstage. This would certainly be one way of understanding the compliance of the Indian artists selling their work under the Palace portal. On the other hand, Rodríguez describes the tourist gaze as "all-consuming" and "inescapable," and the fact that she puts "backstage" and "real" in quotation marks suggests that she doubts the existence of a private world beyond the influence of tourism.

Even the most highly developed tourist sites may include back regions that tourists can never access, and there is no question that people sometimes experience a contrast between their public and private lives. They may even experience their private life as more true or real (although the opposite is also possible). A spatial and experiential distinction between public and private therefore makes sense. However, this distinction is misleading when it comes to the analysis of subjectivity. Rodríguez's own discussion of internalization suggests that public and private spaces are interrelated. Internalization is the process through which people bring outside forces inside. It is internalization, not the omnipresence of tourists themselves, that renders tourism inescapable and all-consuming. Once the objects of the tourist gaze begin to see themselves as tourists do, they subject themselves to its effects, even in the absence of tourists. Outside expectations thus become an integral part of their subject formation, even in their most sheltered and ethnically homogeneous retreats (a point well established in theories of racism and colonialism). Internalization affects not only subjectivity but also how people understand culture and tradition. "As new culture is developed for tourists, the way local peoples tell stories about their traditions to foreigners influences how they talk about and express their own culture to themselves." Through this process, what began as a made-up tourist performance or representation can become locally meaningful and genuinely "traditional" (Bruner 2005, 22, 199–201, 208).

This breakdown of the public/private, outside/inside dichotomy seriously undermines the concept of the authentic elsewhere, because it suggests that the space where Indians are "just being themselves" may not exist. To stick with the performance analogy, imagine stage actors remaining in character after they go home. If it is true that Native Americans internalize the expectations of others, they may acquiesce to tourist stereotypes not just in order to succeed in a tourist market but also as they negotiate their identities as Indians *among other Indians*. Evans-Pritchard (1990, 95–100) provides evidence of this, describing a portal program meeting in which some participants questioned other participants' Indianness. At the same meeting, some artists emphasized how they learned skills from family members in a traditional manner, in contrast to those who learned their craft in technical colleges or jobs, often from non-Indians.

Indians defending, inventing, fabricating, and performing their Indianness in front of other Indians must be understood in the context of federal law that ties special rights to definitions of who an Indian is, the bureaucratic recognition of tribal existence, the economic rewards of being an Indian in a tourist economy, and so forth. But we must also evaluate such instances as part of in-group identity politics. It is impossible to separate these different factors (internal and external, private and public), since identities never exist in vacuums, but always in overlapping social formations and in relation to other identities.

It might be tempting to interpret the fact that Native Americans have internalized outsider expectations about what it means to be Indian as the ultimate indicator of lost authenticity. Internalization is certainly one of the most pernicious effects of colonialism. Yet lamenting the fact that Indians no longer autonomously determine their own cultural identities reveals a fundamental misunderstanding of identity itself, since *all* individuals and groups internalize the expectations of others. Although we often experience our identities as internal and fixed, our identities are always relative and dependent on others. It is misleading to say that when we are among our own we can just be ourselves. Men *learn* how to be men, from other men *and from women*. Germans develop their sense of Germanness based not only on interactions with other Germans but also on how they think people from other nations view them. Catholics develop identities in relationship not only to other Catholics but also to Protestants and people of other faiths (and no faith). It is less significant that Native Americans form identities in relationship to non-Indians than that tourists, critics, and anthropologists expect otherwise, assuming that *real* Indians inhabit a space and time unto themselves. The narrative construction of this authentic elsewhere doubly imperils indigenous peoples, first by discounting their existence in public spaces as inauthentic, and second by acknowledging their authenticity only in an imaginary space that does not exist.

The Politics of Authenticity

What is at stake here is more than a social scientific theory of identity and subjectivity. Reproducing the idea of an authentic elsewhere has significant political implications for indigenous peoples, whose political rights (not to mention social and psychological well-being) often depend upon ideas about cultural authenticity. For example, Elizabeth Povinelli (1999, 21) describes the Australian mandate that Aboriginal land claims be tied to the "real acknowledgement of traditional law and real observance of traditional customs." Courts evaluating land claims must measure Aboriginal claimants and their social practices against an abstract notion of Aboriginal tradition. Povinelli argues that this process brings together two modes of recognition: "recognition is at once a formal acknowledgement of a subaltern group's *being* and of its *being worthy* of national recognition and, at the same time, a formal moment of being inspected, examined, and investigated. I suggest this inspection always already constitutes indigenous persons as failures of indigenousness as such" (23). This is because actual Aborigines are never able to live up to a fantasy version of Aboriginality that locates their cultural authenticity in the precolonial past. In fact, as Povinelli shows, the presence of actual individuals always displaces fantastic traditions to ever-receding horizons. "What was this thing 'Aboriginal tradition' which was never wherever anyone was?" she asks (24).[24]

If "colonial domination worked by inspiring in colonized subjects a desire to identify with their colonizers," then "multicultural domination seems to work, in contrast, by inspiring subaltern and minority subjects to identify with the impossible object of an authentic self-identity" (Povinelli 2002, 6). Povinelli (1999) argues that the impossible demand that Aborigines embody ancient tradition reflects not so much a strategy on the part of Euro-Australians to maintain their power as a genuine desire. The successful maintenance of Aboriginal culture would confirm the goodness of the liberal nation-state and wipe away its shameful colonial history. The politics of recognition, then, does as much for Euro-Australians as for Aborigines.

Povinelli (1999, 37) notes that failures of identity are not particular to Australian Aborigines: "In their nature as socially produced and negotiated abstractions, all identities fail to correspond fully with any particular social subject or group and are propped up or undermined by their relation to other social identities and institutions." In other words, no individual or group can ever per-

The Palace Portal

fectly exemplify masculinity, or Americanness, or Jewishness, or blackness, since all of these are abstract concepts. In this way, the failure of indigenous peoples in Australia or New Mexico to fully embody indigeneity is *exemplary*, not exceptional. However, Povinelli (37) points out that "all failures of identity are not the same; they are not related to state and capital institutional structures in the same way, and they do not produce the same discursive and affective results." For example, the U.S. government issues "Certificate of Degree of Indian Blood" identification cards to Native Americans that guarantee access to certain services and legal privileges but does not in the same way certify masculinity.

More fundamentally, many failures of identity never appear as failures at all. Dominant identities often go unquestioned. Because dominant groups can claim a normative position beyond culture and history (chapter 1), their authenticity seems irrelevant. Authenticity is a concept associated with only certain kinds of groups, often indigenous, that are culturally marked. Debating a group's authenticity therefore highlights its culture and deflects attention away from other circumstances, including politics and economics (e.g., Povinelli 1999, 24). Sometimes this works in favor of indigenous groups, who can employ strategic essentialism to secure political rights. In the case of the portal program, emphasizing the artists' cultural identity displaced a robust legal argument about racial discrimination and ensured Native Americans' exclusive access to a high-profile space. However, it does not take much scrutiny before a group's authenticity becomes suspect, and there are significant risks and limitations associated with the politics of authenticity (e.g., Conklin 1997). Furthermore, groups less able to emphasize a cultural (as opposed to, say, racial) identity have been less successful in taking advantage of multicultural politics (e.g., J. Hooker 2005).

Critiques of "staged authenticity," such as those directed at the portal program, tend to undermine claims to authenticity in places where people actually are while reproducing in their margins the possibility of real tradition where people are not. The halfway deconstruction of authenticity therefore reduces the advantages while increasing the risks of the politics of authenticity for indigenous peoples. Anthropologists interested in supporting subaltern politics should therefore downplay the significance of cultural authenticity altogether.

Akhil Gupta (1998, 229) argues that while critiques of invented traditions have "most often been interpreted as providing the intellectual armory to undermine the claims of indigenous peoples to property rights and native practices," their political and practical implications are more open-ended. Highlighting the invention of tradition breaks the connection between authenticity and temporal depth. "Thus, the possibility of immobilizing movements of resistance or the construction of oppositional identities on the grounds that they are 'invented' is undercut if one maintains that this is a feature of *all* traditions. What matters is not the temporal depth of these identities but their existence." In the case of the portal, this might mean that evaluating its authenticity is less important than understanding it as a complex space in which Native American artists come together (to work, sell, wait, socialize, cooperate, compete, squabble, share, converse, etc.). As Bruner (2005, 209) suggests with respect to two Indonesian tourist performances, "The problem of focusing so narrowly on the quest for authenticity is that one is always looking elsewhere, over the shoulder or around the bend, which prevents one from taking the Ramayana and the *barong* as serious performances that deserve to be studied in their own right." Letting the question of authenticity go might help us not only take the portal market seriously as a social site but also eliminate the need to search for *real* tradition elsewhere, a search that can never fully succeed.

CHAPTER THREE

Heritage and Recognition in the Española Valley

From Santa Fe we head twenty-five miles north on U.S. Highway 84/285, through a high desert landscape of canyons and mesas, to a very different place. The city of Española is smaller and poorer than Santa Fe. Although tourists drive through Española on their way between Santa Fe and Taos, they usually see little more than a congested strip of highway lined with businesses that seemingly lack the character and class of New Mexico's more renowned destinations. One guide book even calls Española "the anti–Santa Fe" (Penland 2004, 122).[1] With a 2010 population just over ten thousand, Española is too big to have the charm of a northern New Mexico village. And although its population is predominantly Hispanic, it was established in the 1880s as a railroad town, a fact that ties it to American industry and modernity. Its dusty mercantile image and working-class character make it hard to romanticize and connect to an ancient New Mexico. As Sylvia Rodríguez puts it, "to the tourist gaze, Española is all class, lower class that is, and no culture, therefore invisible and uninteresting but slow to drive through, on the way from one site of greater attraction to the other" (quoted in Trujillo 2009, 14).[2]

This chapter examines the production and negotiation of public cultural identities in and around Española, how people draw on the past as they position themselves in the present, and how these processes relate to the politics of recognition. The first part of the chapter surveys the cultural geography of the Española valley, a landscape segmented by race and class that has provided the historical resources for Española's self-construction. The second part analyzes the development of a "tricultural" plaza project in Española beginning in the 1990s. Unlike almost every settlement around it, Española had a main street—the mark of Anglo-American enterprise—rather than a plaza. Plazas were the heart of both Pueblo and Spanish town planning (Wilson and Polyzoides 2011), and Española needed one of its own, at least in the mind of a visionary mayor. The final part of the chapter examines a series of efforts in the 1990s to commemorate the Spanish colonization of New Mexico in 1598. The National Park Service and Española's civic leaders presented a depoliticized interpretation of Spanish colonialism that allowed them to avoid controversy. Both the plaza project and the commemorations downplayed the Española valley's Anglo-American history and highlighted its Spanish colonial history. Depoliticization and the creative manipulation of the politics of visibility have garnered national recognition for Española and paved the way for the Northern Rio Grande National Heritage Area.

Rethinking Recognition

The Española case requires and demonstrates the value of moving beyond two assumptions that run through liberal theories of cultural recognition. First, these theories tend to assume that recognition occurs as an exchange between two parties, one dominant and the other subordinate. Hegel's master-slave dialectic is the prototype for this exchange, and in colonial settings "the colonizer" and "the colonized" typically fill these roles. Yet New Mexico's double colonial history complicates the politics of recognition, since Hispanos simultaneously occupy the positions of colonizer and colonized. They appear quasi-indigenous in their relationship with the United States but antagonistic to indigeneity in their relationship with Native Americans. As one resident of Truchas put it, "We've got both the blood of the colonizer and the blood of the colonized in our veins. . . . We're the conquerors and the conquered, the victors and victims" (quoted in Kosek 2006, 50).

The ambiguous position of Nuevomexicanos often produces strange effects. For example, multicultural reforms in settler colonies frequently entail a reassessment of colonial histories and a national discourse of mourning and shame (e.g., Povinelli 2002). But in New Mexico, the federal government actively sought to *commemorate* (in the most positive sense) Spanish colonialism as a way of recognizing the contributions of Hispanics to American history. When Pueblo Indians opposed this project and demanded counter-recognition, agencies such as the National Park Service retreated to a discourse of multicultural "coexistence." The object of recognition thus shifted from a group of people to a region. Meanwhile, *American* colonialism faded into the background. Cultural recognition and political rights became dissociated as the celebration of cultural heritage turned away from political struggles over land and water.

The second problem with many theories of recognition is that, at least half the time, they treat identity and difference as preexisting phenomena waiting to be recognized. Taking a cue from the first wave of postcolonial critics (e.g., Fanon 1967; Memmi [1957] 1991), many advocates of recognition combine essentialist and constructivist understandings of identity: recognize me for who I really am (the essentialist perspective) or else you will damage my self-image and I will become someone I am not (the constructivist perspective). As Patchen Markell (2003, 59) notes of Charles Taylor's (1994) influential treatise on multiculturalism, the constructivist view of identity explains why recognition matters (lack of proper recognition is hurtful), but an essentialist understanding of identity is necessary to distinguish successful recognition from misrecognition. Markell argues that this contradictory conception of identity gives us a false understanding of social life and leads to a political project that can never succeed and may reproduce existing injustices.

Turning our full attention to how identities are produced and negotiated under particular social conditions is ethnographically and politically productive. The material I present in this chapter suggests not only that identities are shaped by the politics of recognition but also that their construction and negotiation can challenge and reconfigure the context of recognition itself. Throughout the chapter I examine the multiple contexts that have shaped and constrained—but not fully determined—cultural production and identity formation in Española. The city and its plaza sit at the center of regional, national, and multinational spheres of influence that are complexly interrelated.

People in Española have crafted public identities in relationship to a wide range of landmarks and symbolic resources scattered throughout the larger Española valley. Racial ideologies, class structures, aesthetic principles, and economic markets influence the value of particular cultural forms within this context. For example, "Spanish colonial" history and folk genres are often privileged over lowrider cars, Indian casinos, strip malls, drug culture, trailer architecture, or railroad lore.[3] These cultural preferences reveal the interplay between regional and national forces. The valorization of Spanish identities and cultural forms, for instance, reflects a long history of Anglo-American racism and the devaluation of all things Mexican. Anthropologists, folklorists, museum curators, and other culture workers, mostly from outside the Española valley, have also contributed to the selective assessment of cultural value.[4] Furthermore, within a liberal multicultural context not all forms of difference are equally recognizable.

The politics of recognition in Española simultaneously stabilizes and destabilizes American nationalism and sovereignty. Española's self-construction takes place within a contested multinational context, challenging an understanding of the politics of recognition as a one-way exchange between a sovereign state and internal, subordinate groups or "national minorities" (Kymlicka 1995, 10). Recognizing the Española valley's cultural distinctiveness *and* its Americanness (affirming that it is different *and* that it belongs) calls into question what it means to be American. Multicultural recognition therefore confirms the instability of identity. It affirms the sovereignty of the United States through appeals for recognition and challenges it by reasserting Pueblo, Spanish, and Mexican claims to the region and its population. In this chapter

The Española Valley

I explore both the hegemonic and subversive dimensions of cultural production in Española, concluding that neither ultimately triumphs.

Race, Class, and Culture in the Española Valley

The town of Española sprang up in 1880 as a stop along a narrow-gauge railroad between Alamosa, Colorado, and Santa Fe.[5] The "Chili Line" made Española a regional center for agricultural commerce. In 1885 a traveler described Española as a "baby city [that] lies in the beautiful valley of the Rio Grande, in the midst of a cluster of hoary old Spanish towns and Indian pueblos." He recounted his encounters with the Mexicans and Indians hanging around town as well as the delightful expeditions he and his wife made in the valley (Harrison 1885, 825, 835). Española has always been integrated into the valley's economy and social networks. More than thirty Pueblos, villages, and hamlets dot the Española valley. Over the course of the twentieth century the city absorbed a half dozen older Hispano communities, and it now overlaps Santa Clara Pueblo and Ohkay Owingeh. The city markets itself as a "tri-cultural hub" from which visitors can explore the surrounding region (Española Valley Chamber of Commerce 2004, 6).

This section begins to map the regional context within which Española's leaders and residents have constructed public cultural identities. Through three vignettes, I survey a set of sites that have served as symbolic resources and points of reference for Española. As anthropologist Michael Trujillo (2009, 3) notes, "Española is centrally located in a regional discursive geography defined by state and popular discourses of the 'Land of Enchantment.' Thus, the valley is steeped in its Nuevomexicano roots and the romanticism that accompanies them." Yet the valley also evokes *dis*enchantment, exposing the brutal underside of romantic fantasy. "Española is a place where discourses of tradition and the most painful aspects of modernity seem to intermingle, boil, and saturate the landscape." Rapid social change has resulted in anomie and social trauma (D. Hall 1995), and the Española valley bears the marks of poverty and drug addiction (Garcia 2010). It is therefore no surprise that the symbolic significance of each of the following sites is equivocal. They reveal a landscape transformed by Spanish and American colonialism and fractured along lines of race and class.

San Gabriel and the Tewa Pueblos

In his fascinating study of ethnic relations and the construction of cultural identities in the Española valley, Michael Trujillo (2009, 1–2) cites a joke: "Who discovered Española?" The answer: "Marco Cholo." The joke masterfully turns a number of assumptions about history, race, and class on their heads. People sometimes credit the Spanish conquistador Juan de Oñate with "discovering" Española in 1598, despite the fact that the town did not come into existence until the 1880s.[6] Alluding not to Oñate but to Marco Polo (the more famous thirteenth-century Venetian traveler), the joke seems to play off the desire to aggrandize and exoticize Española's origins by linking the city to a (southern) European explorer. However, the term "cholo," which has been used for centuries throughout Latin America, subverts this Eurocentric origin story. Although it has various meanings, in general *cholo* refers to an individual of mixed Spanish and Native American ancestry (or to acculturated Indians). It can also imply social and cultural marginalization and lower-class status, illustrating how ideas about racial purity structure class hierarchies in Latin America and the American Southwest. In northern New Mexico, *cholo* denotes a partly Nuevomexicano, partly mainstream American, "shifty way of being that is considered somehow illicit and menacing by those passing through Española" (2). Imagining the founder of Española as a lower-class racial hybrid thus disrupts the narrative of noble, clear-cut identities that dominates the region.[7]

Oñate *did* establish the first Spanish colony in New Mexico just *north* of present-day Española. His party was *not* racially or culturally pure, though. Oñate himself, born in New Spain to a Basque father and an Andalusian mother, embodied Spain's own cultural diversity. He married a woman who was the granddaughter of Hernán Cortés and the great-granddaughter of the Mexica ruler Montezuma. The settlers Oñate led included Spaniards born in Spain, Spaniards born in Mexico, and mestizos, and many of the men partnered with Indian women once they arrived in New Mexico (Trujillo 2009, 44; Wilson 1997, 29).

The colonists reached the confluence of the Rio Grande and Rio Chama in the summer of 1598 and settled in the Tewa village of Yunque Owingeh, which Oñate renamed San Gabriel. He called the village on the opposite side of the river, known as Okhay Owingeh, San Juan Bautista (later San Juan de los Caballeros).[8] The Spaniards occupied existing structures after the Indians abandoned them, voluntarily or involuntarily. One of Oñate's first tasks was to build a church, which must have been simple since it was finished within a few weeks. No one knows the exact location of that church today, but we do know that the colonists later built a more substantial church at San Gabriel named San Miguel. Florence Hawley Ellis discovered remains of this church when she excavated the Yunque Owingeh site between 1959 and 1961.[9] In 1996 the city of Española constructed a representation of this church on its new plaza. Claiming Oñate as the founder of Española and "reconstructing" San Miguel in Española illustrate the temporal and spatial dislocations involved in the production of Española's civic identity.

The Spanish colonists abandoned San Gabriel around 1610 when they moved the capital to Santa Fe, but the site represents one of the first European settlements in the present-day United States, predating Jamestown, Virginia, by a decade. It became a National Historic Landmark in 1964 but has largely been overlooked ever since. Ellis and her crew backfilled their excavation in 1962, and modern homes, outbuildings, fields, and corrals now cover the site. Interest in developing a museum or visitors center at the Yunque Owingeh site has existed since the 1960s. Writer and historian Orlando Romero (1987, 7–9), who would later join the heritage area board, noted that "the concept of San Gabriel means different things to different people." Although "there were disagreements" between Spaniards and Indians at the time of the conquest, "even abuse to the point that the Pueblo Rebellion was clearly justified," alliances that formed after Diego de Vargas re-conquered New Mexico in 1692 led to close relationships between Hispanics and Indians. For Romero, San Gabriel was ultimate-ly a reminder of peaceful coexistence. Yet it is easy to see why Pueblo people might be ambivalent about (if not downright hos-tile toward) commemorating this original site of Spanish coloniza-tion. In 2005 San Juan Pueblo officially returned to its pre-Span-ish name, Ohkay Owingeh.

Five other Tewa-speaking Pueblos occupy the Española val-ley: Nambe, Pojoaque, San Ildefonso, Santa Clara, and Tesuque. All pursue cultural conservation and language revitalization, but some have invested in the culture industry more than others. The Poeh Center at Pojoaque Pueblo exemplifies this kind of cultural development. With its emphasis on the plaza form, adobe archi-tecture, and cultural production, the Poeh Center parallels the Es-pañola plaza project in interesting ways (see Guthrie 2010a, 315–17). The Pueblos attract tourists not only with their ceremonial dances and artistic traditions but also with their casinos, which generally do not trade in images of cultural authenticity. Although outsiders may view casinos as opposed to Indian cultural identity or as a sign of culture loss, the relationship between Indian gam-ing and cultural production is complex (Cattelino 2008). In many cases gaming revenues support tribal infrastructure, strengthen economic and political self-determination, and help to fund cul-tural revitalization projects.[10] Though often excluded from her-itage discourses, casinos are just as much a part of the cultural landscape of the Española valley as are plaza-centered Pueblos, just as much a point of reference for the city's cultural production. They provide important employment opportunities for Hispanos. Santa Clara's Big Rock Casino actually sits in the heart of Espa-ñola on Riverside Drive.

Chimayó

Riverside Drive, which tourists take on their way between Santa Fe and Taos, has replaced Española's first main street (Paseo de Oñate) as the city's main commercial strip. Besides the fast-food restaurants, banks, auto repair shops, and other businesses that line the street, it is well known for the "lowrider" cars that cruise it (Bright 1998; Parsons, Padilla, and Arellano 1999).[11] Española is famous for its lowrider scene, but as a working-class Chicano cultural form, lowriding has done little to help the city associate itself with the region's dominant ("pure" Spanish and Indian) cultural identities. There are, however, dozens of villages outside of Española that date to the Spanish colonial period. Some of the most famous lie along the "High Road" to Taos, a scenic route that motorists reach by turning off Riverside Drive at the Long John Silver's onto Highway 76. Almost immediately they come to Santa Cruz de la Cañada, one of the most important settlements established after Spaniards reconquered New Mexico in 1692. Santa Cruz became the ecclesiastical center of the surrounding valley. Its eighteenth-century adobe church was restored in the 1970s and 1980s. Española has dwarfed the village, though, and a paved road now cuts diagonally through its plaza, which serves principally as a parking lot.

Several miles east of Santa Cruz the highway leads to Chimayó before turning northeast into the mountains toward Córdova, Truchas, and Las Trampas. Chimayó provides an apt example of how "culture" has been produced in the Española valley, how some forms of culture are valorized while others are repressed, and how these processes both reflect and reinforce racial ideologies and class hierarchies (cf. Trujillo 2009, 14–15). Established after the reconquest, Chimayó is a hearth of Hispano art, architecture, and religion. It is known for its weavers and the picturesque Santuario de Chimayó, an early-nineteenth-century chapel believed to be built on healing ground. Every year during Holy Week tens of thousands of Catholics pilgrimage to Chimayó—some of them walking for days—to pray at the chapel and touch the holy dirt found in a hole in the floor (see Trujillo 2009, 57–73; Weigle 2010, 121–23). The santuario has become one of northern New Mexico's premier tourist destinations, and the plaza in front of it now also serves as a parking lot.[12] However, many consider another plaza in the village (Plaza del Cerro) the most intact Spanish colonial plaza in New Mexico (Usner 1995; Wilson and Polyzoides 2011, 69–75, 142–47). It remains virtually hidden, and tourists are discouraged from nosing around.

Yet there are also conspicuous signs of *Chicano* culture in Chimayó, including lowriders. The area between Española and Chimayó is known as the lowrider capital of New Mexico (Bright 1998, 587). Sylvia Rodríguez (1992, 105; cf. Whitecotton 1996, 19) may be correct that "Chicano" and "Hispano" identities are not mutually exclusive (and that "Hispano identity has become 'Chicanoized' through modernization, outmigration, and resistance"), but purists continue to view lowriders as contaminants. Sue Ellen Strale, a resident of Chimayó, put it this way: "You live in this beautifully pure place, and a low-rider passes you slowly on the road and the driver pretends to shoot you. You look in his eyes and see pure evil" (quoted in Weyermann 2000).

Strale was alluding to Chimayó's dark side. Among the social problems prevalent in the Española valley (including high rates of domestic violence, homicide, motor vehicle deaths, and suicide), the most infamous is drug abuse. Since the late 1990s Chimayó has been a center of northern New Mexico's raging heroin epidemic. Rio Arriba County (which includes Española and parts of Chimayó) had the highest rate of illicit drug overdoses of any county in New Mexico (three times the state average), and New Mexico led the nation in per capita deaths from overdoses (its rate, too, several times the national average). Rio Arriba County's overdose rate has been more than ten times the national rate (Trujillo 2009, 76). Although Mexican black tar heroin is the drug of choice in the Española valley, users often combine it with other drugs. Residents of Chimayó have joined forces with state and federal governments to combat this problem, collecting used syringes from arroyos, arresting local drug traffickers, and funding treatment centers and prevention programs (Glendinning 2005). Yet the problem remains entrenched, claiming the lives of multiple generations of addicts (Garcia 2010).

Some middle-class community leaders in the Española valley attribute the drug epidemic to culture loss and "(re)assert their

The Española Valley

vision of tradition and community" (Trujillo 2009, 86). For example, Harry Montoya, the director of a nonprofit organization that works to prevent substance abuse, maintains that "*la cultura cura*—the culture cures. Our belief is that a lot of what's happening in our communities here in northern New Mexico has to do with somewhat of a loss of culture in terms of who the people are." He goes on to say: "The food, the music, I mean that's a beautiful thing of who we are as a people. The dance, the traditions that we have . . . within the Hispano and the Indian cultures. Things that we have done for hundreds of years that have been passed on from generation to generation. And we need to see those as curative factors, resilient factors in terms of this is who we are" (Lowe 1997). Montoya's repeated invocation of "who we are" (or, at least, who we *once were and can be again*) combines the essentialist and constructivist understandings of identity I discussed at the beginning of this chapter.

Michael Trujillo's research on drug use in the Española valley challenges this narrative of culture loss. Trujillo (2009, 91) "met numerous drug users who were highly engaged with the traditional aspects of their culture, such as Spanish-language musicians and matachines dancers. Indeed, some drug users were more engaged with supposed traditional Nuevomexicano culture than the community leaders who propose culture as the cure." Trujillo also discovered that drug users were creatively constructing *new* social worlds (which they sometimes opposed to Nuevomexicano "tradition") and even perceived themselves to be embedded in a culture of drug use (91–92). "Yeah, it's a tradition, a generation man! It's tradition," one drug user declared. Added another: "it's a ritual of tradition for four generations" (95; cf. Garcia 2008, 726).

Brenda Bright (1998, 591) similarly interprets lowriding as a sign of cultural production, not culture loss: "Chicano art forms complemented the production of tourist and ethnic arts—both Hispano and Native—in the Rio Grande valley. Hence the loss of land and increased tourism—the very things that threatened to erode Hispano culture—instead created the conditions under which the Chicano Movement strengthened local conceptions of culture." As one man from Chimayó explained, "It's my culture, man. It's like my inheritance. My family all lowride, so I just keep lowriding myself. It's something that's *traditional*" (583). Drug use and lowriding in the Española valley are evidence of culture loss only if we assume (as many middle-class civic leaders do) that there are only two kinds of (legitimate, authentic) "culture" in northern New Mexico: Spanish and Native American, both conceived in essentialized terms.

The discourse of culture loss plays out within both the anti-politics of culture and the politics of authenticity. Trujillo (2006, 101) notes that substance abuse specialists frequently apply culturalist explanations to indigenous peoples and Latinos. "Economic and social problems often drop out of the discussion and culture loss becomes, in practical isolation, itself the problem." He finds "that economic and other social difficulties explain the valley's" high overdose rates and calls for "a more equitable social and economic structure" (90, 104).[13] Angela Garcia (2010) also attributes the epidemic to dispossession and economic marginalization. Although talk about cultural traits is often depoliticizing, Harry Montoya, who advocates culture as a cure, observes that "the whole Americanization of people has caused a great deal of what I believe is internalized oppression" that must be dealt with in addressing addiction (Lowe 1997). Cultural revitalization can therefore be a form of decolonization. Ironically, though, the narrow conception of culture and essentialized understanding of identity I noted above may reflect a "colonization of consciousness," a form of resistance that reproduces colonial structures and categories (Comaroff and Comaroff 1995). Furthermore, culturalist explanations almost always focus attention on the loss of an agrarian culture, linking land loss, an identity crisis, and substance abuse (e.g., Garcia 2008, 2010; D. Hall 1995, 66). While this narrative has the potential to energize struggles to reclaim land grants, it can also divert attention away from socioeconomic inequalities not directly related to land loss, such as underemployment and inadequate access to health care and other social services. In his outstanding ethnography of forest politics in northern New Mexico,

Jake Kosek (2006, 6–7) notes that pathologizing Hispano culture and lamenting culture loss can distract from poverty and racism.

Even when culturalist explanations of drug use directly address land loss, their political effects can be ambiguous. The anti-politics of culture quickly morphs into the politics of authenticity. Cultural revitalization and claims of cultural continuity can legitimize land grant activism, while evidence of culture loss can have the opposite effect (Trujillo 2006, 99–101; see also Rodríguez 1987, 1990, 1994). For example, a prominent environmentalist told Kosek (2006, xii) that a massive heroin raid in Chimayó in 1999 demonstrated that Hispanos "may have once been traditional, but they've lost that now. . . . The people's culture has been so contaminated by the dominant culture that they've lost any traditional ties to the land." He continued, "This is tremendously sad. . . . What they need to do is reconnect with the land, but I think Monday's raid demonstrated that it may be too late for that." He concluded that because their use of the forest was no longer "traditional" they had forfeited their rights to its resources. Note the backward logic: the drug raid proved culture loss, which invalidated land claims. He did not acknowledge that land dispossession in northern New Mexico was a major cause of the cultural change he lamented.

Los Alamos

On the opposite side of Española from Chimayó, both literally and figuratively, is Los Alamos. In 1943 the U.S. government established a top-secret laboratory fifteen miles southwest of Española on the Pajarito Plateau to consolidate work on the development of an atomic bomb. The town of Los Alamos grew up overnight. After the two bombs were dropped on Japan to end World War II, Los Alamos National Laboratory (LANL) continued to grow, exerting increasing gravitational pull over all of northern New Mexico. Now a center for nuclear weapons development and scientific research, the laboratory employs more than eleven thousand people, many of whom commute from the Española valley. The federal government is the number one employer in the state of New Mexico, and the growth of LANL played an important role in northern New Mexico's shift from an agricultural economy to one based on wage labor.

Although Los Alamos and Española are neighbors, the two towns could not be more different. Alluding to the region's racialized geography, one Nuevomexicana described Los Alamos as "the exact opposite of the rest of northern New Mexico in every way . . . , the white sheep of the family" (quoted in Kosek 2006, 229). According to the 2010 census, Los Alamos's population was 15 percent Hispanic, Española's 87 percent. Average household income was $111,207 for Los Alamos, $48,971 for Española. Los Alamos County is one of the most affluent counties in the United States, while Rio Arriba County (in which Española sits) is one of the poorest. The former boasts the greatest number of PhDs per capita in the United States and far better schools than the latter (for more contrasts, see Kosek 2006, 229, 238; and Masco 2006, 208). These disparities led Chuck Montaño, a longtime LANL employee and an activist, to describe the relationship between Los Alamos and the surrounding communities as "a type of nuclear apartheid" (quoted in Kosek 2006, 239).

The lab has both strong supporters and strong critics, but many New Mexicans are ambivalent about its effects on the region. They rely on LANL for employment and are grateful for the opportunities the lab has brought them, including the ability to make a living and remain in their hometowns and villages. Others consider the lab a colonial institution, a "nuclear maquiladora" that benefits wealthy white outsiders at the expense of poor people of color (Masco 2006, 160–214; see also Kosek 2006, 19–20, 239–43). They resent the federal appropriation of land and natural resources and point out that Hispanos and Indians are far more likely to hold low-paying service jobs than lucrative science posts, a fact the lab attributes to the rarity of "minorities" with advanced degrees in the sciences (Masco 2006, 359–60 n. 30). Growing concerns about the environmental costs of New Mexico's nuclear economy add to local anxieties. The image of poor Nuevomexicanos scavenging in the Los Alamos dump in order to reclaim items contaminated by radiation (202–3) illustrates the region's social and environmental inequalities.

Despite black-and-white (or, as Chuck Montaño put it, "brown and white" [Kosek 2006, 240]) contrasts, Los Alamos and the rest of northern New Mexico "are intimately linked through flows of labor, radiation, and formations of nature. . . . By tracing these flows of knowledge, labor, and materials under the metal fences and across the officially sanctioned imaginations of these often-opposed places," Kosek (2006, 231) demonstrates "the many ways that they are in fact co-constituted colonial geographies." I want to focus here on the co-constitution of cultural identities. Ultramodern Los Alamos has largely ignored New Mexico's cult of tradition. Its presence threatens New Mexico's tourist image and antimodern appeal (Masco 2006, 217–28). Yet its gleaming self-image owes as much to its location as to its investment in science and technology, since one reason it appears so futuristic is because everything around it appears so ancient. Since 1943 Los Alamos scientists have enjoyed leaving the laboratory to explore "traditional" New Mexico. Bandelier National Monument, which includes Ancestral Puebloan ruins excavated by the Museum of New Mexico, and Hispano villages such as Chimayó have always been popular destinations (Kosek 2006, 235–36).[14] Willie Atencio, a former member of the Northern Rio Grande National Heritage Area board, used to give tours of churches to visiting scientists interested in the region, mediating between international and local worlds, between science and religion.

Perhaps more interesting is the way in which people living outside of Los Alamos have helped to reproduce this discourse of tradition and modernity and its temporal logic. Don Usner (1995, 4), who grew up in Los Alamos and Chimayó, recalled that "it was always a wonderful trip back in time and back to the earth to come to Chimayó." A LANL employee from Truchas told Kosek (2006, 253) that Los Alamos "is the opposite of where I come from. . . . We split wood, they split atoms. We have traditional knowledge, they are nuclear scientists. We are native to the landscape, they are transplants." And Joseph Masco (2006,

166) quotes another Nuevomexicano who contrasted Truchas and Los Alamos: "One is living in the 19th century, the other in the 22nd. In Truchas, people are just trying to get by, making a living off the land. In Los Alamos, you have people who are thinking about space travel, which would be incomprehensible to the villagers in Truchas. They need to focus on putting food on the table."

All three of these speakers traditionalize northern New Mexican villages, associating them with the past and projecting Los Alamos into the future. Yet as I will show in the next chapter, none of these villages are stuck in the nineteenth century. Wage labor on a regional scale long ago superseded a land-based economy. In fact, the very journey between village and laboratory that reveals sharp contrasts between wealth and poverty is testament to the region's transformation. Ironically, then, the more villages were integrated into a capitalist, military-industrial economy the more they became symbols of tradition. Descriptions of preindustrial village life are less factual statements than part of the discursive construction of northern New Mexico.

Española has been caught somewhere between the city on the hill and the villages in the valley. It is older (and less "modern") than Los Alamos but younger (and less "traditional") than the Pueblos and Spanish colonial settlements. Two years before the establishment of Los Alamos National Laboratory the rail line that made Española a mercantile hub was abandoned, signaling an economic downgrading and impending identity crisis. As northern New Mexico transitioned from an agricultural to a tourist economy, Española's railroad origins became a liability. The valorization of Pueblo and Spanish colonial "folk" cultures by Anglo scholars, artists, and preservationists left Española marginalized in the region's cultural economy. As Santa Fe and Taos attracted increasing numbers of tourists throughout the twentieth century, Española began to fall off the map, sometimes literally.[15] The city has increasingly found itself in the economic and cultural shadow of its neighbors, as well as the butt of regional jokes (Cordova 1990; Peterson 1984; Trujillo 2009, 15–18).[16] Within this context

The Española Valley

Española began an ambitious plaza project in the late 1980s and attempted to remake its public image.

Española's Tricultural Plaza

The Española plaza project has selectively appropriated and re-made some of the valley's symbolic resources while ignoring others, advancing a cohesive discourse of tricultural coexistence. The plaza project was the brainchild of Richard Lucero, a visionary, indefatigable, and controversial mayor, whose perseverance and enthusiasm helped turn a personal dream into a civic reality. He told me that it was in 1968, during his first mayoral term, that he first came up with the idea for a plaza in Española (R. Lucero 2003). Lucero lost and reclaimed his position in the years to come, but from 1986 to 1994 and 1998 to 2006 he presided over city government, using his significant political clout to broker deals on behalf of the city.

A strong advocate of cultural conservation, Lucero envisioned the Española plaza as a center for economic development based on culture and history. It would "give our artists and crafts people a place to market their products, provide the historical preservation and recognition of our three cultures and become a very strong tourist attraction, thereby becoming the financial 'boost' we *must* have" (Plaza de Española Foundation 1992). Thanks to the support of Senator Pete Domenici (a close ally of Richard Lucero) and other members of New Mexico's congressional delegation, the project received its first federal funding in 1989 through the Economic Development Administration. The city established a nonprofit organization called the Plaza de Española Foundation to handle fund-raising efforts. Other plaza funding came from state and private sources.[17]

The plaza form itself was highly symbolic. Lucero (2003) told me that plazas represent public spaces in which people can come together, interact with one another, and build community. They symbolize cultural identity and exchange, he said: a people's identity is manifested in their plaza, where they celebrate all their important community events. As the plaza brochure noted, "In both

Pueblo Indian and Spanish communities, a centrally-located plaza has traditionally afforded citizens a place for social, cultural and commercial exchange. With this in mind, the residents of Española have set about to build such a plaza" (Plaza de Española Foundation 1995).

The plaza has not yet become the everyday center of community designers envisioned. Only a trickle of tourists and locals visit the plaza except for special events. This is partly due to the plaza's siting and historical context. It occupies an eleven-acre lot on the west side of the Rio Grande, in the city's old downtown mercantile district (near where the rail depot once stood). Two major highways converge just east of the site, making the plaza seem hemmed in by traffic. It is difficult to reach by foot and thus is not integrated with the rest of the town, whereas traditional plazas constituted the center of Indian and Spanish villages. Given Española's origins as a railroad town, its history of automobile-oriented town planning, and the fact that the plaza was created near the end of the twentieth century rather than several hundred years earlier, it is probably inevitable that the plaza would function more like an urban park than a traditional plaza. For these reasons plaza director Lou Baker (2003) conceived of the space as a downtown area rather than plaza, but the idea of a plaza remains dominant in Española.

The plaza's incompletion has also contributed to its underuse. The original site plan, designed by Santa Fe architect Bernabe Romero, was extraordinarily ambitious (see fig. 10). The city initially estimated that the entire project could cost up to thirty million dollars but was able to raise only a fraction of that. In addition to the cultural and historical centers I discuss in the next section, plaza proponents discussed building an amphitheater, library, hotel, and restaurant, as well as meeting rooms, outdoor patios, artist studios, and commercial centers. Most of these structures remain unbuilt. When I asked Richard Lucero (2003) what he hoped the plaza would be like in twenty-five years, he said he hoped it would be completed and that people would use it, "sitting in the benches and talking like they used to. People walk-

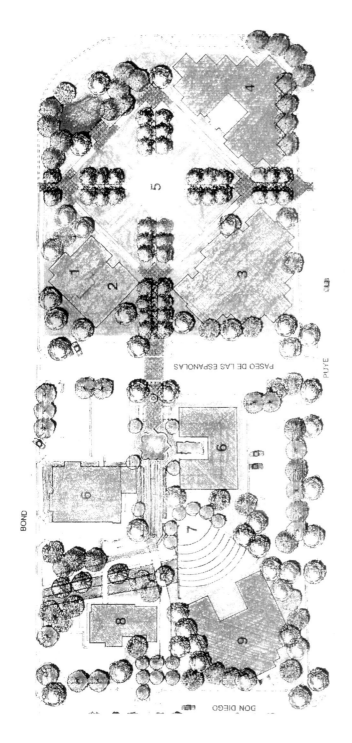

Fig. 10. Plaza de Española master plan by Bernabe Romero (detail). Major structures include (1) Misión, (2) Convento, (3) Spanish Cultural Center, (4) Native American Center, (6) commercial centers, (7) amphitheater, (8) Bond House, and (9) Commemorative Spanish Colonization Center. The fountains and waterfall stretch between the two commercial centers (the uppermost of which was the post office). Source: Plaza de Española Foundation 1992.

Fig. 11. Española plaza, showing the Convento (*far left*), Misión, and gazebo.

ing in the plaza, people going there to have a cup of coffee with their neighbors, with their friends. . . . Having their fiestas there, having family reunions there, having weddings there, having all these things, all the things that make us a people."

In 2003 the city completed a Veterans' Memorial Wall that was not part of the original plaza plan. It honors veterans from the entire Española valley and may turn out to be one of the most meaningful features of the plaza for local citizens. The completion of a gazebo at the center of the plaza in 2008 partially relieved the plaza's vast emptiness (see fig. 11).[18] In recent years exhibits in the Bond House and Misión and offices and shops in the Convento (all of which I discuss below) have brought more traffic to the plaza. And in 2010 the Northern New Mexico Regional Art Center relocated from Los Alamos to the Española plaza. The nonprofit organization has opened a gift shop and gallery in the Convento, begun offering art classes in the old post office (a building that predated the plaza and closed in 2009), and partnered with

The Española Valley

the city to support arts programming. These recent developments have increased the plaza's vitality and suggest its potential.

Triculturalism on the Plaza

The plaza project proceeded from the assumption that three "cultures" (Native American, Spanish, and Anglo) inhabit the Española valley and that they "have lived in harmony for hundreds of years" (A. Lucero and Reeves 1990, 12).[19] Maintaining sharp boundaries between these groups required emphasizing long-term cultural continuity. According to an article about the plaza project in a city newsletter (A. Lucero and Reeves 1990, 12), "The Native Americans who have lived here for centuries are still observing their culture" through art and dance. "They live with the customs and traditions of their ancestors" and "welcome us into their homes today as they did in the days of the early settlers." Similarly, "the Spanish Culture is still lived here in the Española Valley as in no other place in the nation. The customs and traditions brought with the early colonizers are practiced here today." The article singled out language, religion, and art. "The pride of the Spanish settler still remains in today's Spanish families of the Española Valley. This Spanish culture must be preserved in our beloved Española." Finally, "the Anglo Culture is still thriving in our valley" (in case anyone was concerned about its disappearance). "The Anglo came here and brought commerce and industry to our community. They established themselves here, and many families still remain. The Anglo-American has co-mingled with the Spanish and Native Americans and today observes many of the same customs and traditions of those two cultures." Note how the article figures Indians and Nuevomexicanos as tradition bearers (especially artists) whose cultures have changed little, if at all, in hundreds of years. Anglo culture (industrial capitalism) may still exist in the valley, but Anglos themselves have "co-mingled" with and adopted the cultures of Indians and Hispanos. No mention is made of Indians and Hispanos intermingling with one another or integrating into a capitalist American system. This contrast between tenacious, culturally pure Indians and Hispanos and vanishing Anglos foreshadows the plaza project's subversiveness, as I will show.

The plaza prospectus reproduced this tricultural discourse, emphasizing the place of Indians and Nuevomexicanos in the United States: "The Native American culture is the richest asset that New Mexico shares with the United States of America. The Spanish Culture of New Mexico has changed little in 400 years, in its language and customs. Therefore, it remains a rich part of American History" (Plaza de Española Foundation 1992). Both the newsletter and prospectus put Native Americans to work, welcoming strangers (including colonizers) into their homes before becoming national resources. The "therefore" in this statement also requires unpacking, since it seems to destabilize the meaning of "American." It might reflect the politics of difference: Hispanos remain different enough to warrant national recognition (just as the *Americanness* of Indians and Hispanos makes the plaza project worthy of federal funding). But if we understand "American" to refer here to the United States, asserting that a four-hundred-year-old *Spanish* culture remains a part of *American* history challenges the sovereignty of the United States as an Anglo nation-state established in 1776. If we understand "American" in its hemispheric sense, it challenges the supremacy of the United States. The plaza project initiates all of these processes, affirming and destabilizing the sovereignty of the United States at the same time.

Ground-breaking ceremonies on the plaza in 1990 rehearsed the tricultural theme and confirmed Española's national significance. Attendees included Senator Domenici, Congressman Bill Richardson (who would go on to become governor of New Mexico), Secretary of the Interior Manuel Lujan (a New Mexico native whose niece Kathy Córdova became the chair of the heritage area board), and several state legislators. The *Santa Fe New Mexican* reported that "throughout the three-hour groundbreaking ceremony, speakers stressed unity of the Hispanic, Anglo and Indian cultures that populate the Española Valley, pride in the region's 400-year-old history and the economic benefits the Plaza de Española will bring to the region." The event included a trilingual mass

Fig. 12. The Bond House.

and speeches in English, Spanish, and Tewa. One speaker insisted: "We are not a melting pot of cultures in the Española Valley, we are a rich mosaic with each culture preserved." Traditional music and a performance by a Matachines troupe heightened the festive atmosphere of this "old-fashioned community gathering" (Woods 1990). This kind of multicultural public ritual, with its obligatory set of cultural performances, carefully balanced inclusion of both Indians and Nuevomexicanos, and religiosity, has become a fine-tuned genre in northern New Mexico, perfected on the Española plaza (e.g., May 1998).

Triculturalism was to be more than just abstract rhetoric: the plaza's site plan called for individual buildings representing each of Española's three cultures. The building that was supposed to serve as "a historical museum for the preservation of the Anglo culture and the mercantile business system" (Plaza de Española Foundation 1992) already existed. Known as the Bond House, it sat on a hill overlooking the main plaza area (see fig. 12). Brothers Frank and George Bond came to Española soon after the arrival of the railroad and established a mercantile business in the early 1880s. Frank and his wife built a two-room adobe house in 1887 that grew with their family. The city bought the house in the 1950s after the death of the Bonds' son and used it as a city hall until the 1970s. By this time the house was quite large and, with its unique combination of adobe construction and Victorian features, replete with architectural interest. It was placed on New Mexico's Register of Cultural Properties in 1978 and the National Register of Historic Places in 1980.

In the 1980s a group of local history enthusiasts who called themselves the San Gabriel Historical Society (after New Mexico's first capital) developed an exhibit for the Bond House on Española's mercantile period and the Bond legacy. The city contributed some funds to operate the house as a museum, but that money had dried up by 1990. Meanwhile, the historical society, concerned about the house's deterioration, began advocating for its preservation and renovation. The society believed the preservation of the Bond House would be one way to ensure the city did not forget its history. "Española is strictly a railroad town," said one member. "There was no town here at all before that" (quoted in Navarro 1997). The Bond House was completely restored in 2000, and since then a variety of exhibits have been mounted inside of it, some but not all focusing on Española's mercantile history.[20]

Ironically, Frank Bond hardly embodied the spirit of cooperation and harmonious coexistence that the Española plaza celebrates. Savvy businessmen, the Bonds acquired large land interests and enjoyed successful careers as sheep ranchers and merchants. The Bonds became middlemen between wool sellers and buyers, strengthening the region's ties to a national market economy. They extended lines of credit to small-scale sheepherders who then became indebted and lost their flocks when markets fluctuated. "By the late 1880s, the Bond Company directly owned twenty-five thousand sheep and was handling more than two hundred thousand more indirectly each year" (Kosek 2006, 16). It took advantage of Forest Service grazing regulations at the expense of Hispanos (94), who were reduced "to the equivalent of livestock sharecroppers who bore all the risk and reaped few of the profits. The result was devastating to both the local economy and the landscape" (17; see also Deutsch 1987, 22–23). Not surprisingly, the city of Española has not incorporated this history of exploitation and economic transformation into the plaza's public narrative.

Three other buildings planned for the plaza, a Native American Center, a Spanish Cultural Center, and a Commemorative Spanish Colonization Center, have never been built. The first two would have informed visitors about Native American and Spanish colonial history, language, art, dance, food, and culture (Plaza de Española Foundation 1992). The Commemorative Spanish Colonization Center "would include museums, a research center and a cultural center. It would also be a place to hold cultural events and to provide an interpretation of the story of the Spanish colonization" (Ragan 1996b).

Two other elements of the original plaza plan were constructed during the 1990s. The first was a re-creation of the "Arches of the Alhambra" combined with a fountain and waterfall (see fig. 13). The arches commemorate Spain's defeat of the Moors and Columbus's voyage in 1492, two world-historical events that paved the way for the Spanish conquest of New Mexico. They thus symbolize European colonial dominance and a culturally and religiously purified Spain in the heart of the Española valley. However, water restrictions have frequently left the fountain and waterfall dry, diminishing the ensemble's grandeur. The second new element on the plaza, and perhaps the most intriguing building in Española, is the Misión-Convento, to which I now turn.

The Misión-Convento

The crown jewel of the Española plaza is the Misión-Convento, an impressive adobe structure completed in 1996. The right half of the building, the Misión, is a representation of San Miguel, the cruciform church Spaniards built at San Gabriel in 1598 (see fig. 14). The left half is called the Convento. During the Spanish colonial period, conventos housed friars, provided storage space, and

Fig. 13. The Arches of the Alhambra with waterfall and fountain.

Fig. 14. The Española Misión.

offered protection against hostile Indians. The Convento on the Española plaza provides office and retail space, while the Misión is a museum and special event venue.

Richard Lucero and his colleagues first suggested rebuilding the church of San Miguel on its original site, but San Juan Pueblo (now Ohkay Owingeh) rejected this proposal due to concerns about increased tourist traffic through the reservation and the appropriateness of reconstructing the church. So Lucero resolved to build a representation of the church on the new Española plaza, about five miles south of the site of San Gabriel. This relocation appropriates some of the region's most important history for the city of Española. The plaza itself virtually becomes a re-creation—or perhaps an updated version—of San Gabriel, the site of New Mexico's founding. According to plaza developers, reconstructing the church of San Miguel was important and entirely appropriate for the plaza. Several people I talked to, including Bernabe Romero (the building's architect) and Nick Salazar (the chair of the Plaza de Española Foundation), told me they believed the Misión, like the church of San Miguel, symbolized the coming together of Hispanic and Pueblo cultures and was thus an ideal anchor for the tricultural plaza.

Romero based his design on archaeological evidence. An architectural historian with the National Park Service worked with the city to extrapolate from the wall foundations Florence Hawley Ellis uncovered at the San Gabriel site. But since the foundations indicated only "shape, dimensions, orientation and door locations," all above-ground details and proportions were speculative. The Misión departs from the original church in the orientation of its facade, omission of a side door, use of concrete support beams, and the addition of windows, a convento, and an undocumented freestanding porch (Wilson 1998).

Romero and Lucero both told me that the building should be considered a "representation" of San Miguel. Romero was justifiably proud of his work on the plaza. He covered an entire table in his office with drawings and plans of the plaza and Misión-Convento when I went to meet him. He described the Misión as a conceptual design based on common sense. Lucero said the building was as accurate as they could make it, although it was probably bigger than the original. Architectural historian Chris Wilson (1998) called the Misión "a 'contemporary interpretation' inspired by that first Spanish chapel" and commended Romero's "striking" design.

The Misión quickly became more than a *representation*, though; many people refer to it as a "replica" or "reconstruction" of San Miguel. "I'd like to go out on a limb and say that, if we brought back the people who lived here 400 years ago, they wouldn't be able to tell the difference," said the vice-chairman of the Plaza de Española Foundation (quoted in Ragan 1996a).[21] So much confusion was there about the project that a few descriptions even portrayed the Misión as a *restoration* of the original church of San Miguel and the Española plaza as the site of the original San Gabriel settlement (Dejevsky 1998; Hagan 1988). Officially naming the building "La Misión de San Miguel de San Gabriel" did not clarify matters, nor did embedding a slab near its front door with the building's construction date (1996) encrypted in roman numerals: "SAN GABRIEL / MCMXCVI." By this point the Misión had become the perfect simulacrum, displacing and appropriating the originality of San Miguel. Commentators thus applied to the Misión three of the four understandings of authenticity Edward Bruner (2005, 149–50) identifies in historical sites: authenticity as a credible and convincing reproduction (Lucero and Romero's position), authenticity as historically accurate (the vice-chairman's position), and authenticity as the original. Exaggerating the Misión's historical pedigree granted Española greater historical depth and legitimated its status as the new San Gabriel. Relocating the foundational site of New Mexico's Spanish colonial history to the plaza also helped to render Española a different kind of American city, one worthy of national recognition.

Plaza promoters promised to build the Misión using both traditional materials and community labor. "Local people will come together to rebuild the chapel just as it was originally done," imagined the mayor (Hagan 1988). To kick off this project, Senator Domenici, Congressman Richardson, and other dignitaries at the plaza ground-breaking ceremony in 1990 donned overalls and helped make a few adobe bricks for the Misión-Convento (Woods 1990).[22] Lumber and adobe bricks were later donated, and volunteers helped landscape the plaza, but otherwise the construction of the Misión-Convento was little like the construction of the church of San Miguel. Bernabe Romero told me that instead of using community labor they had to hire a contractor and construction firm to erect the building due to insurance requirements (see Ragan 1996a). Rina Swentzell (2003b), an architectural historian from Santa Clara Pueblo, found the whole idea amusing: "wouldn't it have been interesting if it had been built in the original way. . . . We'll just get the San Juan kids and the women out there and get them building that place again and let's show the community what actually did happen."

Public Religion on the Plaza?

Perhaps the most significant difference between San Miguel and the Misión is that the Misión is not a church. Just as a court challenge in the 1970s led the Museum of New Mexico to classify the portal program as a living exhibit and educational program rather than an open market, a legal challenge forced the city of Española to clarify the meaning of the Misión. In 1992 Tony Scarborough, an Española lawyer and former state supreme court justice, charged that the planned Misión violated the separation of church and state enshrined in the U.S. Constitution. The American Civil Liberties Union (ACLU) agreed, suggesting that the use of public funds to build the Misión-Convento on public land raised "a glaring constitutional issue." Scarborough also objected to the celebration of a Christian mass—even a trilingual one—at the ground-breaking ceremony in 1990 (Roy 1992a).

A lawyer for the city responded, "This is not going to be a consecrated church. It's a museum. It is intended to be an exact replica of the first chapel in San Juan. . . . In the late 16th century, chapels served as a community center and played an important part in many of New Mexico's plazas" (Roy 1992a). The city subsequently made it clear that the Misión would be a museum for religious art, not a church. In a laudatory editorial, the *Albuquerque Journal* noted that "even though the mission will give visitors the feeling of standing inside a historic adobe church, the building will be used for art, not religion" ("Española Project Downtown Savior" 1996). Others found justification for the Misión in history. Nick Salazar told me that he, the mayor, and another plaza supporter went to the plaza early one morning surreptitiously to install the cross (a potential lightning rod for controversy) on top of the Misión. Bernabe Romero, the building's architect, made no apologies: the cross was historical, he said. The ACLU backed down, stating that so long as the Misión was nondenominational and no religious services were held there, they would not oppose the project. But simply calling the Misión a historical monument would not be enough, an attorney for the organization said. "We'll be looking at how they build it, what they put in it and how it is used" (Roy 1993a).

This legal battle began over the separation of government and religion, a principle the city never challenged. Although no one involved in the debate explicitly evoked the politics of recognition, governmental acknowledgment and support was precisely what was at issue, and not just at the city level. Federal funding had already reached the plaza, and state and national politicians had publicly supported the project. The Misión thus indirectly tested the limits of recognition under liberal multiculturalism: How much cultural difference (in this case, public religion) can the state tolerate? While it was possible to recognize the cultural and historical aspects of Catholicism, the religious aspects were strictly off limits. Yet excluding Catholic religion would mean cutting the heart out of Nuevomexicano culture and history, which is what politicians sought to recognize.[23]

The city was thus torn between the sixteenth and twentieth centuries, between authenticity and the law. By describing the Misión as a replica and museum, the city distinguished it from the original.[24] Arguing that churches had a secular function and that they were part of New Mexico history, on the other hand, justified the liberal recognition of churches, highlighted the similarities between the Misión and San Miguel, and helped to reclaim the Misión's authenticity as a *secular* structure. "The city probably would be criticized by the architectural and historical communities if the chapel were not included," remarked the Española lawyer, making no mention of *religious* communities (Roy 1992a). The city thus attempted to comply with the law *and* to defend the Misión's authenticity. The building's ambiguous status made this possible. Early press coverage referred to it as both a "chapel" and a "chapel museum," both a "mission" and a "mission museum."

Secularism and Subversion in the Church/Museum

In 2003 the city finally substantiated its claim that the Misión was a museum when it installed a permanent art exhibition in the interior. However, rather than clarifying the meaning of this officially secular copy of a church, this intriguing project further complicates it. Fourteen coats of arms representing the Spanish settlers who came with Oñate in 1598 now hang on the walls of the nave. But the focal point of the project is five elaborately carved wooden

Fig. 15. Reredos inside the Misión.

frames modeled after reredos, altar screens that stand at the front of churches and contain paintings of saints (see figs. 15 and 16).

The director and lead artist of the project was Clare Villa, who lives a few miles north of Española in Alcalde.[25] Villa (2003a) told me that in painting the reredos she borrowed motifs from colonial churches in northern New Mexico and used traditional colors and techniques in order to make the artwork seem familiar. She wanted visitors to get a feeling for how churches in New Mexico may have looked in the eighteenth century, how the church of San Miguel may have looked. Villa decorated the top of one reredo with Native American motifs and another with European motifs. The tallest screen (which stands twenty-six feet high) is adorned with a (speculative) painting of the church of San Miguel. An interpretive sign in front of that reredo reads: "The beautiful *Misión y Convento* located on the *Plaza de Española* is based on the design and history of the Spanish community of San Gabriel de Yunque which was originally built on what is now the San Juan Pueblo." The sign goes on to refer to the Misión as a reconstruc-

Fig. 16. A reredo with saints mounted on the wall.

tion and "magnificent reproduction [that] stands as a monumental remembrance of the founding and colonization of the first Spanish settlement in *Nuevo México* in 1598."

Unlike traditional reredos, though, the striking altar screens in the Misión frame not images of saints but eighteen paintings of historic churches in northern New Mexico and twelve paintings of scenes from New Mexico history. Sculptures of the churches' patron saints stand next to the paintings. The historical scenes depict the turning points in New Mexico history, including Spanish exploration and settlement, the Pueblo Revolt, the reconquest, trade with the United States, and statehood.

The Misión art project complicates the meaning of the building, which simultaneously complies with and subverts the constitutional separation of church and state. Clare Villa (2003b) acknowledged that the interior of the Misión "obviously bolsters people's religion, and it bolsters the Christian religion . . . because all the stuff in it is Catholic." But the reason for this is not that the city is endorsing Catholicism. "The museum is highly leaning towards the Catholic religion, but it's leaning that way in a historic way because historically you can't change history," Villa explained to me. "Those are the folks that came in. And so those are the churches they built." The project not only historicizes religion but also turns it into an object of cultural interest. The art and ritual of New Mexico's "folk" Catholicism quickly attract anthropological interest. Villa (2003a) noted that although everything in the Misión is religious, it is *ethnically* religious, implying that it is worthy of public interpretation and governmental recognition.

However, if the Misión secularizes religion, it simultaneously sacralizes history and culture by placing paintings of churches and historical scenes within a religious context. Framed by the reredos in the church/museum, the paintings become objects of veneration. I asked Villa if the art project turns the Misión into a shrine to local churches. "Yeah, definitely," she answered. "That's a good way to put it" (Villa 2003b). The Española Misión thus complies with the constitutional separation of church and state by emphasizing the cultural and historical (rather than religious) significance of churches, but then it reincorporates history and culture into a religious framework, reclaiming the sacredness of churches and advancing an implicitly Christian historiography of New Mexico.[26] The Misión project destabilizes the concept of "heritage" as an innocuous and apolitical object suitable for public recognition by challenging the conceptual distinctions and constitutional principles upon which cultural recognition relies.

The Misión-Convento may be not only a subversive heritage site but also an *anti*-heritage site. Sitting in Richard Lucero's Country Farm Supply office, where he did most of his business as mayor, I asked him to describe the Misión. "It's not a church and it's not a museum," he said flatly. "What it really is is a compass." The Misión is a place where visitors can learn something about New Mexico history before venturing into the countryside to see it in person. It "wasn't supposed to be a destination point" itself (Lucero 2003). The Native American Center planned for the plaza was also supposed to be a compass, guiding visitors to the surrounding Pueblos (Plaza de Española Foundation 1992). This compass metaphor suggests a centrifugal force at play on the plaza, where centripetal forces generally dominate. The plaza draws the region's Indian and Spanish colonial heritage to its center. Yet redirecting tourists outward affirms the reciprocal relationship between city and region, legitimizing Española's claim to be "the heart of northern New Mexico" (Española Valley Chamber of Commerce 2009). The Misión is less self-referential than the Palace of the Governors. Despite its status as a "replica" of San Miguel, it diverts attention away from itself and shirks the status of a heritage attraction.[27]

Notes from the Field

MARCH 17, 2003

Bus tour of the Northern Rio Grande National Heritage Area

The National Park Service held a workshop in Santa Fe on collaborative conservation that drew participants from all over the country. Heritage areas received a lot of attention, and Ernest Ortega organized a bus tour of the NRGNHA.

Our first stop was San Gabriel de Yunque Owingeh, New Mexico's first Spanish capital. Herman Agoyo, a former governor of San Juan Pueblo, talked about the history of San Gabriel, the excavation of the church there, and his hopes to build a heritage center to interpret the site. He bent over and picked up a potsherd that Bob Powers, an NPS archaeologist, dated on the spot to the 1200s or 1300s. Ernest told the group that we were next going to Española, "where a replica of the San Gabriel plaza is being reconstructed—or constructed." On the plaza, Samuel Delgado talked about Española's history, the Misión, and the veterans' memorial. The director of another heritage area said he was glad to see the veterans' wall because heritage areas are about living people today, not about the past. Our third stop was the church at Santa Cruz, where Willie Atencio talked to the group about architectural preservation and the artwork inside the church. He repeated what I had heard him say before: "This is a living church, not a museum."

Finally, we stopped at the Santuario de Chimayó. Father Roca, a well-known Franciscan priest in his eighties, charmed the group with his sense of humor, stories, and deep faith.

The four tour guides brought the sites to life. Yet no one commented on the divergent manifestations of heritage evident as we moved from an empty field where a church once stood to a reconstruction of that church that is not a church but a museum to two churches that *are* churches, not museums, but that have museum qualities.

New Mexico's natural beauty left the final impression on the tour. As we drove back from Chimayó, the storm clouds broke and the setting sun spectacularly illuminated the high desert landscape.

The Plaza and Its Discontents

Not everyone in Española supported the plaza project. Some critics, including several city councilors, thought the project was a poor use of limited resources.[28] One resident wondered why tourists would come see a plaza in Española when they could see plazas in Santa Fe and Taos. She believed the city should invest its money instead in a project that would more directly benefit Española's "little people," such as bringing a Wal-Mart or other discount store to town (Roy 1992b). A Super Wal-Mart did open in Española in 1999. Rampant gentrification in Santa Fe and Taos and the fate of their plazas also made many Españolans uneasy. Orlando Romero (1990) warned the city about the negative impacts of tourism. Española had been able to maintain its integrity while Santa Fe was inundated with change, he wrote. If the city followed Santa Fe's lead it "could be plunging into an abyss from which it may never be able to extricate itself." Better to be like Pecos and other New Mexico towns that had declared, "We don't want to become another Santa Fe!"[29]

Some critics questioned the city's decision to tear down several buildings, one of which dated to the nineteenth century, in order to make way for its new plaza. "What is the difference between a preservationist and a demolitionist in Española?" one editorialist asked. "The City of Española recently demolished the People's Department Store to make way for the construction of a phony, ersatz, imitation, never-before-existed, tourist-trapping, gee I-wish-we-had-one-of-those 'Historic Plaza Project!' The People's Department Store was the best example of American mercantile era architecture in Española!" (McCalmont 1990). Part of the People's building was a vestige of Española's first mercantile store, established in the 1880s by the Bond family (see also "History Ignored?" 1999). Bernabe Romero, the architect who designed the plaza and the Misión-Convento, told me that the mercantile buildings were in poor condition and architecturally unremarkable. Richard Lucero (2003) said they were in ruins and that the decision to tear them down was not a hard one.[30]

Whether or not more buildings on the plaza were worth saving, preserving and interpreting the city's mercantile past has been an uphill battle. Española's original main street (Paseo de Oñate), which runs into the plaza on its east side, provides an apt example. In 1993 the Española Main Street program, based on a National Trust for Historic Preservation model, began operations. Its goal was "to redevelop the historic downtown area of Española as the commercial hub of northern New Mexico" in order to rekindle a sense of community. This redevelopment would produce "an attractive combination of restored historic properties and complementary new building and public spaces where people from throughout rural northern New Mexico could meet and gather," work and shop (Española MainStreet n.d.).

During the 1990s, the Main Street program and plaza project both sought to develop spaces that would bring people together, invigorate the local economy, and promote regional history. They both looked to the past for inspiration, but while the former celebrated Española's mercantile origins, the latter reimagined Española as a city founded before American colonization. Juxtaposing two different models of town planning, these contemporary projects enjoyed unequal success. The Main Street program has never made much progress, and today numerous boarded-up buildings and vacant lots line Paseo de Oñate. In contrast, the plaza project kicked off with great fanfare and received national attention, although inadequate funding has also impeded its development. Creating a new tricultural city center (indeed, *re*-creating the site of New Mexico's founding) proved more exciting than revitalizing an outmoded downtown district, hardly a unique undertaking.

A Twist on the Politics of Visibility

With the plaza project, Española has invested more in drawing the region's Spanish colonial heritage to its center than in commemorating its own railroad history. Plans to display a train engine or create a railroad museum on the plaza have never materialized. The city has gained national recognition by reinventing itself as a site of difference within the United States. In some ways, Española has followed in the footsteps of Santa Fe, which has marketed itself as the "City Different" since the early 1900s. Both cities have cultivated exotic public images by at least partially erasing the imprint of Anglo-Americans. They have also combined unabashed fabrication with claims of historical authenticity.[31] Española's ability to pull this off is particularly impressive given its relatively recent origins. When I asked Bernabe Romero about the logic of tearing down old buildings to create a plaza commemorating history, he sympathized with preservationism but cited Santa Fe's invented self-image, rigid historic design ordinance, and passion for fake adobe architecture. It's our turn to create history, he stated.

When Española's turn came around, though, its engagement with the politics of visibility was potentially subversive. In chapter 1, I argued that rendering twentieth-century Anglos invisible at the Palace of the Governors contributed to the construction of a normative (Anglo) American modernity in New Mexico. In Española, where 84 percent of the residents identified themselves as Hispanic in the 1990 and 2000 censuses, the plaza project basically reflects a Nuevomexicano perspective that does not normalize Anglo-Americans.[32] It makes sense that these residents might want to see some physical manifestation of their heritage at the

The Española Valley

(heretofore missing) symbolic center of their city. Indeed, to the extent that it downplays the city's railroad history and challenges liberal norms regarding religion, the plaza project could be read as a reassertion of Indian and Hispano dominance in northern New Mexico. True, it has always been fairly apolitical, promoting an innocuous discourse of tricultural harmony. American colonization is not openly critiqued on the plaza, nor are Anglos entirely displaced from it. However, "subordinated populations may focus on cultural preservation as a means of obliquely addressing more deeply political themes" (Horton 2010, 91; see also Nieto-Phillips 2004, 175–76). In other words, the absence of explicit political critique does not necessarily indicate acquiescence.

Still, it is important not to overstate the plaza project's subversiveness. It poses little threat to existing power relations in the Española valley. So harmless did it appear in 1991 that the director of Los Alamos National Laboratory wrote a congratulatory letter to Nick Salazar, the president of the Plaza de Española Foundation, "to wholeheartedly endorse your efforts to build a Plaza in Española" and to offer the laboratory's support in its development (Plaza de Española Foundation 1992). Perhaps most significantly, the plaza project has reproduced a hegemonic discourse about race, class, and identity that was itself a product of American colonization. Like the "culture as cure" model of substance abuse prevention, the celebration of "Spanish" and "Native American" cultures on the plaza operates within, not outside of, a colonial context.

Commemorating Colonization

One reason efforts to promote Española's railroad past never gained much ground on the plaza project was timing: interest in New Mexico's Hispanic heritage surged in the 1990s. Two anniversaries drew attention to and produced an explosion of discourse about Spanish colonization: 1992 marked the five hundredth anniversary of Columbus's arrival in the New World, and 1998 was the four hundredth anniversary of Juan de Oñate's colonization of New Mexico. The Española plaza project broke ground with its sights set on the first anniversary and then geared up again for the second. A growing sense of displacement and disenfranchisement among Nuevomexicanos also fueled a Hispanic revival. In order to deal with Anglo-American dominance, Hispanos pursued two strategies: identifying with their ancestors the colonizers (which led to a revitalization of Spanish American identity) and identifying themselves as the colonized (which led to a discourse of Nuevomexicano indigeneity). If reveling in the glorious past was psychologically soothing, highlighting present-day subjugation and demanding recognition were politically productive.

Spanish American identity first coalesced around the turn of the twentieth century after Anglos began settling in New Mexico. Finding themselves demoted in the new colonial hierarchy, elite Nuevomexicanos began distinguishing themselves from "Mexicans," whom Anglos considered mongrels unfit for self-government (P. Mitchell 2005; Montgomery 2002; Nieto-Phillips 2004). This strategy reasserted racial purity and Native American inferiority (Archuleta 2007; Gómez 2007).[33] Anglos looking for ways to govern a region with a Hispanic majority, disrupt alliances between Hispanics and Indians, and secure statehood supported Nuevomexicanos' claims to Spanishness in "a rhetorical compromise" (Gómez 2005, 24–38; Montgomery 2002, 11). Laura Gómez (2005, 13) shows that Nuevomexicanos were "off-white" in the American racial system. Their claims to whiteness "functioned simultaneously to challenge white supremacy (with the insistence of the expansion of the white category to include Mexicans under certain social conditions) and to buttress white supremacy (with Mexicans themselves functioning as a wedge racial group that reproduced the subordination of Pueblo Indians, Blacks, and nomadic Indians)."[34]

Sarah Horton (2002, 59) argues that if "Spanish American identity was formed in response to the passing of New Mexico to Anglo control," its intensification in the 1990s "may be read as a response to an ever-progressing Hispanic dispossession." As one *New York Times* article explained, Hispanics clung to the

The Española Valley

Spanish colonial past "out of insecurities over losing their language, culture and political and demographic dominance." Anglos had overtaken Hispanics in population size. "Spanish no longer echoes around Santa Fe as the 10th generation of Spanish descendants has assimilated to the point of losing its ancestral language" (Brooke 1998). Like the Santa Fe fiesta (Horton 2010), the Oñate quadricentennial entailed "a reinvigoration of Spanish-ness that aimed to collapse the gap between the conquistador past and a less glorious present" (Horton 2002, 49), repressing the reality of subjugation (Trujillo 2009, 46). As in the early twentieth century, identification with Spanish colonizers in the 1990s sometimes involved claims to whiteness and pure European descent (Gonzales 2007, 229; Rodríguez 2001, 205–6). As Samuel Delgado put it, "We may not have been born in Spain, but Spain was born in us" (quoted in McGuire 2000). In both time periods, resistance to Anglo-American hegemony through the reassertion of Spanish identity both challenged and reproduced Anglo racial ideologies.

Although the articulation of Spanish American identity in the 1990s had much in common with its articulation in the early 1900s, by the end of the century a sense of victimization and growing concerns about culture loss introduced a new dynamic to regional identity politics. Nuevomexicanos were also able to express their grievances, as an endangered minority, in terms of recognition.

In debates over recognition, Hispanos identified as victims of Anglo-American colonization. Activists critiqued Anglocentric histories of New Mexico that either vilified or completely ignored Hispanics (e.g., Horton 2002, 51; Ortega 2003; López 1998a). The New Mexican Hispanic Culture Preservation League, founded in 1998 in Albuquerque by Millie Santillanes, sought "to Preserve the heritage, Spanish language and the history of Hispanic New Mexico, to promote the education and understanding of the contributions of Hispanics to the development of New Mexico and the nation, to protect the history of the New Mexican Hispanic heritage and culture." Its mission statement emphasizes restoring "the TRUTH and PRIDE of our New Mexican Hispanic

Culture" (NMHCPL 2010). Originally called the Spanish American Anti-Defamation League, the organization "saw itself as countering a hegemonic disregard for the history of Spanish culture and achievements in the public schools and in the media, which members argued caused poor self-esteem and self-hatred among Hispanos" (Horton 2002, 51).

This link between public image and psychological well-being relates directly to the politics of recognition. A few years before New Mexico's quadricentennial, Canadian philosopher Charles Taylor (1994, 25–26) argued that "a person or group of people can suffer real damage, real distortion, if the people or society around them mirror back to them a confining or demeaning or contemptible picture of themselves. Nonrecognition or misrecognition can inflict harm, can be a form of oppression, imprisoning someone in a false, distorted, and reduced mode of being." As examples, Taylor cited women, blacks, and colonized people, whose internalized inferiority prevents them from achieving their full potential in society. "Due recognition," he maintained, "is not just a courtesy we owe people. It is a vital human need."

In his sensitive portrait of the Española valley, Douglas Kent Hall (1995, 47) documents the outward and inward violence resulting from nonrecognition. "One tragic aspect of life in northern New Mexico is the displaced and sadly wasted passions of many of its young men. In their veins still runs a trickle of blood from the conquistadors. Like their ancestors they hunger for recognition; they want to be noticed, to have something that will affirm their worth." In 1995, Hall found that "the world that might once have acknowledged that heritage has faded. So they hang out; they fight; they drink; they shoot up; they fall into useless routines. They run afoul of the law. They die in the streets. They crash and burn."

Yet recognition has its own problems. Like Taylor, Spanish American activists in the 1990s drew on both essentialist and constructivist understandings of identity to explain the importance of recognition. Millie Santillanes lamented the fact that "our own kids want to be *mestizos*, . . . to claim their Indian ancestry over their Spanish ancestry." Young people go to college and learn "horrid things about the Spanish. . . . That happened to my eldest daughter, when she went to the university, all of a sudden she wanted to be a Chicana. She says, 'Look at me, look at my skin color. I'm not Spanish'" (quoted in Horton 2002, 52; cf. Trujillo 2009, 53). These comments reveal both the enduring fantasy of racial purity and the impact of the Chicano movement in New Mexico. Santillanes implied that her daughter was *not* mixed but *wanted* to be. More fundamentally, they reveal the belief that people *really are* one thing (the essentialist view of identity) but without proper recognition they can become something *else* (the constructivist view).

This contradictory understanding of identity, which runs through both liberal theories of recognition and lived experience, was not the only impediment to the successful recognition of Spanish Americans in New Mexico. Even if Hispanos could be recognized for who they *really* were, they still had to face their own status as colonizers. In fact, the more Spanish they appeared, the less indigenous they seemed. The two strategies they employed for dealing with Anglo dominance (identifying as both the colonizers and the colonized) thus worked at cross-purposes. Their predicament was a contemporary manifestation of what John Bodine (1968) called the "tri-ethnic trap." Even more significant was the fact that Native Americans were also demanding recognition in the 1990s. Commemorating Columbus, Oñate, and the contribution of Hispanics to American history offended many Indians, who responded by vilifying the conquistadores and celebrating their own cultural survival (e.g., Reyna 1992). This, however, left many Hispanics feeling victimized and misunderstood. More than a debate about the past, the Oñate quadricentennial became part of "ethnosymbolic warfare" in present-day New Mexico (Gonzales 2007, 219), and the combatants took the issues personally. Recognition and injury were closely linked in this debate, and properly recognizing everyone seemed impossible.[35]

Notes from the Field

APRIL 24, 2003

Northern Rio Grande National Heritage Area board meeting, the
Bond House, Española

In a discussion about recruiting new board members, one particular name was controversial. Sam Delgado said he was not comfortable with that person and suggested an alternative. Kathy Córdova noted that the alternative lived in Albuquerque, which is outside the heritage area, but Sam stated that he was originally from a village within the heritage area. José Villa asked Sam why he didn't like the first person. "Well, personally I don't like the way he promotes our history. It's as he learned it at the University of New Mexico and it's not like what we believe it to be. It's just like, I look at him like a *turista* [tourist]." Sam stated that the Hispanic Culture Preservation League felt the same way. José asked if this person was Hispanic.

> SD: Es Chicano. Es Chicano. [He's Chicano.]
> JV: Well that's good.
> SD: Es Chicano.
> JV: That's a big plus.
> SD: No es Nuevomexicano. [He's not Nuevomexicano.] He's a Chicano . . .
> JV: That's what I am . . .
> SD: . . . from Colorado.
> JV: . . . so be careful. [laughs]

Sam reiterated his concern about how New Mexico history is taught at the university level. What counts more, he asked, being a resident or having one's heart in New Mexico?

The discussion moved on, and the board began planning its next meeting. José remarked that they might need more time to meet "if we start talking about whether northern New Mexico Hispanics are more qualified than others." People laughed and began joking. Michael Garcia said, "Well, we're all northern New Mexico Hispanics, so can we vote now? We don't have to discuss it [at the next meeting]." More laughter, but José stated that he was not a northern New Mexico Hispanic. "According to [Sam], I'm unqualified because I'm not from here, and so I don't have a *corazón* [heart]. I'm a Mexican because my father came from Mexico. I'm Indian because my father's an Indian." Sam protested: he was in no way opposed to Chicanos, but he himself did not want to be classified as one. Chicanos and Nuevomexicanos were different groups with different experiences, he explained. José emphasized his respect for Nuevomexicanos, and the conversation again moved on to another topic.

Later in the meeting, though, José brought up Chicanos again, passionately recounting his involvement in the Chicano movement in California. Sam worked in California for more than thirty years and differentiated between people like José who claimed Chicano identity for themselves and people like himself who were labeled Chicano against their will. At this point Michael jumped back into the conversation. He recalled going from Peñasco to the University of New Mexico in Albuquerque. "You know, when I left here, went to UNM, I was Spanish American, that's what I was always taught." He began attending meetings and before long was identifying as Chicano. "And then after awhile I come back home and I thought there was something wrong with being Spanish American. . . . When I went to UNM, it was a way of organizing the different groups with one name that we gave ourselves. It was okay to be Chicano because that's the name that we gave ourselves." Despite this personal testimony about fluid identities, the debate went on for several more minutes and ended tensely.

A National Park Service Study

In 1988 Congress passed the Spanish Colonization Commemorative Act (P.L. 100-559), which authorized the secretary of the interior to study Spanish colonialism in New Mexico and make recommendations regarding resource preservation, interpretation, and the establishment of visitor centers. National Park Service staff in Santa Fe and Denver carried out the study and published an eighty-two-page report in 1991 titled "Alternative Concepts for Commemorating Spanish Colonization." The report treated Spanish colonization sympathetically, not surprising given Congress's request. Scholars involved in the project "cautioned the team about past mistakes that have resulted in the perpetuation of stereotypes, myths, and misconceptions about this period of American history" (NPS 1991, 14). One "misconception" was probably the Spanish "black legend," the idea that Spanish conquistadores brutally mistreated Native Americans (for a discussion of the black legend by one member of the study team, see Sánchez 1990).

With a linear historical overview that began with the arrival of Spaniards, the report privileged a Western view of New Mexico's past. It addressed Pueblo reactions and resistance to European conquest but interpreted the Pueblo Revolt of 1680—one of the most important indigenous uprisings in North American history—mostly in terms of its effects on the second phase of Spanish colonialism (NPS 1991, 10, 16). The report also asserted that Spanish colonial practices were less destructive than English ones: "Pueblo Indian cultures have persisted despite waves of acculturation by Spain, Mexico, and the United States," and "in many cases their heritage survives largely intact" (12). These claims oversimplify complex encounters and omit Pueblo perspectives on Spanish colonization.

Nevertheless, the report's authors aimed for neutrality. They assumed that it was possible to interpret "the complete story of Spanish colonization" (NPS 1991, iv), as if there was only *one*, and hoped "to improve the accuracy and objectivity with which the story is told" (43). The authors even imagined an objective stance toward conquest: "Conquest of one group by another, whether ultimately perceived as positive or negative, has occurred repeatedly throughout history and throughout the world. The Spanish conquest of New Mexico was no exception" (14–15). This nonstatement neutralized Spanish conquest through abstraction and implied that it may one day be possible to reach consensus and judge Spanish colonization once and for all. This ultimate moment seems unlikely ever to arrive in New Mexico, where Hispanics and Native Americans (among others) have fundamentally opposed views of European colonization. Although neutrality may be impossible, the ideal of objectivity defused and displaced political controversy.

Another depoliticizing dimension of the report was its focus on physical manifestations of Spanish colonialism. The report inventoried historical and archaeological sites in New Mexico. This made sense for an agency primarily concerned with managing places, but it effectively concretized and contained Spanish colonization, deflecting attention away from its enduring social and political effects.[36]

Addressing the period between 1540 (Coronado's expedition) and 1821 (Mexican independence), the "Alternative Concepts" report could almost have ignored New Mexico's *second* colonization altogether. However, if not for American acquisition the U.S. government would have had no reason to study and commemorate Spanish colonialism in New Mexico. The first task was therefore to reclaim New Mexico and its past for the United States: "Spanish colonization in New Mexico is not foreign history but rather an integral part of United States history" (14). Glossing over the political and military circumstances of American colonization, the report emphasized cultural exchange.[37] It stressed Anglos' superficial influence in the Southwest and the persistence of a distinctive Hispanic culture. Many southwestern families still "maintain Hispanic lifeways, traditions, kinship patterns, [and] settlement and land-use patterns . . . , and even among Anglo families, innumerable Spanish words are used in everyday speech." Downplaying Americanization and elevating Hispanic influence symbolically reversed—and sanitized—the colonial process. This same procedure was evident on the Española plaza.

Yet the Park Service report was also subversive, directly challenging Anglocentric American nationalism. "American culture derives from both an English and a Spanish colonial heritage," the authors stated. "The Spanish colonies were a major contributor to American culture, and this study seeks to recognize that contribution" (NPS 1991, 12–13). Recognition here thus involves *political* incorporation and the affirmation of *cultural* distinctiveness. The report simultaneously confirmed the political dominance of the United States and destabilized a hegemonic understanding of American culture.

The final part of this report described seven combinable commemorative strategies: conducting more research, improving interpretation, developing a commemorative center, interpreting a living history scene, identifying tour routes, establishing new units of the national park system, and improving assistance to local sites (NPS 1991, 43–65).[38] All of these were consistent with the establishment of a national heritage area, and work on the Northern Rio Grande National Heritage Area began in the late 1990s. The "Alternative Concepts" report served as the feasibility study for the heritage area, and the Northern Rio Grande National Heritage Area Act of 2006 cited its findings. But the heritage area was a broader project. Between the beginning and end of the 1990s the Park Service shifted its commemorative focus from Spanish colonization to the *coexistence* of Indians and Hispanics. The reasons for this will soon become clear.

Convivencia *on the Plaza*

The "Alternative Concepts" report cited the Española plaza as an example of projects commemorating Spanish colonization (NPS 1991, 50–51). Two years earlier the Columbus Quincentenary Commission, established by Congress, also endorsed the plaza project, and organizers began referring to the plaza as the "New Mexico Quincentenary Commemorative Plaza."[39] Plaza promoters proudly advertised this national recognition (Plaza de Española Foundation 1995).

Yet the plaza project emphasized the Española valley's tricultural heritage more than Spanish colonization. Mayor Lucero (2003) told me that the building originally called the Commemorative Spanish Colonization Center (which remains unbuilt) should be renamed the "Blending of Cultures Center," because "colonization" did not accurately describe the relationship between Spaniards and Indians. Instead of colonization, which implied destruction and enculturation, he preferred *convivencia*, or living together and sharing. Had the Spanish truly colonized the Pueblos, he reasoned, the Indians would have been wiped out, not still practicing their native religion.

These two approaches to Spanish colonialism (commemorating colonization versus celebrating coexistence) have also found expression in the Española fiesta, which began in the 1930s. Whereas the Santa Fe fiesta commemorates Diego de Vargas's "peaceful" reconquest of New Mexico, Española's fiesta honors Juan de Oñate. The "Caballeros de Oñate," men impersonating Oñate and his military party, commemorate the Spanish settlement of New Mexico and promote Hispanic-Christian culture. Some fiesta promoters, however, have advocated a softer approach. In 1986 Lucero explained that "Fiesta is also a time to celebrate the tri-cultures that every day work together on unity. And it's a time for forgiveness. We can't go to the Indian communities and try to make up for what the early Spaniards did to them. But we can work for harmony and peace now" (quoted in Shockley 1986). "Convivencia" was the theme of the 1991 fiesta's grand parade (Velasquez 1991). And in 2001 a group of teenagers took over the Española fiesta, stripped Oñate of his sword and armor, and honored the valley's mestizo population, changes Lucero applauded (Sharpe 2001; Stone 2001).[40] Triculturalism has always prevailed on the plaza over colonial triumphalism, and for this reason the plaza has avoided some of the intense controversy surrounding Oñate.

The Last Conquistador

As the four hundredth anniversary of Spanish colonization approached, it became increasingly difficult for New Mexicans to avoid Oñate. Some considered Oñate a hero and others a villain. The conquistador's most infamous act followed the murder of his nephew and a dozen other Spaniards by the residents of Acoma Pueblo in 1598. In order to demonstrate the might of Spain and squelch the rebellion, Oñate sent troops from San Gabriel to punish the Acomas. The Spanish massacred hundreds of Indians atop Acoma Mesa and imprisoned and tried hundreds more. Oñate demanded that all the children be handed over for a Christian upbringing, sentenced all the adults to twenty years of servitude, and decreed that all the men would have one foot chopped off (Simmons 1991, 132–46). Oñate was subsequently recalled to Mexico City and convicted of cruelty toward the Indians. He was banished from New Mexico but eventually cleared of all charges.

New Mexicans continue to debate the details, context, and significance of the Acoma affair (including whether Oñate's amputation orders were actually carried out). Many remember the sixteenth century as if it were yesterday. I once rode from Española to a meeting in Taos with two members of the heritage area board, Samuel Delgado (who proudly identifies himself as a Spanish American) and José Villa (who is equally proud of his mixed Spanish and Indian ancestry). The two of them got into a pointed discussion about how many Indians' feet Oñate chopped off (most records say twenty-four) and the reliability of oral versus written history. Delgado, who coordinated Española's quadricentennial (or *cuarto centenario*) celebration in 1998, never misses an opportunity to defend Oñate's reputation and the honor of Spanish colonial heritage. At the time of the quadricentennial, he wrote a letter to the editor of the *Rio Grande Sun* in which he lamented "the negative forces trying to create negative feelings amongst Hispanics and our pueblo Indian brothers and sisters." Delgado (1998) noted several positive dimensions of the colonial relationship between the Spanish and the Indians and concluded that the Spanish black legend "still exists and is pushing stronger than ever to separate us from our rich 400-year heritage. We have co-existed for 400 years—Let us commemorate the positive contributions by both cultures and the wisdom we have gained from the negative."

Celebrating the legacy of Spanish colonization proved to be too controversial with Oñate at the center of attention, however.

Fig. 17. *The Last Conquistador* by Reynaldo Rivera at the Oñate Monument and Visitors Center, Alcalde.

Quadricentennial commemorations produced tensions statewide, erupting dramatically in the Española valley. The Oñate Monument and Visitors Center, built with county, state, and federal funds, opened in 1994 a few miles up the road from Española in Alcalde, just north of Ohkay Owingeh.[41] Its main attraction is an outdoor statue of Juan de Oñate sculpted by Reynaldo "Sonny" Rivera of Albuquerque and completed for the quincentennial (see fig. 17). The twelve-foot-high bronze statue, titled *The Last Conquistador*, depicts a heroic Oñate mounted on a larger-than-life horse (Loewen 1999, 119; Sharpe 1992; Stone 2003). Chris Wilson (1997, 318) remarks that "the monument shows no apparent signs of regret nor any desire for contemporary reconciliation. To place this glorification of the conquistador who so brutally suppressed the Acoma uprising of 1599 in the Española Valley north of Santa Fe, where six thousand Tewa Pueblo Indians live today, displays a monumental insensitivity" (cf. Simmons 2003).

The center and monument were controversial from the start. In 1991 vandals sawed down the billboard announcing the new monument (Sharpe 1991). Then in January 1998, just as the state was gearing up for its quadricentennial, protesters sawed off the statue's right foot at the ankle.[42] An anonymous group of "Native Americans and native New Mexicans" acting "on behalf of our brothers and sisters of Acoma pueblo" claimed responsibility for the amputation in a letter to local media outlets. According to the note, Oñate's atrocities at Acoma had left enduring scars. "We see no glory in celebrating Onate's fourth centennial, and we do not want our faces rubbed in it. If you must speak of his expedition, speak the truth in all its entirety" (Diaz 1998; "Group: We Have Oñate's Foot" 1998). An anonymous letter to the *Santa Fe Reporter* described the amputation as a demand for counter-recognition: "New Mexico was poised for a grand celebration of the Cuartocentenario and we could not let that happen without voicing our existence. Outside of 'Indian art' and 'gaming,' we have become an invisible people, even to ourselves. Our Hispanic brothers have forgotten on whose land they dwell." Colonizers had disrupted indigenous lifeways and imposed their own beliefs to such an extent that "many of our people have forgotten how to live. Our actions were to redirect the thinking of those who have forgotten us" ("Proud Actions" 1998).

Some people doubted the protesters were actually Indians or Hispanos and speculated they may even have been from out of state (e.g., Diaz 1998). Juan Estevan Arellano, the director of the Oñate Center, suspected the culprits may have been environmental extremists opposed to the center's work on land grants and water rights. "There's no animosity between Hispanos and Native

Americans around here, we're brothers," he remarked. "Most of the people around here are mestizo, they've got Indian blood. I'm mestizo myself" (quoted in Lentz 1998). Arellano observed that Anglos were most vocal in opposing Oñate. "What we are seeing now is that the Anglos are trying to revive the Black Legend. . . . They are trying to create a schism between Native Americans and the Indo-Hispanos, so they can exploit it" (López 1998a). The vandals were never identified and the severed foot was never found, so the incident remains a mystery.[43] One thing is for certain: blaming outsiders for the amputation protected the myth of regional multicultural harmony, in which Hispanos were particularly invested.

After the amputation the statue's foot was quickly recast and reattached, costing $10,000 (the entire statue was valued at $108,000) (Diaz 1998; Hummels 1998). "In a sense, so long as the statue is complete, the story it tells is incomplete," argues James Loewen. "The statue honors Oñate, but honoring Oñate this way tells only one side of what he did" (Loewen 1999, 121; cf. Simmons 2003).[44] Ironically, Oñate became better known *after* the well-publicized amputation.

Incommensurable Understandings of the Past

The cuarto centenario revealed conflicting interpretations of New Mexico history and radically different ways of relating to the past that complicated the politics of recognition. In El Paso, Albuquerque, Santa Fe, and the Española valley, debates over Oñate were heated and drawn out. For many Hispanos, Oñate was a courageous leader and founding father. Many regretted his cruelty (which they believed was outweighed by his accomplishments and benevolent intentions—or matched by Indian brutality) but also dismissed Indian grievances. Some argued that Native American communities were not entirely peaceful before the conquest, so it was unfair to claim that the Spanish had destroyed utopian societies (Gonzales 2007, 227). "I think he was a hell of a man," said Reynaldo Rivera, the statue's artist (quoted in Hummels 1998). For many Indians, on the other hand, Oñate inflicted immeasurable harm on Pueblo communities. As one academic put it, "it's like asking the Jewish people to celebrate Hitler" (Baldauf 1998). A former governor of Sandia Pueblo actually compared Oñate to Hitler, describing him as a ruthless and bloodthirsty killer (Hummels 1998; see also Rolwing 1998).

The polarized debate resulted in a "war of statues" (Geyer 1998) and competing demands for recognition. In 1996 the San Juan Pueblo tribal council introduced a proposal to create a statue of Po'pay, the San Juan man who led the 1680 Pueblo Revolt, to be New Mexico's second and final contribution to the National Statuary Hall in the U.S. Capitol in Washington. Po'pay was the antithesis of Oñate and was almost as divisive. While many Pueblo people revered him as a freedom fighter, Hispanos decried his brutality toward priests and settlers. Despite protests, the state legislature approved the proposal, and a marble statue by Cliff Fragua of Jemez Pueblo was installed in 2005 (see Archuleta 2007; Delgado 2004; Sando and Agoyo 2005).

Some moderates advocated a more nuanced interpretation of Oñate's character and deeds (see T. Chávez 1998; López 1998b; Trujillo 2005, 136). Commentators also challenged the essentialized racial categories that the cuarto centenario reinvigorated (e.g., "Proud Actions" 1998). Juan Estevan Arellano described the Oñate Center as an "Indo-Hispano cultural center" and drew attention to the long history of racial mixing in New Mexico (López 1998a), which blurred racial boundaries and helped to establish Hispanic indigeneity (see Trujillo 2009, 47–48). Jake Kosek (2006, 58) argues that the notion of mestizaje disrupts the myth of triculturalism but notes that "these claims of mixed blood are made carefully." Racial boundaries "are still strongly reinforced and strictly policed, even by those who claim *mestizo* origins." Claims to indigeneity are especially contentious given their currency in struggles over land and water. In Albuquerque and elsewhere, constituencies on both sides of the debate marginalized Chicanos attempting to mediate between Indians and Nuevomexicanos (Gonzales 2007, 227–29). In general, reconciliation seemed impossible as the polarized debate both reflected and reinforced New Mexico's oppositional ethno-racial structure.

Sometimes people fought over the correct view of a single shared history. The group claiming to have cut off the statue's foot in Alcalde wrote: "This land was ours before the Conquistadors, Mexicans or Anglos came here. We know the history of this place before their time, and we have not forgotten it since their arrival" ("Group: We Have Oñate's Foot" 1998). In Española, Mayor Lucero (2003) told me that dealing with Oñate was unavoidable. "You can't change history," he said. "We don't change it to please ourselves." Lou Baker (2003), the former director of the Española plaza, also thought it was wrong to avoid the violent history of Spanish colonization "because history is history, right, wrong, or indifferent. . . . We can't change history because we want to be politically correct."[45] Yet the Española plaza project reinvents the city's history, and its proponents have demonstrated savvy and sensitivity in dealing with controversial issues.[46]

Other times, people abandoned the idea that there was one single New Mexican history and argued instead about *multiple* histories. In Albuquerque, after it became clear that no one sculpture or monument (nor the exclusion of a monument altogether) would satisfy everyone, the Arts Board proposed a combined effort involving both Hispanic and Pueblo artists. Millie Santillanes (1998), the leader the movement to commemorate Oñate in Albuquerque, objected to this multicultural compromise: "This is not about fairness, it's about history, our history, not the rich, multi-ethnic history of our state. That is a different work of art." She later stated that if those opposed to the Oñate monument "want their own statue, I don't care what it is. I won't fight it. . . . But don't interfere with our culture and our history" (quoted in Zoretich 1999). Tony Romero (1998) also disliked the idea of a multicultural monument: "why clutter it up with other histories?" he asked.

Many Hispanos did not understand how Oñate's treatment of the Acomas four hundred years earlier could still be hurtful. "Give me a break," complained Estevan Arellano (the champion of mestizaje). "It was 400 years ago. It's OK to hold a grudge, but for 400 years?" (quoted in Brooke 1998). Elizabeth Archul-

Fig. 18. Figures in *La Jornada* (Reynaldo Rivera and Betty Sabo) viewed from within *Numbe Whageh* (Nora Naranjo-Morse), on the grounds of the Albuquerque Museum.

eta (2007, 328, 332) points out that many Hispanics hold their own grudge when it comes to the Spanish priests killed during the Pueblo Revolt, recasting their ancestors as victims of Pueblo aggression. Nevertheless, Pueblo communities often reckon time differently than non-Indians do, as the ultimate result of Albuquerque's cuarto centenario commemoration illustrates. The memorial consists of two parts, a collection of life-size bronze figures by Betty Sabo and Reynaldo "Sonny" Rivera (the creator of the Alcalde statue) called *La Jornada* (The Journey), and an earthwork by Santa Clara Pueblo artist Nora Naranjo-Morse called *The Environment* or *Numbe Whageh* (Our Center Place) (see fig. 18). The pair was installed outside the Albuquerque Museum in 2005. *La Jornada* includes a line of settlers and livestock traversing rugged terrain, led by a standing Oñate. It emphasizes settlement over conquest. *Numbe Whageh* features a spiral walkway within a hilly landscape planted with native vegetation that includes boul-

The Española Valley

ders with Pueblo markings. Naranjo-Morse created the piece with the first encounter between Pueblo people and Spaniards in mind (Freise 2007, 240), but the installation contains no explicit reference to Spanish colonization.

Kathy Freise (2007, 235) argues that both *La Jornada* and *Numbe Whageh* are tied to the past but that the latter also gestures to the future. Yet it is hard to compare the two halves of the memorial, given how visually and conceptually different they are. One half is linear, representational, and focused on human achievement, while the other is circular, abstract, and focused on the natural environment. And this is precisely my point: the two works reflect not just different ideas about Spanish colonization but also radically different *ways of thinking* about Spanish colonization, time, and place. "Echoing the lines along which the arguments about the memorial played out, it is appropriate that the two components stand side by side, removed from one another, sharing a space but not an aesthetic. They run parallel to one another, no easy relationship between them," Freise suggests (233). She goes on to argue that the two halves of the memorial "are set into a kind of permanent negotiation with one another, affiliated with history and memory." They "mirror the ways in which any notion of a collective, unified narrative about how people live in this time and place [has] been disrupted" (251). It is unclear whether this permanent negotiation between incommensurable perspectives can ever be resolved. After the cuarto centenario, viewing New Mexico history objectively seemed impossible.

"We Kept the Bottle in a Paper Bag": 150 Years of American Rule

While Indians and Nuevomexicanos were arguing about the interpretation and commemoration of Spanish colonization in the 1990s, Anglos mostly stayed out of the fray. Meanwhile, two anniversaries associated with *American* colonization slipped by virtually unnoticed. The uneven attention paid to New Mexico's double colonial history reflected the politics of visibility and reinforced American hegemony in the region.

In 1996, as the state was gearing up for the cuarto centenario, the 150th anniversary of Stephen Kearny's occupation of Santa Fe was basically a non-event, despite its national and international significance. Stephanie Kearny, the general's great-granddaughter, did not want to let the anniversary pass, so she, "two of her sisters, two historians, and a reporter discreetly gathered in Santa Fe's central plaza and sipped champagne from plastic cups. Ms. Kearny, an Albuquerque financial consultant, said, 'We kept the bottle in a paper bag because we were afraid of being thrown in jail'" (Brooke 1998).

Larry Calloway (1996b), a columnist for the *Albuquerque Journal*, commented on the lack of recognition in 1996: "New Mexico seems, on the official level, ashamed to be part of the United States. If this weren't true, then surely the state would be preparing for a big flag-waving sesquicentennial ceremony." He continued: "Many cutting-edge historians see the Mexican-American war and the doctrine of Manifest Destiny as shameful. Many see the concluding Treaty of Guadalupe Hidalgo as fraudulent. And they teach this attitude in the schools." Calloway (1996a) noted that the cuarto centenario commemoration received hundreds of thousands of dollars of state funding and the support of New Mexico's congressional delegation, which was "fair if you have the votes. But it also distorts New Mexico values to fund the quadricentennial of the Spanish occupation of Santa Fe and shun the sesquicentennial of the American occupation of Santa Fe."

Sylvia Rodríguez (2001, 209) argues that Calloway ignored "the enchantment factor, which had managed to remove Kearny from public view well before the Chicano movement or revisionist historiography." New Mexico's romantic tourist image depended equally on the visibility of Native Americans and Hispanics and the *invisibility* of Anglos. I would carry the argument even further. While Calloway implied that Anglos were victims of political correctness, national shame, and their own minority status (which was quickly changing), I believe that lack of recognition here (and Anglo invisibility more generally) powerfully *strengthened* the political position of Anglos in New Mexico and helped to maintain their dominant, not subordinate, status. If there *had* been a

Kearny commemoration, land grant activists would surely have protested. Hispanics and Native Americans may even have joined forces. This reaction would have threatened (Anglo) American hegemony, at least discursively. Instead, while Kearny's descendants discreetly sipped champagne on the plaza, Anglos mostly remained in the shadows, watching as the war between Indians and Hispanos waged.

Two years later, 1998 marked not only the 400th anniversary of Spanish colonization but also the 150th anniversary of the Treaty of Guadalupe Hidalgo and the 100th anniversary of the Spanish-American War (both of which enlarged U.S. possessions as the Spanish empire shrank). Some commentators contrasted the brutality of Spanish and American colonization. For example, Samuel Delgado observed that not much is heard about the cruel *American* practice of "attacking Indian camps, killing everyone in sight, chasing them all over the country, and resettling them with slogans like 'The only good Indian is a dead Indian.'" Manifest Destiny applied to both Hispanics and Indians, he noted (Delgado 1998; see also Gonzales 2007, 223; López 1998a). Others used this coincidence to draw attention to the land grant struggle in New Mexico (Kosek 2006, 55).

Yet this attempt to shift attention from Spanish to American colonization largely failed. Native Americans rejected the argument that Nuevomexicanos were victims of the United States. The group that claimed responsibility for cutting off the Oñate statue's foot wrote: "Isn't the Treaty of Guadalupe Hidalgo really people whining about land taken unlawfully—people who took land themselves? We have little or no sympathy there" ("Proud Actions" 1998; see also Gonzales 2007, 227). Not surprisingly, some Anglos threw their support behind the Indians (e.g., Wood 1998; cf. Brandtner de Martinez 1998). A retired Anglo Forest Service official commented to Jake Kosek (2006, 58): "I am not sure why these people [Hispanos] think they have the right to this land. Their ancestors stole more land than we ever stole from them. . . . Besides, they are not natives, they are immigrants just like I am." This counterargument enabled Anglos to step out of the spotlight

Fig. 19. "Spanish Settlement of the Southwest 1598" commemorative stamp. © 1998 United States Postal Service. All rights reserved. Used with permission.

and self-righteously shift the role of colonizer back onto Hispanics. Despite the efforts of activists such as Delgado, a critique of U.S. colonization was quickly sucked back into a debate about Spanish colonization.[47]

A Commemorative Stamp for Española

One of the most interesting quadricentennial projects, which succeeded in completely dodging Oñate, takes us back to the Española plaza. The U.S. Postal Service (usps) wanted to commemorate the four hundredth anniversary of the Camino Real de Tierra Adentro (the royal road from Mexico City into New Mexico) and the founding of the Spanish colony at San Gabriel. The usps rejected several possible stamp images outright. Oñate was too controversial, a mounted conquistador too militant, the church at Taos Pueblo or Ranchos de Taos inappropriate for a commercial product. It finally found an acceptable image: a photograph of Española's brand-new Misión-Convento (see fig. 19) taken by Susan Hazen-Hammond of Santa Fe (Amick 1999, 176–79).[48]

Not surprisingly, featuring an image of the Misión-Convento on a stamp commemorating "Spanish Settlement of the Southwest 1598" added to the confusion about the Misión's historicity. Postal Service statements referred to the building as a "replica," but several newspapers reported that the stamp depicted the original church of San Miguel. Hazen-Hammond's attempt to capture the "timeless" quality of New Mexico architecture (Armijo 1998) thus proved effective. Press coverage consistently omitted the name of the building's designer. "To view this stamp in a more historically accurate light allows us to acknowledge the artistic contribution of the architect, Bernabe Romero, and to appreciate the building as a heartfelt expression of contemporary pride in the Hispanic heritage of the Southwest," wrote Chris Wilson (1998). Romero himself was happy with the stamp and believed attention should be focused not on the building but on the four-hundred-year legacy of Spanish colonization in New Mexico.

Had the original church still been standing, it might not have made it onto the stamp anyway. Some postal officials were concerned that depicting a church on a commemorative stamp might be interpreted as promoting Christianity. Hazen-Hammond did some background research and assured the USPS's research firm that the Misión was a public, secular building. Wilson (1998) would have preferred that the image of "an authentic Spanish colonial building" appear on the stamp, such as the church at Acoma Pueblo or the church in Las Trampas. Given the importance of Catholicism to Spanish colonization, depicting a church would have been entirely appropriate, he argued. (This is the "it's historical, not religious" argument.) "The use instead of the Española community center—constructed and operated with public funds, but modeled on a church, topped by a cross and named La Misión—raises more vexing questions about the separation of church and state." In any case, someone unfamiliar with the building featured on the stamp would have no way of knowing it was not a church.[49]

Senator Domenici commended the USPS for paying tribute "to the cultural, political and social contributions of Hispanics in the

Fig. 20. Eagle dancers from San Juan Pueblo perform at the stamp
dedication ceremony. Photograph by Susan Hazen-Hammond, © 1998.

United States" (Amick 1999, 177). But the first-day-of-issue ceremony on the Española plaza in July 1998 was predictably "a celebration of the blending of the Spanish and the Indian cultures in
northern New Mexico" (see fig. 20). It included all the typical elements of a multicultural Española plaza ceremony: an invocation
in Tewa, a benediction in Spanish, and mariachi, Matachines, and
Pueblo eagle dance performances. "On behalf of the eight northern pueblos, it's an honor for us to be here for the stamp dedication," said the governor of San Juan Pueblo. "It commemorates
the re-establishment of historical ties and the spiritual merging of
the two cultures. We are here to celebrate who we've become as a
result of the two cultures" (Johnson 1998).

Senator Domenici and the governor of New Mexico attended
the first-day-of-issue ceremony, which included the National An-
them and the Pledge of Allegiance, first in Spanish, then in English
(Johnson 1998). The event coincided with Española's annual fiesta in 1998, and the plaza was decked out in red, white, and blue
balloons. A British newspaper observed that the stamp represents

The Española Valley

an assertion of federal authority in New Mexico, whose relationship to the United States has been a tenuous one. The article noted that the Spanish settled the area more than two centuries before New Mexico became a state and that the cuarto centenario arguably "has nothing to do with the United States" (Dejevsky 1998).

"New Mexico USA"

The Española valley has always been a multinational region where national identities are flexible and overlapping and where sovereignties are contested and unstable. Spanish colonization, Mexican independence, and American colonization added layers of complexity to changing indigenous conceptions of territory and belonging. Native Americans continue to assert and negotiate the limits of their sovereignty in multiple arenas. In the 1960s Chicano nationalists reimagined the American Southwest as Aztlán, the spiritual homeland of the Aztecs (J. R. Chávez 1984; Kosek 2006, 220–22). Land grant activists today still invoke the terms of the Treaty of Guadalupe Hidalgo, an international agreement, in making land claims. Joseph Masco (2006) argues that even Los Alamos National Laboratory, established to strengthen national security, has rendered northern New Mexico a more fractured national space.[50] Nuclear scientists faced with the responsibility of managing nuclear waste for ten thousand years have been forced to imagine a future in which New Mexico is no longer part of the United States (197–201).

The cuarto centenario celebration highlighted this multinational context. For example, the flags of Spain, Mexico, the United States, and New Mexico flew at the Oñate Monument and Visitors Center in Alcalde (López 1998a), where Oñate virtually became the founder not only of New Mexico but also of all subsequent polities. The same flags, in addition to the flag of the Eight Northern Pueblos, were raised on the Española plaza for its dedication in 1990 (Roy 1990c). In 1998 Spanish dignitaries and soldiers traveled to New Mexico to participate in several commemorations of Spanish colonization culminating at the Palace of the Governors (Brooke 1998; Horton 2010, 65–66). Considering that

Fig. 21. American flags on the plaza, Veterans Day 2003.

the territory long ago passed from Spanish to Mexican to American hands, this nostalgic reenactment of Spanish glory must have been tinged with dramatic irony.

New Mexicans frequently have to remind people from other parts of the country that New Mexico is part of the United States (the state's license plates read "New Mexico USA").[51] The cuarto centenario celebrations and the development of the Española plaza provided opportunities for acknowledging New Mexico's Americanness. New Mexico's congressional delegates helped secure federal funding for the plaza and made trips to Española to participate in plaza ceremonies, signaling that the plaza was indeed an American project. The American flag raised for the plaza's dedication in 1990 had flown over the U.S. Capitol (Eichstaedt 1990; Woods 1990). Recognizing—or claiming—New Mexican space and time as American allowed the federal government to reaffirm its territorial sovereignty and appropriate the pre-American past, expanding the base and deepening the roots of U.S. nationalism. In this sense the politics of recognition stabilized American identity and sovereignty in a contested borderland.

The Española Valley

Fig. 22. Dedication of the Veterans' Memorial Wall, 2003.

The dedication of the Veterans' Memorial Wall on the Española plaza in November 2003, like the issuance of the Spanish
Settlement stamp in 1998, struck me as a ritual that confirmed
the plaza's status as an American national space. It was a cold
and drizzly Veterans Day, and the plaza, abuzz with activity, was
encircled by bright American flags that stood out dramatically
against the brown earth and gray sky (see figs. 21 and 22). The
two-hour ceremony included an eagle dance by members of San
Juan Pueblo (of course), but unlike other plaza ceremonies it was
full of patriotic military pomp. As I looked out onto a sea of two
thousand brown faces—most of them veterans from the Española valley with their families—I realized how much these men and
women had invested in their country. Indians and Hispanics have
long and proud histories of serving in the U.S. military, and New
Mexicans in particular have made great sacrifices for the United
States in war.[52]

Yet many New Mexican veterans have complicated relationships to the United States. "We are good enough citizens to be sent
to war but not good enough to be treated as citizens," one veter-

an told Jake Kosek (2006, 220). Said another: "They will let us fight and die for the country, but they will not let us graze a cow or collect firewood on the national forest." In writing about Florida Seminole veterans, Jessica Cattelino (2004, 262–63) argues for a theory of "overlapping citizenship" that takes into account the social and political meaning of veterans' multiple identities. "Seminole service in the United States military simultaneously incorporates Seminoles into the institutions, symbols, and rituals of the United States and provides a socially recognized mechanism for perpetuating Seminole pride and polity." More research on the social significance of military service among Hispanics and Native Americans in New Mexico might reveal similar dynamics. It would certainly be a mistake to interpret the dedication of the memorial on the Española plaza as even a temporary resolution or consolidation of citizenship and identity in New Mexico, which have been contentious since the 1800s (Gómez 2007).

Cattelino (2004, 273) maintains that Indians serving in the U.S. military have "forced American publics and policymakers to consider the limits and meanings of U.S. citizenship." Similarly, recognizing the place of Indians and Hispanics in the United States as culturally distinct citizens raises important questions about what it means to be American. The assertion of Hispanic *American* heritage subverts the dominant view of the United States as an Anglo-American nation (Trujillo 2009, 38). Far from settling questions of identity in northern New Mexico (or the United States), the politics of recognition therefore reflects and confirms the instability of identity.

Nuevomexicanos have transgressed Anglo nationalism and challenged U.S. sovereignty in creative ways. For example, the dedication of the Española plaza in 1990 inspired Connie Valdez, the president of Northern New Mexico Community College, to declare: "The establishment (of the United States) took place in the Española Valley in 1598, contrary to what the history books say. . . . The first capital of the United States is found in Yunge Owinge in San Juan Pueblo de los Caballeros. . . . It is time we celebrate and give proper recognition to this Valley for the proud heritage and culture that it embodies" (quoted in Woods 1990). Valdez intriguingly reversed the logic of nationalistic rhetoric. Instead of the United States appropriating this region's pre-American history as part of its own past, the region claimed the United States, without surrendering its cultural distinctiveness. By 2009 Española had so successfully reinvented itself as the new San Gabriel that mayor Joseph Maestas was able to describe *Española* as "the first Capital City in America" (Española Valley Chamber of Commerce 2009, 2).

In the 1998 cuarto centenario debate, people compared both Po'pay and Oñate to George Washington (as revolutionary or founding father), depending on their position. Either way, the analogy suggests that U.S. history is the framework within which New Mexican history is interpreted, that American heroes are the measure of Spanish and Indian ones.[53] But historian Marc Simmons turned the comparison around. Oñate deserved the title "the George Washington of New Mexico," but "since our Don Juan came first, perhaps we should properly refer to our president as 'The Oñate of the United States'" (quoted in Gonzales 2007, 220). In Simmons's formulation, New Mexico becomes the measure of the United States.

The relationship between the politics of recognition and American sovereignty is equally complex. Patchen Markell (2003, 24–25) notes that states can pursue sovereignty "through the establishment of an official pluralism that at once affirms differences and governs them, reducing a threateningly open field of social plurality to a relatively orderly catalog of identities." States that dole out recognition are themselves recognized in the process: recognition "furthers the state's project of rendering the social world 'legible' and governable: to appeal to the state *for* the recognition of one's own identity—to present oneself as knowable—is already to offer the state the reciprocal recognition of its sovereignty that it demands" (31). Yet Markell insists that state sovereignty is never a complete project.

In the Española valley, the federal government's recognition of enduring multinational claims and identities simultaneously reinforces and destabilizes American sovereignty. On the one hand, it renders a disorderly region more manageable and confirms—through political ritual—the government's beneficent control of the region. In the ceremonies on the Española plaza, the United States is supreme among all those represented (note the Pledge of Allegiance to the flag of the United States, in both Spanish and English). On the other hand, the United States has gained legitimacy by acknowledging, not suppressing, the enduring legacy of Pueblo, Spanish, and Mexican polities in New Mexico. It may be supreme, but American politicians have shared the stage with officials representing other governments and territories both within and far from the United States. The politics of recognition in the Española valley illustrates what Jessica Cattelino (2008) calls "sovereign interdependencies," or the way in which polities negotiate their sovereignty in relationship to and in collaboration with one another. The intercontinental scale of recognition also challenges the equation of the United States with "America," revealing the United States' geographical smallness and historical recentness. It is ultimately impossible to separate the colonialist and multiculturalist, hegemonic and subversive forces at play here. Recognition involves their ongoing negotiation.

From the Española Plaza to the Northern
Rio Grande National Heritage Area

Knowing that Richard Lucero was one of the NRGNHA's strongest supporters, I asked him about its relationship to the Española plaza project. He told me they were one and the same. Developing a national heritage area would be one way to secure congressional funding for the preservation of Spanish colonial heritage in northern New Mexico, one of the plaza project's principal aims. The heritage area represented a geographically expanded version of the plaza. The region, rather than the plaza, was the destination, Lucero (2003) stressed, returning to his compass metaphor. The plaza project and heritage area movement certainly have much in common, including the promotion of New Mexico's Native American and Hispanic cultures and a nonthreatening discourse of multicultural coexistence in which the Spanish settler plays a more prominent role than the conquistador. I often heard Ernest Ortega talk about the need for the NRGNHA to avoid the "Oñate syndrome," although he was also opposed to "sugarcoating" New Mexico history. The Española plaza project thus provides a geographical and political foundation for the national heritage area initiative, which represents a national attempt to make room for this region of cultural difference in the United States at large. The Española plaza was also the unofficial headquarters of the heritage area in its early years.[54]

The establishment of the Northern Rio Grande National Heritage Area provides another key opportunity for negotiating the place of New Mexico in the United States and, more broadly, the meaning of "America" itself. I asked several people if they thought the heritage area designation was an attempt by the federal government to consolidate its claim to a contested region once and for all. Was the recognition of Indian and Nuevomexicano heritage as *American* heritage a neocolonial act? "Not at all. Not at all!" exclaimed Orlando Romero (2003). "Because the reality is, it *is* American heritage" in the hemispheric sense of "American." He did not buy my argument about American colonialism and implied that my conception of America was too narrow. "I see myself as an American: a Latin American, a South American and an American from all the way up, from Canada all the way down to Mexico before there were borders."

Ernest Ortega (2003) and I discussed why the U.S. government should commemorate the Spanish colonization of the Southwest. Ortega earned a master's degree in Spanish colonial history, taught high school history, and then worked for the National Park Service for more than thirty years in various locations, beginning and ending in New Mexico. He began by arguing that what happened in New Mexico before 1848 had a direct bearing on U.S. history because the United States acquired the territory. The descendants of the people living there are now American citizens. He then stressed the need for recognition: "Take a look at American history books, and it is all presented from an eastern seaboard perspective, east to west. . . . Our American history does not tell the American Indian story. . . . It doesn't tell the Spanish story." Ortega then made a subtle shift, using "America" to refer to a much larger territory: "I'm not talking United States history, I'm talking American history; we're in that American continent." Because most American history books only present U.S. history, he thought the National Park Service's efforts to commemorate intercontinental history were important. Our conversation made it clear that the ambiguity of the term "American" makes it a tool for both asserting and challenging the United States' hemispheric dominance.

Finally, I talked about the heritage area's national implications with Pablo Sedillo (2003), a native New Mexican and field representative for Senator Jeff Bingaman, who first sponsored the Northern Rio Grande National Heritage Area legislation. He suggested that one goal of the national heritage area is "to let people know of the richness and the contributions of this area to the nation, and to settle the whole question of loyalty and unity once and for all." Nuevomexicanos' use of Spanish and their cultural difference called this loyalty into question. "Remember, we fought; we did not want to be part of the United States." When New Mexico did become an American territory, the government was uneager to grant New Mexico statehood, treated New Mexicans as second-class citizens, and pressured them to "forget that you speak Spanish, forget your culture. You're now Americans; now you must assimilate to the American way of life." Sedillo remarked that some New Mexicans still equate "Americanos" with "Anglos" or foreigners. He believed that this strong Hispanic identity has led outsiders to believe that New Mexicans "don't want to change and be part of the mainstream."

In bringing together the politics of loyalty and equality, Sedillo identified a cyclical process in which political rights are based on cultural identity (see also Nieto-Phillips 2004). Yet rather than call for a more inclusive federal government or point out that forced assimilation can backfire, Sedillo (2003) took the conversation in a different direction. In response to the demand that

The Española Valley

New Mexicans assimilate to the American way of life, Sedillo asserted that "we feel that our practices, our customs and traditions and mores *are* the American way of life, and when we talk about America, it's encompassing the entire nation." Contrary to the view that New Mexicans do not want to integrate, "I submit to you that we are part of the mainstream." Sedillo pushed the argument about Americanos even further: "all those of us that live in the hemisphere are Americanos." Of those people, more speak Spanish than English, and for this reason the United States should be more inclusive of Hispanics. Sedillo's argument, though, subverts the usual temporal logic of recognition. Sedillo seemed less interested in describing a *future* state that recognizes minorities than a state that is already multicultural, whether it likes it or not. He asserted that New Mexicans are *already* culturally American by refiguring the very idea of America (and the American mainstream). The problem, therefore, is not so much the misrecognition or nonrecognition of New Mexicans but the misrecognition of America.

Negotiating difference and belonging in the Española valley and elsewhere in northern New Mexico is an ongoing and open-ended process that necessarily implicates broader national identities and sovereignties. The Northern Rio Grande National Heritage Area clearly has the potential to advance hegemonic or subversive views of culture, history, and identity. If the material I have presented in this chapter is any kind of indicator, it may well do both.

CHAPTER FOUR

The Politics of Preservation in Las Trampas

One of the paintings in the Española Misión is of the church of San José de Gracia in the mountain village of Las Trampas, which lies along the High Road between Santa Fe and Taos. Las Trampas has captivated the imagination of Anglo-Americans since they began arriving in New Mexico in the nineteenth century. Especially since the 1960s, writers have described the adobe church as one of the finest, most important, and best-preserved Spanish colonial mission churches in the Southwest, a textbook example of eighteenth-century New Mexican ecclesiastical architecture. They have extolled the village and its mountain setting, praising Las Trampas as a typical Spanish American agricultural community, one of the most interesting and least spoiled in northern New Mexico. With fewer than one hundred residents today, the village has no tourist facilities but is nevertheless a popular stop along a well-traveled route.

The first time I visited Las Trampas I was like many tourists, driving the High Road (a two-lane highway) and stopping in all the villages along the way: Chimayó, Truchas, Ranchos de Taos. It was the end of August 2000, and I enjoyed the climb into the Sangre de Cristo Mountains, where pigmy forests of piñon and juniper gave way to ponderosa pines and then to firs and aspens. Adobe structures, pasturelands, and hilltop crosses dotted the settled landscape, but the road also cut through spectacular swaths of Bureau of Land Management and Forest Service lands, where the presence of humans was less visible (see fig. 23). "The highlight of

Fig. 23. The high desert along the High Road.

the trip," I wrote in my journal, "was the church of San José de Gracia in Las Trampas" (see figs. 24 and 25). "I was really blown away by the simple and charming beauty of this adobe church," which was "perfectly picturesque against the blue sky. The inside was light, with an ancient wood floor, painted ceiling beams, and outstanding altar and nave paintings. I spent time reading about the church's features and history, and in general being awed by its beauty and peacefulness." Like many who had come before me, I found the church incomparable as an example of Spanish colonial architecture.

I knew from my guidebook that Las Trampas was famous, but I did not know that it had been the focus of preservation campaigns by Anglos throughout the twentieth century. In this chapter I analyze how outsiders have represented Las Trampas and their efforts to preserve the church, the village's architecture and settlement pattern, and village life itself. These cultural conservation campaigns, which began in the 1920s, were part of the larger romantic movement that developed in Santa Fe and guided the restoration of the Palace of the Governors. In Las Trampas, howev-

Fig. 24. San José de Gracia Catholic Church.

er, we see more clearly the psychological, political, and economic dimensions of Anglo antimodernism.

I show how preservationist discourse, as a systematic way of thinking, speaking, and acting, has helped to perpetuate a colonial order. It is easy to find overt colonial activity in northern New Mexico, from the breakup of Hispanic land grants (R. Ortiz 1980; Briggs and Van Ness 1987; Ebright 1994) and the ongoing political and economic marginalization of Nuevomexicanos to missionary and governmental campaigns to Americanize Hispanic villages (Deutsch 1987, 63–86, 107–26). The colonial nature of preservation campaigns in Las Trampas is less obvious, though, since preservationists generally *celebrated* Nuevomexicanos' religious devotion, artistic traditions, communitarian values, and pastoral way of life and had little personal involvement in the economic and political changes that undermined the viability of northern New Mexican villages. Neither their words nor their actions, then, explicitly advanced Anglo-American interests. Quite the contrary, these antimodernists often criticized the cultural foundation of their own society.

Fig. 25. The interior of San José de Gracia.

Yet I argue that preservationist discourse brought together the cultural, economic, and political dimensions of American colonialism. To begin with, outsiders have dominated the representation of Las Trampas, and their patronizing and primitivistic descriptions have influenced Anglo-American engagements with northern New Mexico. Trampaseños are rarely quoted in texts about the village, and seldom have they had the ability to represent themselves in a sustained way to a broad audience. This chapter is inevitably embedded in this politics of representation. Yet it is not "about" Las Trampas in the same way that previous chapters were about the Palace of the Governors or the Española valley. It does not offer a view of Las Trampas from the inside but rather examines how outsiders have constructed the village. In fact, villagers and their "voices" are almost entirely missing from the chapter. At the end of the chapter I consider my role as an anthropologist in the discursive construction of Las Trampas. I conclude somewhat uncomfortably with a discussion of power and resistance, representation and recognition, not in the ethnographic present but in what I call the counter-ethnographic present. First, though, I explore the colonialist nature of preservation in Las Trampas.

The Discursive Construction of Las Trampas

Anglos have tended to represent Las Trampas in one of two ways: as a timeless, traditional, and self-sufficient agricultural community or as a dying village that is hemorrhaging residents and cultural integrity. The image of the village as isolated and unchanging is stunningly disconnected from reality, since American colonization has transformed its economy. The second view, while seemingly more realistic, builds on the first view and a simplistic understanding of migration patterns. Commentators have interpreted out-migration as an alarming new development and indicator of collapse, when in fact seasonal migration has been a part of villagers' economic repertoire and a technique for *maintaining* village life since the nineteenth century. Although I provide evidence in this chapter that challenges both of these images, my principal goal is not to present a more accurate portrait of Las Trampas. Rather, I am interested in the characteristics and effects of these two discourses, which tell us more about Anglo preservationists than about Las Trampas but which have nevertheless profoundly affected the village.

In this way my analysis resembles Edward Said's critique of Orientalism. The relevance of Said's work should not be surprising, since "the Southwest *is* America's Orient" (Babcock 1997, 264; see also Gutiérrez 2002). Drawing on Michel Foucault's theory of discourse, Said (1978, 3, 5–6) defines Orientalism as a "corporate institution for dealing with the Orient . . . by making statements about it, authorizing views of it, describing it, by teaching it, settling it, ruling over it: in short, Orientalism as a Western style for dominating, restructuring, and having authority over the Orient." His investigation "deals principally, not with a correspondence between Orientalism and the Orient, but with the internal consistency of Orientalism and its ideas about the Orient . . . despite or beyond any correspondence, or lack thereof, with a 'real' Orient." Yet Said goes on to urge us "never to assume that the structure of Orientalism is nothing more than a structure of lies or of myths which, were the truth about them to be told, would simply blow away. . . . Orientalism is more particularly valuable as a sign of European-Atlantic power over the Orient than it is as a veridic discourse about the Orient." Its durability is linked to its political efficacy. "After all, any system of ideas that can remain unchanged" for so long "must be something more formidable than a mere collection of lies. Orientalism, therefore, is not an airy European fantasy about the Orient but a created body of theory and practice in which, for many generations, there has been a considerable material investment."

James Ferguson (1994, 25–26) takes a similar approach in his study of development discourse in Lesotho (a country completely surrounded by South Africa). He analyzes a 1975 World Bank report that portrayed Lesotho as "a traditional subsistence peasant society" that was "virtually untouched by modern economic development." From a scholarly point of view this characterization seems outlandish, since Lesotho had served as a labor reserve for South Africa for more than a century and had been transformed by economic development. Yet Ferguson maintains that "what is needed is not so much a correction or setting straight of the discourse of the 'development' industry in Lesotho . . . as a way of accounting for it, and of showing what it does" (28). He argues that this discourse constructs Lesotho as a perfect candidate for the kind of intervention the World Bank and other development agencies specialize in and then guides the actual implementation of development programs (28, 73–74). The development apparatus in Lesotho has powerful, unintended, and often unperceived effects. While it fails to promote economic growth, it succeeds in "depoliticizing everything it touches, everywhere whisking political realities out of sight" (xv). In particular, development depoliticizes poverty (converting it into a technical problem) and the state, which appears to be a neutral instrument for policy implementation (256).

There are significant similarities, but also differences, between Lesotho and Las Trampas. In New Mexico, efforts to "develop" and Americanize Nuevomexicano communities began in the 1800s, but a counter-movement became increasingly prominent in the twentieth century. Whereas "tradition" usually appears as an obstacle in development discourse (an impediment to modernization), antimodernists in New Mexico positively valued (some) Hispanic cultural traditions. Preservationists were only *partially* opposed to development in Las Trampas. As we will see, they often celebrated the village's cultural integrity but decried its economic inefficiency. Modernist projects that advocated change and antimodernist projects that opposed it were often entangled in contradictory ways that rendered both ineffective.

Yet just as in Lesotho, the discursive construction of Las Trampas has had powerful, unintended effects. Both images of Las Trampas—as timeless and traditional or decaying and contaminated—serve Anglo interests. Descriptions of the village as traditional and unchanging reassure Anglos that an alternative to the modern world still exists and that, therefore, American colonization must not have been totally destructive. They avert feelings of colonial guilt through a process of denial and justify policies that ensure underdevelopment and entrenched poverty in Nuevomexicano villages. The second narrative about Las Trampas builds upon the first. In this version, a village that was once self-sufficient and noble is in ruins, losing residents and culture as the outside world overwhelms it. If the first discourse is romantic, the second is tragic, casting villagers as pathetic victims. Anglo preservationists, with their wisdom, foresight, and technical expertise, respond to this crisis by swooping in to save the villagers from the ravages of modernity and sometimes from themselves. Its effect, then, is to justify a coordinated intervention into village life.

While the discourse of tradition depends upon imperialist denial, the discourse of loss reveals a deep imperialist nostalgia, a mourning for what colonialism has transformed or destroyed. Renato Rosaldo (1993, 69–70) has analyzed colonizers' propensity to long for the very forms of life they have intentionally altered and to regret that the "traditional" societies they have subjected to their civilizing mission have been changed in the process. Imperialist nostalgia, he argues, enables colonial agents to assume a pose of "innocent yearning" and to conceal their complicity in often brutal domination. In other words, it casts the colonizers as innocent bystanders. This stance is evident in New Mexico when preservationists blame villagers for their culture loss and launch cultural conservation campaigns on their behalf. In these instances, preservationists appear to work *against* (the cultural effects of) colonialism and modernity, and each success enables Americans to avoid fully facing the destructive nature of their own society.

The alleviation of colonial guilt is important even though most preservationists were not personally responsible for the social and economic changes they mourned. They did not consider themselves to be members of Nuevomexicano communities but identified with the dominant American society, despite their disenchantment. Celebrating the village's endurance or rescuing its cultural heritage therefore helped preservationists distance themselves from the aspects of their own society they found most loathsome. Resolving preservationists' contradictory attitudes toward their own society enabled them to remain a part of that society without challenging the economic and political foundations of American colonialism. Their work in the cultural realm therefore helped to justify the status quo. And while their colonial involvement was mostly at the level of culture, it helped to sustain a much broader set of colonial conditions.

Anglos seldom acknowledged the relationship between mode of production and cultural survival and tended to treat culture and economics as if they were totally separate.[1] It was always the *cultural* significance of agricultural village life (the social relationships, values, landscape patterns, religion, architecture) that mattered most, not the economics of farming or ranching. So separate were culture and economics in preservationist discourse that when Anglos did address the village's material basis, they typically recommended modernizing agricultural practices in order to *preserve* art, architecture, folklife, and religious life. Doubts about preserving a preindustrial way of life in the age of industrial or postindustrial capitalism rarely deterred them.[2] In fact, talking about culture was a way of *not* talking about the breakup of land grants, access to natural resources, the systematic marginalization of Nuevomexicanos, or other factors that severely undermined the viability of the village. Preservationists were always much more willing to support cultural conservation than Hispanos' material struggles.[3]

To the extent that focusing on culture deflected attention away from land politics, preservationist discourse helped to *mystify* colonial domination (cf. Rodríguez 1989). This does not mean that land politics are any more significant (or real) than cultural politics. Despite the fact — in part *because* of the fact — that preservationists consistently sought to separate culture from political economy, social scientists cannot do so. There is nothing apolitical about the anti-politics of culture. And as we have seen before, the anti-politics of culture quickly morphs into the politics of authenticity in northern New Mexico. Nuevomexicanos seeking to regain access to land and natural resources have found it useful to emphasize their traditional cultural heritage and connection to the land in order to win Anglo support. Moreover, for many Nuevomexicanos today land has as much cultural significance as economic significance, if not more. Even the *loss* of land has become a central dimension of Nuevomexicano identity (Garcia 2008; Kosek 2006, 30–61). For all of these reasons we will need to pay attention to the relationship between nature and culture, the material and immaterial, in the work of preservationists in Las Trampas.

An Island in the Storm?

Twelve families from Santa Fe established the village of Santo Tomás Apóstol del Río de Las Trampas in 1751 after Governor Tomás Vélez Capuchín granted them 46,000 acres of land. Eking out a living on the frontier was hard, but the village prospered, growing to 63 families (278 people) by 1776. In 1760 the bishop of Durango granted Las Trampas a license to build a chapel within the fortified village walls. The villagers raised funds for the construction of the church, which they completed around 1780 (Bunting 1970; Dominguez 1956, 99; Hillerman 1970; Kessell 1980, 101–7; Pratt and Gavin 1991).[4]

The church's history and architectural features inspired Anglo observers. They marveled at the four-foot-thick adobe walls, twin bell towers, an outdoor/indoor choir loft, nineteenth-century religious folk art, and a transverse clerestory window that dramatically illuminated the front altar. Everyone recognized that the church was the center of the villagers' life, "a symbol of their religion and their tradition and whole cultural identity" (Sweeney 1988, 15). Some writers described the village's adobe houses and the long, narrow plots of land that stretched between the river and the *acequias* (earthen irrigation ditches). The acequia system in Las Trampas was still basically intact, including flumes made of hollowed-out logs that carried water over arroyos.[5] All of this — the vernacular architecture, settlement pattern, cultural landscape, and traditional village life — was typical, characteristic, picturesque, charming (for thorough descriptions of the church and village, see Batson 1998; Bunting 1964, 62–67; Bunting 1970; Dominguez 1956; Pratt and Gavin 1991; Wilson and Polyzoides 2011, 162–69).

A Timeless Utopia

"Time stood still in Las Trampas," the *Santa Fe New Mexican* mused in 1966 (MacGregor 1966, 8). A National Park Service report acknowledged that Las Trampas is famous for "the impression of changeless cultural continuity" (NPS 1967a, 1). Like other Nuevomexicano villages (Montgomery 2002, 163–64; Weigle 2010, 117–18), Las Trampas was known for its "medieval" culture. Writers described the village as a relic of seventeenth-century Spain or eighteenth-century colonial New Mexico (WPA [1940] 1989, 289; Calvin 1948, 18). Architect Nathaniel Owings (1966) called the village a "lovely, fragile, surviving example of the past." In 1947 an admirer argued that Las Trampas surpassed anything in Santa Fe in antiquarian value "because it is a timeless town untouched by the vandal called 'Modern.'" He went on to remark that "the little plaza struggles along as if there had never been an Hidalgo treaty, a Kearney, a century of American occupation. 1846 or 1946, it does not phase Trampas in the least. There are more traditions, more legends, more ecclesiastical gems in this little village than practically in the whole state combined" (Crocchiola 1947).[6]

Much to the delight of Anglos, the picturesque village contained no bars, gas stations, neon signs, hot dog stands, "come-on zoos," or other tourist accommodations (Conron 1968, 28; "Threat to Las Trampas" 1967). According to architectural historian Bainbridge Bunting (1961, 2; 1970, 38), the church of San José de Gracia had "escaped the grotesque efforts at 'modernization' under Bishop Lamy" in the nineteenth century and had not been "molested" by progress. Likewise, the houses, though some had been abandoned, had "been spared the disfiguration of aluminum windows and hollow-core front doors." More importantly, tradition still guided the agrarian life of the village. Replastering the adobe church and maintaining the acequia system were cooperative, community affairs (NPS 1967b; Sax 1986, 1412). Tony Hillerman (1970, 20) likened the drive from Santa Fe to Las Trampas to a trip back in time from the Space Age to the "Age of Faith."

William Brown (1963), a National Park Service historian, described Las Trampas on a National Survey of Historic Sites and Buildings form as "one of the finest examples of Spanish-American agricultural communities in the United States," closer to the eighteenth than the twentieth century. The small Hispano communities of northern New Mexico, he wrote, are "almost untouched by Anglo influence, their agricultural techniques . . . free from the mechanization that characterizes Anglo farming in the lowlands. Crops are harvested by hand, with goats and horses stamping out the grain in the primitive manner." Brown emphasized the villages' self-sufficiency, homogeneity, and strong sense of community. "As in days gone by the church is the center of communal life. Every phase of agriculture is observed with religious ceremony and ritual." Young people were leaving the villages, "but the older generations carry on their agricultural and pastoral pursuits in a unique way of life — one that is picturesque even as it slowly fades away."

Reassuring accounts of village life constitute an enduring tradition in and of themselves. A 1983 magazine article titled "Islands in the Storm" painted an idyllic portrait of Las Trampas that completely ignored the village's harsh material conditions and social crises, reporting that the village was free of social stratification and welfare dependency, insulated from economic depression, and sustained by community spirit that required only the ringing of the church bell to summon citizens to cooperative labor (Gaines 1983; cf. deBuys and Harris 1990, 90).

The Regional Community

Many writers attributed Las Trampas's timelessness to it is geographic, cultural, and economic isolation. Yet Anglos severely underestimated the extent to which Las Trampas was both integrated into a larger regional economy and transformed by American colonization.[7] The reality of life in New Mexico's Hispano villages contrasted sharply with the utopian vision Anglo newcomers relished. In an important study of Anglo-Hispanic relations in New Mexico and Colorado in the late nineteenth and early twentieth centuries, Sarah Deutsch (1987, 40) points out that Nuevomexicano villages were never isolated, static, or self-sufficient, and the fact that they appeared so was testament to the villagers' adaptive regional strategies.

Even before American conquest, villagers migrated seasonally to supplement their subsistence economy (Deutsch 1987, 9, 16–17, 40). American colonization initially expanded the economic opportunities available to villagers, who left home on a seasonal basis to work on the railroad, in sugar beet fields, in coal mines, or on cattle and sheep ranches from New Mexico to Wyoming. Maintaining their ties to villages while taking advantage of new opportunities far from home, Nuevomexicanos established a regional community between 1880 and 1914 (40). Even when entire families moved permanently to northern Colorado, "colonizing" a new area and establishing modified versions of their home villages, economic and kinship ties remained significant. This new regional community represented an "extension of community links, village by village, like runners from a plant, to encompass an entire region. No longer could the village exist or be understood apart from its laboring migrants, and the migrants, too, had inseparable and essential links to the village" (35). As we will see, Anglo preservationists interpreted out-migration in the twentieth century as a clear indication of the villages' decline, but Deutsch shows that seasonal migration represented a new mode of expansion (not dissolution) that enabled the *survival* of Hispanic villages and cultural traits (30–40). Jake Kosek (2006, 116) adds that "Hispano identity, community, and ties to the land were strategically formed in relation to this migration, not as an antithesis of it."

After World War II, employment in Los Alamos National Laboratory was another way Nuevomexicanos could maintain ties to their villages and land by (temporarily) leaving them. Immigration to California expanded "the *manito* nation" even farther ("manito" is an affectionate term for northern New Mexicans, short for *hermanito*, "little brother") (D. Hall 1995, 68). Sarah Horton (2010, 187) shows that Hispanos reconstituted New Mexican communities in California. Like their predecessors, these "diasporic Hispanos" often "viewed emigration as a temporary solution to limited economic opportunities." They maintained kinship ties to northern New Mexico, formed hometown clubs while away, visited New Mexico regularly, and moved back home upon retirement. Out-migration has actually intensified Hispano nationalism and facilitated cultural conservation, since it has provided Nuevomexicanos with increased economic security and the time, resources, and interest to invest in cultural activities back home (184–92; see also D. Hall 1995, 208–9).[8]

Deutsch (1987, 8) challenges portrayals of Nuevomexicanos as passive victims of American colonization. Yet she also warns against downplaying Anglo racism and oppression: "Chicanos and Anglos both tried to control the interaction on this frontier, and both discovered the limits of the control they achieved." She shows that the regional community served both Hispanic and Anglo interests (40, 207) and that racist employment practices and government policies severely limited Nuevomexicano initiative. The breakup of Hispanic land grants had the most devastating and long-lasting effect on village economies, making migratory wage labor all the more essential since it drastically impeded Hispanos' ability to subsist off the land. If Anglo preservationists tended to ignore or misunderstand Nuevomexicanos' regional migration patterns, they also typically overlooked the economic, political, and cultural significance of land dispossession.

The Breakup of the Las Trampas Grant

The story of the Las Trampas land grant illustrates the machinations that disintegrated the land grant system. As Malcolm Ebright (1994, 145) puts it, the Las Trampas grant, one of the oldest continuously occupied community land grants in northern New Mexico, survived on the periphery of the colony against incredible odds until Anglo lawyers assaulted it in the early 1900s. A protocol appended to the 1848 Treaty of Guadalupe Hidalgo affirmed the legality of Mexican land grants, and in 1860 Congress specifically confirmed the Las Trampas grant to the village of Las Trampas, acknowledging it as a community grant. Yet Anglo-American law was largely incompatible with communal property rights. In 1900, David Martínez Jr., a grant heir who needed money to pay debts, initiated a suit to partition the grant so that he could sell his share. He was joined by four other descendants of the original grantees, but other grant heirs were not properly informed of the suit. Plaintiffs were thus able to force a sale of the grant without the knowledge of the other owners. The court found that only 650 acres of the grant constituted private land, and the rest was sold, eventually to Frank Bond of Española for about $17,000. The lawyers/speculators profited most from the transaction while villagers received only about $25 each for their share of the community lands. In fact, most of the villagers did not even realize that the grant had been sold and thus continued using the land. They were caught up in a foreign legal system that they did not understand and in which they exerted little power (deBuys 1985, 175–85; Ebright 1994, 151–55).

Bond deeded the grant in 1907 to the Las Trampas Lumber Company of Albuquerque, which filed a quiet title suit to determine exactly what land it owned. More land grant heirs were named in this suit, which involved a new survey of the grant revealing about 7,000 acres of private land, but the suit was settled out of court. Under the terms of the settlement, which Santa Fe attorneys Charles Catron and Alois B. Renehan drafted amid shady dealings, the villagers received deeds to their private lands, right-of-way easements for irrigation ditches, and use rights to common lands for grazing and small wood gathering. The lumber company retained timber rights on the grant. The lawyers led the settlers to believe their heirs would retain use rights in perpetuity, but unbeknownst to them Renehan ensured that the court did not officially record the use-right agreements so that if the company sold the grant, the buyer would not have to respect them (deBuys 1985, 185–90; Ebright 1994, 155–60).

The final phase of the saga began in 1925 and has yet to be completely resolved. In that year the Las Trampas Lumber Company, on the verge of bankruptcy, began negotiating with the federal government to sell the grant. Despite evidence that the settlers were still using the common lands (evidence that they retained use rights to it), the U.S. Forest Service bought the grant in 1926 in a three-way trade, adding it to Carson National Forest. The national forest now completely surrounded the village. After investigation, the Forest Service, a multi-use land management agency, concluded that the use agreements were without effect. The federal government, then, turned out to be the last accomplice in the drawn-out dispossession of Las Trampas land grant heirs (deBuys 1985, 190; Ebright 1994, 160–68; Forrest 1998, 159–66, 187–88; Frei 1982).

Since the 1920s the Forest Service has accommodated and excluded traditional users depending on political and environmental conditions. Conflict between land grant activists and the agency produced militant protests during the 1960s, and to this day land grant heirs continue to negotiate with the Forest Service over grazing and wood-gathering policies (deBuys 1985; Kosek 2006). In recent decades the involvement of environmentalists (mostly wealthy Anglos) has made the conflict even more contentious (Kosek 2006, 128–38; Masco 2006, 185–87; Varela 2001). Nuevomexicanos often find they are more successful in negotiating this conflict if they conform to an idealized image of traditional, indigenous land users with a rich but endangered cultural heritage than if they adopt more militant tactics or organize around class. This strategic essentialism demonstrates the ability of subalterns to manipulate a hegemonic cultural system but also carries significant political risks (Kosek 2006, 128–40; Pulido 1996, 174–75, 204–5).

Antimodernist Yearning

Given this history of migration and dispossession, how could Anglos continue throughout the twentieth century to describe Las Trampas as an untouched, timeless, self-sufficient agricultural community? Their view of the village was idealistic and highly selective. Antimodernists began congregating in Santa Fe and Taos in the early 1900s. In Pueblo and Hispanic communities they found an alternative to the dehumanizing materialism of urban industrial society. Hispanic villagers seemed to live in harmony with each other and with nature, exemplifying rural values such as communalism, honesty, virtuousness, frugality, and piety. Romantics hoped to preserve an earlier set of American values in the villages of northern New Mexico and helped to shape a century of social policy (Forrest 1998, 33–37, 42, 53, 61–62, 103; see also Deutsch 1987, 190).

Anglo newcomers such as Mary Austin, Frank Applegate, Mabel Dodge Luhan, and Edgar Lee Hewett orchestrated revivals of Spanish and Indian artistic traditions, collecting and creating a market for folk art in the name of preservation (Mullin 2001). Austin and Applegate established the Spanish Colonial Arts Society in 1925 and helped organize Santa Fe's first Spanish Market that same year. They helped to define traditional Hispanic art, much as the Museum of New Mexico regulated the authenticity of Indian art (Forrest 1998, 44–54; Lovato 2004, 80–81; Montgomery 2002, 158–89). In Taos, art colonists promoted cultural and environmental conservation, revived native arts and ritual practices, and opposed visible manifestations of modernization and assimilation in order to preserve a "traditional" look. Sylvia Rodríguez (1989, 88–90) argues that these efforts, combined with federal policy and tourism promotion, "helped to further entrench and perpetuate . . . conditions of segregation and underdevelopment. . . . The art colony converted inequality and backwardness into marketable assets and promoted the perpetuation of those conditions by which these 'assets' were sustained" (cf. Montgomery 2002, 188).

Anglos also became interested in New Mexico's vernacular architecture, especially its mission churches, the basis of Santa Fe's new style of architecture (Chauvenet 1985). Austin facilitated the purchase of the Santuario de Chimayó in 1929 to preserve it as a place of worship and a religious museum (Forrest 1998, 54). In the 1920s and early 1930s the Society for the Preservation and Restoration of New Mexico Mission Churches restored adobe churches at several Pueblos and in Las Trampas. The society consisted of the same cadre of Anglo-Americans active in Santa Fe, including John Gaw Meem, its architect (Kessell 1980, 22–30; Wilson 1997, 237–44). The much-delayed restoration work in Trampas finally began in 1931 and was completed the following year. B. A. Reuter supervised the work, which included installing a new asphalt roof, and prodded the villagers to help out. "Excuse making, and the shifting of responsibility has become a fine art" in Las Trampas, he reported, going on to acknowledge that "there were seemingly justifiable impediments to their self interest in the work." These impediments would have included the disastrous and destabilizing effects of the Great Depression on village life (Chauvenet 1985, 50–51).

The Hispanic New Deal

In her outstanding history of the Hispanic New Deal in New Mexico, Suzanne Forrest (1998, 17) shows that, contrary to the myth of self-sufficiency, Nuevomexicano villages were on the verge of collapse during the Depression (see also Weigle 1975). Opportunities for wage labor disappeared in the 1930s, virtually bringing an end to the regional system that had sustained the villages for decades. Between the 1920s and 1930s the number of seasonal migrants dropped from 7,000–10,000 to 2,000, and migrants earned about one third of what they had earned before (Deutsch 1987, 164). The contraction of employment opportunities and hostile policies toward migrants in Colorado forced Hispanos to retreat to overcrowded villages and worn-out land. Under extreme stress, villages became destitute despite their close social networks and adaptability. By 1934, 60 percent of villagers in northern New Mexico were receiving government aid, and in some villages every family appeared to be on relief rolls (Forrest 1998, 79, 101). New Deal programs in New Mexico aimed to improve agriculture, develop home-based industries, improve child and health care, strengthen vocational and cultural education, and preserve cultural traditions.

Influenced by the progressive views of antimodernist intellectuals, the Hispanic New Deal preserved villages, supported Hispanic culture, strengthened group identity, and prevented complete assimilation. Yet cultural conservation projects, like earlier assimilationist campaigns, were a new form of Anglo supervision that undermined village autonomy. Preservationists imposed their own taste, managed authenticity, and promoted a return to the Spanish colonial past (Deutsch 1987, 188–99; Forrest 1998, 178–79). "By the late 1930s, Hispanic control over both their cultural development and their strategies of resistance and confrontation had been severely if not completely eroded, in part at least, by federal government intrusion at virtually every level of their community. This was, perhaps the ultimate Anglo conquest" (Deutsch 1987, 208–9). New Deal cultural policy also had lasting economic and political effects. Crafts provided a meager supplemental income for some Nuevomexicanos but never equaled what they had earned as migrant laborers. Meanwhile, antimodernists romanticized Nuevomexicano poverty, and their support of craft but not industrial or commercial training helped to maintain a low-income population and a marginalized, inexpensive labor force (Deutsch 1987, 193–95; cf. Mullin 2001, 123).

Despite government investment, agricultural production continued to decrease in northern New Mexico, successful cottage industries were limited, villages remained dependent on welfare, and poverty was intransigent (Forrest 1998, 88–89, 151, 178–79). Some New Deal programs were ineffective because they did not change existing economic circumstances, while others were cut off because they threatened to do so. Commercial ranchers vigorously opposed sweeping land reforms that would have involved reserving large sections of grant lands for the exclusive use of inhabitants (Forrest 1998, 157; see also Deutsch 1987, 185–86). "It was extremely unrealistic to expect the Anglo mainstream to approve the subsidized, collective farms and policies which were intended to sustain Hispanic farmers at a subsistence level of living," Forrest argues, "but it was even more unrealistic to expect the farmers, themselves, to forfeit control over their lives for the well meaning but paternalistic and Utopian schemes of the government planners" (177). More broadly, the Hispanic New Deal unsuccessfully attempted to reverse nationwide trends. New Deal planners sought to promote communalism, small subsistence farming, village handcrafts, and centralized planning in New Mexico when the trend in American agriculture was toward private ownership and land speculation, consolidation of farms, mechanization, and individual initiative. Hispanos were not unaware of these developments in the larger society, all of which undercut traditional agricultural practices (174–77; see also deBuys 1985, 308).

New Deal programs were also contradictory. On the one hand planners wanted to preserve the preindustrial, communitarian way of life of northern New Mexico's Hispanic villages, but on the other hand they wanted to rationalize village economies and improve their efficiency. The architects of the Hispanic New Deal thus "found themselves battling on a practical level the very forces they hoped, on an intellectual level, to preserve." This involved distinguishing "between 'good' and 'bad' aspects of Hispanic ethnicity. Purporting to value cultural pluralism they extolled the virtues of Hispanic arts, crafts, music, and folklore but worked mightily to eradicate" superstition, irresponsibility, docility, and ignorance among Hispanics (Forrest 1998, 62, 103, 177).

The paradoxical attempt to prevent and promote change simultaneously has continued to typify Anglo interventions in the life of Las Trampas and other Nuevomexicano villages. Forrest (1998, 181) notes that interest in helping villagers has "welled up at approximately thirty-year intervals, lasted seven to ten years, then drained away in a period of reaction and disillusionment." After World War II curtailed the New Deal, the next period of intense interest in northern New Mexico's Hispano villages came in the 1960s, the era to which I now turn. Preservationists achieved only some of their goals in the 1960s. The movement in the late 1990s to establish the Northern Rio Grande National Heritage Area picked up where those efforts left off. In all three periods the tension between preservation and reform had important political consequences.

Notes from the Field

JUNE 19, 2003

Northern Rio Grande National Heritage Area partners workshop, the Old Santa Fe Trail Building, Santa Fe

The National Park Service and NRGNHA board held an all-day workshop at the Park Service's Old Santa Fe Trail building, a grand Pueblo-Spanish Revival Style adobe constructed in the 1930s by the Civilian Conservation Corps and Work Projects Administration. I had been volunteering there for several months, helping the NRGNHA board with filing, typing, and correspondence. More than sixty people attended the workshop, including representatives of nonprofit organizations, the NPS, the Bureau of Land Management, the U.S. Forest Service, New Mexico's congressional delegates, and city, county, state, and tribal governments. The mix of activists, educators, planners, preservationists, archaeologists, and historians produced stimulating conversation. Participants broke into small groups focused on preservation, education, cultural programming, and economic development. Proposed actions included inventorying heritage resources in the region, recording oral histories, and adding representatives of land grant and acequia organizations to the heritage area board. The workshop demonstrated considerable interest in the heritage area, even though designation and implementation were still several years off.

The Village, the Highway, and the Threat of Modernity

In 1963 a council made up of representatives from various federal and state agencies published a report on the Embudo watershed in north-central New Mexico, which includes Las Trampas. The study painted a bleak picture of northern New Mexico's Hispanic villages. Economic opportunities had continuously diminished, and 17 percent of men were unemployed, more than twice the state rate. The populations of both Rio Arriba and Taos Counties were decreasing, especially as people between the ages of eighteen and sixty-five left to find work.[9] And compared with the state, the region also had high infant mortality rates, inadequate access to health care, problems with sanitation and water supply, elevated high school dropout rates, and low numbers of graduates planning on entering college (ICADP and NMSPO 1963, 26–34).

The situation in Las Trampas was typical of that in surrounding villages. Taxation, forced land sales, and land speculation had reduced the Las Trampas grant from 46,000 acres to a mere 210 acres of cropland, plus grazing and timber allotments in the national forest, often of poor quality. Overgrazing had depleted natural resources and degraded the environment (MacGregor 1966, 5, 8). According to the Embudo report, the village economy had shifted from one based on farming supplemented by wage labor to one in which farming was supplementary. Only one elderly man lived in the village year-round; the other men left home for seasonal wage labor throughout the West. Vacant and abandoned houses were testament to depopulation and entrenched poverty. If not for welfare payments and close ties to the land, Las Trampas and other villages in northern New Mexico would probably be almost completely depopulated (ICADP and NMSPO 1963, 77–79). This bleak picture led John Conron (1967a, 3) to conclude that Las Trampas "maintains a way of life which appears to be no longer possible in twentieth century America." A participant in the Embudo study, Conron was a modernist-trained architect who migrated to New Mexico from Boston in the 1950s (Wilson 1997, 253). The ambiguity—and kernel of hope—in his assessment left the door open for another round of cultural conservation and economic development efforts.

The Embudo report was a first step in this direction (see also van Dresser 1972), and it reflected the same opposing desires that characterized New Deal programs. On the one hand the authors lamented cultural change and advocated preserving the built environment and strengthening the traditional character of small villages. "The houses and structures built in the last several years are already [in 1963] showing the signs of outside, 20th century influence," the authors noted with regret. A new church in the village of Vadito exemplified "the disintegration of the architectural heritage" of the region, even though parishioners themselves built it (ICADP and NMSPO 1963, 122).[10] On the other hand, the report called for modernization. It recommended improving and intensifying agricultural production (especially for export), making better use of natural resources, and developing cottage industries (79, 113–14). The authors worried that the villagers' "wasteful and primitive" agricultural practices would make it difficult to bring them into the life of the nation (132).

Given these contradictory perspectives, it is not surprising that the report recognized the United States as both the cause of and solution to the region's problems. "The watershed's problems owe their creation to the in-rush of changes which followed in the wake of the American annexation," the authors acknowledged. "It's obviously foolish to rely on eighteenth-century patterns to solve the twentieth-century difficulties of the watershed. It's only by going forward and bringing the watershed and its people fully into the life of today's United States that the problems arising from the breakdown of the old Spanish Colonial society can be successfully solved" (ICADP and NMSPO 1963, 116).

The idea of preserving eighteenth-century villages by bringing them into the twentieth century did not seem to strike the authors as paradoxical. They had already begun to see tourism as a way to integrate preservation and reform, although their emphasis on recreational rather than heritage tourism minimized this integration. The report's top-down approach to development and sometimes patronizing tone also contradicted its emphasis on cultural sensitivity and local collaboration (ICADP and NMSPO 1963, 110–11).[11] Even the authors themselves seemed to doubt their own vision: "With the new paved roads and the desire for increased economic improvement, it is doubtful that this centuries-old heritage can withstand the new pressures without deterioration" (122).

A New Threat

It took the threat of a new highway to rally support for a new round of preservation efforts and social engineering in northern New Mexico. In the summer of 1966 the State Highway Department announced plans to pave and widen Highway 76 between Truchas and Peñasco. At that time the highway was a graded country road, precarious after storms and often impassable in the winter. It was the only road that passed through Las Trampas, and villagers were desperate for a safer school bus route and better access to the outside world. Plans called for the improved road to run within a few feet of the churchyard in Las Trampas and to cut through a nineteenth-century schoolhouse (MacGregor 1966, 8–9).

Word of the project soon got out, and newspapers began publishing impassioned articles and editorials on Las Trampas and this new threat to northern New Mexico's architectural and cultural heritage. Architect Nathaniel Owings (1970, 30) was not surprised when someone mailed him a six-page article from the *Santa Fe New Mexican* on the topic: "Every mail brought word of new intrusion, defacement, dismemberment of the remote, the fragile, the beautiful; of threats to or actual destruction of irreplaceable remnants of Spanish-American colonial culture in our Southwest—and, of course, always in the name of progress." Owings, who became a major player in the Trampas campaign, was a part-time resident of Pojoaque (just north of Santa Fe) and a founding partner of the Chicago firm Skidmore, Owings, and Merrill, which has built some of the tallest buildings in the world.

Writers predicted the highway project would not only damage the church's "lovely setting and primitive charm" but also "seriously impair the fragile architectural and environmental values of the picturesque Spanish colonial settlement," spoiling its historic character ("Threat to Las Trampas" 1966; "Preservation Law Saves Historic Town" 1967). John Conron (1967a, 8) insisted that "action must be taken now or the on-rushing twentieth century will absorb, and thus destroy, this fine example of the Spanish heritage which has made such a distinctive place of northern New Mexico. What remains of this way of life is rapidly being suppressed under the pressure of new economic needs and desires, as well as by the advent of tourism."

A 1967 National Park Service report on the controversy noted "a lurking dread" in architectural publications on Las Trampas (NPS 1967a, 4). Anxious calls for preservation suggest that the greatest threat in the road project may not have been to the church of San José de Gracia or to the village but to the preservationists themselves. When historical resources face destruction, preservationists often respond as if their own identity, sense of decorum, or class sensibility were under assault. The proposed highway through Las Trampas threatened to expose Anglos to the destructiveness of American colonization, producing feelings of imperialist guilt. No preservationist seemed to consider the possibility that the improved road might actually help *sustain* the village. For political progressives who considered themselves friends of Spanish Americans and Pueblo Indians the further deterioration of Nuevomexicano communities was intolerable. Their response was thus swift and powerful.

A National Historic Landmark

The residents of Las Trampas themselves overwhelmingly favored the new road (Brown 1967, 8; Gallegos 1966), a position that contradicted the image of traditional villagers content in their isolation (cf. Handler 1988, 151–52). "We don't live isolated the way we do because we want to," one remarked. "We don't have the ways and means to improve." The villagers argued that San José de Gracia was never in danger and that if it had been they would have been the first to protect it. In any case, while the church was hundreds of years old, most of the other structures in the village were much more recent. According to Delfido Lopez, older residents said that the village looked nothing like it did when they were children. And perhaps most importantly, the Trampaseños were tired of being characterized as quaint and backward (Bottoroff 1966; cf. Owings 1970, 32).

The state government acknowledged the villagers' strong support for the road improvement, but preservationists ratcheted the debate up to the national level, where the issues became more abstract and the villagers themselves had little power. Whose heritage was at stake, and who stood to benefit from the preservation of the village? Nathaniel Owings (1966) assured the governor that "the church is of national significance and of the highest architectural and historic merit." The *New Mexican* argued that "not only the property owners of Las Trampas, but the state of New Mexico and the entire nation" stood to gain from the preservation of the village ("Threat to Las Trampas" 1966). The New Mexico Arts Commission and the American Association of Architects stated that buildings such as San José de Gracia "belong really not only to us, but to the entire United States" and commended the villagers for their "contribution to the architectural heritage of America, for which the entire nation owes them gratitude" ("Commendation for the Citizens of Las Trampas" 1969).

The road crisis ended after Secretary of the Interior Stewart Udall intervened. Nathaniel Owings happened to be a member of the Advisory Board on National Parks, Historic Sites, Buildings, and Monuments. In October 1966 the Advisory Board discussed the Las Trampas case and persuaded Udall to write a letter to Governor Jack Campbell requesting that he defer a decision on the project until the Park Service could "undertake studies to assess the national significance of Las Trampas and to explore appropriate means by which the historical and architectural character of the village could best be preserved against the inroads of modern development" (Owings 1970, 31–32). Campbell agreed to the request and omitted a 2,200-foot stretch through the village from the improvement project (Scott 1966).

The National Park Service then prepared a report on the village and various preservation options. Meanwhile, a group of preservationists including Conron, Owings, architect John McHugh, and Park Service veteran David Jones formed the Las Trampas Foundation. Their intention was to act on behalf of the village, which lacked any formal governing body, and, supposedly, to give voice to its residents (Conron 1967b, 1; "Las Trampas, New Mexico" 1967). A few Trampaseños joined them, at least nominally: "brave souls, risking local banishment," according to Owings (1970, 33). "Dedicated to the protection of the village and the encouragement of its economy" and to "safeguarding the heritage of the community," the foundation helped nominate the village to become a National Historic Landmark (Conron 1967b, 1). The Advisory Board then recommended designation to Secretary Udall, who granted landmark status in record time. The village of Las Trampas thus became a National Historic Landmark (NHL) on May 28, 1967. The church of San José de Gracia received its own NHL designation in 1970. Designating a living village a historic landmark defied conventional measures of significance, but the Park Service felt that the village's typicality merited recognition, especially when "cultural values" were taken into consideration (Brown 1967, 3–4, 6).

National Historic Landmark designation brought Las Trampas under the protection of the newly enacted National Historic Preservation Act of 1966. Secretary Udall informed the governor of New Mexico and the secretary of transportation of this protective legislation, which, among other things, requires a review of how federally funded projects will affect historic properties. The designation thus tied up highway funding until the preservationists approved the project. The issue was finally settled in June 1967 when the Bureau of Public Roads, Highway Department, Las Trampas Foundation, and National Park Service agreed upon the "Treaty of Santa Fe." The agreement called for a scaled-down, less intrusive highway through the village that would provide residents with a reliable year-round road without spoiling the village's historic character or aesthetic qualities (Conron 1968, 30–31; Owings 1970, 34; "Preservation Law Saves Historic Town" 1967).[12] Conron (1968, 31) considered the resolution a 75 percent victory for preservationists.

Saving the Villagers from Themselves

Preservationists were continuously vexed by the opposition they encountered in Las Trampas itself. "The stage was set for conflict," the National Park Service noted impartially. On the one hand were the villagers, "torn between tradition and present need" and "tired of being quaint and archaic." On the other were "the well-meaning but . . . intruding Anglos" intent on saving "the old way of life (at the very least its visible forms)" (NPS 1967a, 3). Trampaseños were understandably suspicious and resentful of outsider interventions: "We do not want anyone bossing us around and telling us what to do on our own property; we just want people to leave us alone as we were before," they explained at one meeting. Why did the Las Trampas Foundation get involved in the first place, and why did its members not consult with residents before seeking landmark status, they wondered (Chauvenet 1985, 57). Delfido Lopez put it this way: "If my place was historical and I didn't like it that way, I don't see how the historical society could stop me from changing it. That's how we feel about our village." Perhaps the preservationists should try tearing up the pavement around the Palace of the Governors to see how visitors like driving through mud and deep holes to get there, he suggested (Bottoroff 1966).

The *Santa Fe New Mexican* was sympathetic with the villagers and called for the state to help maintain structures with great public value such as the church in Trampas: "It is not enough to encourage the villagers from the sidelines with free advice and gratuitous meddling" ("Must Pay for Privilege" 1966). The preservationists, however, failed to understand the villagers' resistance and even seemed hurt by it. Conron (1968, 30) thought the villagers mistakenly believed the Las Trampas Foundation opposed progress. "It must be admitted," he wrote, "that we of the Foundation did not explain clearly and fully our position."

Owings (1970, 30, 32) reported that "we had assumed that the villagers themselves would of course wish to preserve the church and churchyard in which their fathers, mothers and grandparents had been buried," but "to our great surprise, we were in error." He recalled that the newspapers took sport in poking fun at the do-gooder preservationists. So "those of us who were concerned decided to do what we could to 'save the villagers from themselves,' as one of us put it, 'for they know not what they are doing.' We did this with a sense of great uneasiness. Was this perhaps arrogance?" Owings blissfully ignored the larger economic and historical context of the village's troubles. He acknowledged that the village's landholdings had been vastly reduced over the years and that "it is evident that pressures had long been exerted." But he went on to remark, "The nature of these pressures and how the acreage came to be reduced to this pathetic figure I do not know; this is not part of our story. Undoubtedly it had to do with foreclosures for taxes and ignorance of true boundaries. But the village is surrounded by a national forest, so to a degree the villagers still have the benefit and use of the vast original acreage." In fact, in the same essay he cites an article from the *Santa Fe New Mexican* that carefully summarized the plight of the village and the breakup of the Las Trampas land grant.

In addition to dismissing the economic, environmental, and political factors that left Las Trampas so debilitated, Owings aestheticized the village and his relationship to it. He recalled having made pilgrimages to the village since 1931. "In recent years, my wife and I have had many a luncheon alfresco, chilled wine resting in the sparkling spring as we perched high above the church, its straw-gold-crusted, blunt-edged adobe walls sparkling in the sun and our luncheon basket balanced on the flume of hollowed-out logs that guides the stream across the gully dividing our hillside from the plaza" (Owings 1970, 30). Leisurely exploring the region around Las Trampas on pleasure trips, converting the village's irrigation system into a personal dining area, and casting a controlling gaze over the church scene from *their* hillside vantage point, the Owingses epitomized colonial sightseers. No wonder

Las Trampas

the people of Las Trampas were suspicious of the well-intentioned preservationists swooping in to save them from themselves.[13]

"A Happy Summer"

The denouement of the two-year highway controversy found the preservationists reassured in their beliefs about culture and tradition in Las Trampas and the redemptive power of their own intervention. According to Owings, the residents of Las Trampas were unhappy about the long delay in the road improvement and so, in the spirit of reconciliation, the Las Trampas Foundation offered to finance a restoration of the church. After a few long, involved meetings, the villagers agreed. The work involved constructing a new roof for the church, reconstructing the church's twin bell towers (which John Gaw Meem designed based on two historic photographs), and applying a new coat of mud plaster to the building's exterior. Everyone in the village participated in the work, but the contribution of women in replastering the church particularly impressed Owings (Owings 1970, 34–35; see also MacGregor 1967; "New Lease on Life" 1967).[14]

Indeed, the sight of the entire community turning out to repair the church was reward enough for the preservationists. Owings wrote: "It had been a happy summer, with the entire village working—young and old, men and women, boys and girls—constantly supplied with succulent watermelons at critical moments by Davy Jones. All was happy, friction was forgotten and the threat of the highway's coming through was no longer a subject of discussion." Father Roca held a special mass in the church to celebrate all the work that had been done, and again Owings was impressed to see the entire village come together to worship. Owings noted that the priest assured the villagers that they "had no reason to fear the Las Trampas Foundation or that anything would be done to damage their village or their church. There was no helicopter, he said, large enough to carry the church away." In actuality, the villagers had every reason to be suspicious of the outsiders. After the service, some thirty-five villagers adjourned to the schoolhouse. "The Las Trampas Foundation had provided a cake

Fig. 26. The church and plaza as viewed from across the improved highway.

baked in the exact form and detail of the church—everything edible except the ladder to the roof." So, in the end, the preservationists were able to consume the church whole. The road was completed by wintertime (see fig. 26), and Owings (1970, 35) vouched that Las Trampas "seemed especially fresh and neat and charmingly beautiful as a New Mexican village should look."

The Politics of Adobe

The use of soft (mud) plaster instead of hard (cement) plaster in the 1967 restoration of San José de Gracia was highly significant. Other adobe churches in northern New Mexico—most recently the famous church at Ranchos de Taos—had "succumbed" to hard plastering (see V. Hooker 1977). Owings (1970, 34) admitted that the preservationists "stood in mortal fear of the fate that had befallen Ranchos de Taos." He was thoroughly pleased with the end result in Las Trampas: "The surfaces were almost as hard as glass, with a texture like homemade bread crust—the entirety so beautiful, so aesthetically satisfying, that it left the question of a cement surface too odious to consider." Mud plaster (a mixture of clay, sand, straw, and water) must be touched up every year and completely redone every few years, depending on conditions. Replastering an entire church is an enormous task for communities, especially those with declining populations. Cement plaster is more expensive but requires less frequent maintenance. Although many preservationists advocate the use of mud plaster, both types of plaster require monitoring and maintenance, and no consensus has emerged as to which is technically better (Wilson 1997, 241).

Locals and newcomers to New Mexico alike have praised the aesthetic and social qualities of adobe construction. Mud plaster is associated with tradition and hand craftsmanship, while cement plaster evokes technical progress and modernization. Anita Rodríguez, a native New Mexican who supervised the replastering of the Las Trampas church in 1986, called adobe a "living architecture" that "represents a living culture" (Sweeney 1988). When the church was remudded a few years later, the *Santa Fe New Mexican* reported that "fresh mud plaster is applied by hand, lovingly sculpted and contoured over the existing mud so that the building has truly become a sculpture, more organic with each remodeling. By its very nature, a mud-plastered adobe structure is destined to be a work in progress" (Dahl 1989). The *New Mexican* described the 1967 replastering of San José de Gracia as hot, hard work made worthwhile by an "old fashioned pioneer spirit of cooperation." The replastering is "a task of love for the church and community and is one of the things that bonds the people together in a time when many villages have lost their sense of community" (MacGregor 1967). A Northern Rio Grande National Heritage Area board member with extensive experience in adobe church preservation told me that "people have their roots in adobe."

For many outside observers, the ritual of remudding an adobe church was as important as the preservation of the church's physical structure. Owings (1970, 34) called the replastering of San José de Gracia in 1967 "a chain reaction of an ancient tradition. . . . The use of adobe, creating the need for rhythmic renewal, and the festival of community effort toward that renewal every several years . . . are benefits of the preservation of custom. Like life itself, the ritual of renewal must be preserved." This spectacle of community cooperation satisfied Anglo observers. A testament to the endurance of custom and the health of the community, the scene reassured preservationists that the village had survived the threat of modernity and assuaged any imperialist shame they may have felt. They could also take credit for this success story. After all, they were the ones who campaigned to save the church, financed its restoration, and publicized the replastering. All this suggests that the preservationists had as much, if not more, to gain from the protection and restoration of San José de Gracia as the villagers who worshipped there. And their stake in the restoration was not merely aesthetic but also political and psychological.

A Living National Monument

The highway threat was averted, but the long-term fate of the village remained uncertain. Preservationists had a larger vision. In 1966 John Conron wrote a proposal on behalf of the New Mexico Society of Architects that recommended purchasing the entire Las Trampas valley and turning it over to the National Park Service to manage as a living national monument or national historic site. Conron (1967a, 5) hoped to preserve the visual impact of the whole setting. "As the viewer approaches from the enclosing ridges, the tight little valley with its farms and winding stream, its church, plaza, and surrounding clusters of homes will thus be seen as a coherent unit." Conron and his colleagues really envisioned creating an exhibit of how a Spanish colonial village *should* look. This would require preserving some buildings, restoring others, and removing the mobile homes that had crept into the valley (Chauvenet 1985, 56; Conron 1986).

Within this picturesque setting it would also be possible "to preserve and display Spanish Colonial traditions, arts and crafts" (Conron 1967a, 2). It was crucial that Las Trampas remain an active agricultural community where people lived. Conron envisioned giving "life tenancy to the present Spanish American land owners and offer[ing] them the opportunity to participate in the raising and marketing of demonstration or experimental crops." As residents died, monument administrators could "seek new Spanish American residents, concentrating upon young people who would be interested in carrying out agricultural experiments in the valley" (6). Presumably Conron wanted Nuevomexicanos to inhabit the village/monument because of their ethnic and cultural identity. The entire proposal was apolitical and never mentioned the villagers' land rights. Authenticity, however, was an implicit concern: "In spite of obvious difficulties, a means should be found to preserve an entire community and have it occupied by Spanish Americans, some of whom (at least) are engaged in activities which are not tourist oriented" (3).

Yet the problem of retaining the villagers was intractable, and the preservationists were unable to deal—conceptually or practically—with the relationship between culture and economics. Nathaniel Owings (1970, 32–33; 1973, 224) dreamed of enabling the villagers to return to a nineteenth-century economy, including sheep raising and wool production, but he made no mention of land politics. John Conron (1968, 28), on the other hand, argued that cultural conservation depended upon economic change. The Trampaseños, he noted, wanted to continue living in the village but also wanted the amenities of the modern world such as refrigerators and television. "The challenge becomes one of integration; integration of an ancient community into the flow of the 20th century, without either the destruction of the culture by the usual contemporary garishness, or the freezing of the culture by the imposition of a Williamsburg type of death."[15] Conron believed that "history should be allowed to continue" and that the villagers should be able "to use 20th-century tools in the expansion of their economy. What we hope to do is to use the best of now, and to extend the value of then" (see also "Las Trampas, New Mexico" 1967). Toward this end he proposed regulating agricultural production, adopting new farming methods and marketing practices, and introducing higher-income crops. Subsistence farming was not part of the plan (Conron 1967a, 5). The architects imagined Las Trampas becoming a model "that other villages could follow to achieve a mainstream-America economic viability that yet would not homogenize them and destroy those still vital elements of cultural substance and form that give them character and distinction" (NPS 1967a, 4). Separating culture and economics, they never addressed the contradiction between preservation and modernization.

William Brown, a National Park Service historian, wrote a "suitability-feasibility critique" of the New Mexico Society of Architects' proposal. Brown (1967, 2–3) sympathized with the desire to preserve Las Trampas as a living national monument. "We are dealing with a rapidly dying species of culture—one about to be overwhelmed by values derived from a dominant industrial-urban-secular culture," he wrote, reiterating a common twentieth-century narrative of tragedy, loss, and death. Brown also agreed that the significance of Las Trampas lay in both the built environment and the people. The village's "Shangri-La isolation" had "sufficiently delayed the start of cultural change to allow, with proper controls quickly applied, salvage of the more salient characteristics of Spanish-American village life, even as it evolves." He believed the best approach might therefore be a program of "controlled evolution," which would involve providing the villagers with alternatives "to a headlong rush into that brand of 20th century life that destroys *all* old values and evidences, that would make their village just another characterless highway satellite, and of their lives a disillusioned emptiness."

Yet Brown (1967, 8–12) ultimately argued that it would be legally, politically, logistically, and financially impossible to turn Las Trampas into a living national monument. The Trampaseños were clearly opposed to heavy-handed interventions. Brown fundamentally opposed "putting people into a mold—whether or not they have chosen it themselves; whether or not it is, in some grand design, beneficial to them." Cultural disintegration "is tragic, in this day of rapid evolution toward a world-wide industrial-urban-secular order, because we hate to see unique forms of human society die; we feel a loss in the world." But cultural adaptability and change are natural, functional, and necessary for survival, he concluded. Brown later mused that "the people in traditional communities have to fight their own war." But "we can help preserve the habitat in which traditional activities can occur. Mostly we can do this by controlling the pace . . . of developmental activity. We can help provide, or maintain, an environment where cultural choice can be made by the people involved. We must leave them in control" (quoted in Sax 1986, 1413). Reducing the scale of the highway through Las Trampas, for instance, required the involvement of powerful outsiders but ostensibly helped villagers maintain their traditional way of life (Sax 1986, 1413). Yet attempts to restrict development in northern New Mexico have more effectively perpetuated economic marginalization than protected cultural choices. Truly protecting a cultural environment in northern New Mexico would require a radical redistribution of land and political rights, which few cultural conservationists ever considered.

The National Park Service packaged Conron's proposal, Brown's critique, and several other commentaries, none by Nuevomexicanos, into a report for the agency's Advisory Board.[16] All the contributors agreed on the value of preserving Las Trampas "as an exemplar of Spanish colonial architecture, village form, and culture" and helping "the people of places rich in traditions of freedom and independence . . . preserve and enhance their way of life" (NPS 1967a, i, iii). The Advisory Board ultimately followed Brown's suggestion and recommended designating the village a National Historic Landmark rather than a national monument. This meant that the village would remain in private hands and not become a part of the national park system, which the government manages. Although the Park Service did not pursue a more ambitious cultural conservation program in Las Trampas, the 1967 report presents a stunning plan for social engineering. It represents an important link in the twentieth-century history of efforts by outsiders to preserve northern New Mexico's Hispano villages, harkening back to New Deal programs and foreshadowing the heritage area movement that began in the 1990s.

Representing the Villagers

Anglo commentators anxiously speculated about whether or not Nuevomexicanos *wanted* to remain in their rural villages and maintain their cultural distinctiveness. John Conron (1967a, 9) felt confident that "many of the Spanish Americans of this region do not want to become middle class citizens of industrialized America. They have had the opportunity to become so and have rejected it. Instead they believe in the desirability of their traditional way of life" (cf. deBuys 1985, 270–71). In contrast, the 1963 Embudo report, in which Conron participated, noted that young people of northern New Mexico are drawn to cities, and Hispanic New Mexicans have adopted American material culture, technology, and values. Assuming they would reject participation in American society "in favor of clinging to the materially unrewarding old ways of subsistence and isolation is contrary to all available evidence and the American ethic of equality and opportunity" (ICADP and NMSPO 1963, 134; cf. Deutsch 1987, 188–89).[17] William Brown (1967, 10) wondered whether the villagers wished to maintain a distinct ethnic identity as *Spanish* Americans and whether young people educated in the valley and drawn to jobs in Los Alamos or Albuquerque considered a "traditional way of life (with selected infusions of 20th-century Americana) superior to the dominant Anglo way of life that surrounds them." He suspected that these young people viewed "their remote village with nostalgia but with no intent to return."

This speculative discussion about what Nuevomexicanos wanted oversimplified the situation and cast the debate in polarizing terms. Conron overemphasized Hispano traditionalism and ignored the fact that opportunities to become "middle class citizens" had always been severely limited for Nuevomexicanos (partly due to the efforts of Anglo antimodernists). Brown and the authors of the Embudo report, on the other hand, underestimated Hispanos' ties to rural village life. Historically, few Nuevomexicanos chose *either* isolation *or* integration, cultural distinctiveness or assimilation. Rather, they creatively adapted to changing circumstances, took advantage of new opportunities, and coped with hostile economic and political forces in ways that allowed (and required) them to do *both*.

Perhaps more significantly, debates about the future of Las Trampas systematically excluded Nuevomexicano voices. Instead, outsiders assumed the right to speak for the villagers and represent their needs and desires. Yet the villagers were by no means powerless in determining their own future. They were able to exert enough political pressure to keep the highway project afloat despite considerable opposition. Moreover, as I will suggest later on, silence can also be subversive.

The National Heritage Area Model

The proposal to turn Las Trampas into a living national monument was ahead of its time. The National Park Service was generally "in the business of preserving remnants of live nature and dead cultures" (Sax 1986, 1389; for a similar initiative see Mac-Cannell 1992, 172–80). The idea of managing an area in which people still live was not completely unprecedented or untested, but it had little institutional support in the 1960s. Partnership parks, where land protection is based on development controls rather than outright acquisition and where people continue to live, began to catch on in the 1970s, but these parks still remain exceptional within the national park system.[18] But the concept of "heritage" itself was beginning to expand to include intangible culture, living populations, the culture and history of underrepresented groups, large geographical regions, and both the distant and recent past (Handler 1987, 128).

National heritage areas, first introduced in 1984, represent the fullest realization of attempts to integrate living communities into park-like units (Barrett 2003; Eugster 2003). In fact, the Las Trampas proposal presaged the Northern Rio Grande National Heritage Area initiative in scope and spirit. The 1967 NPS report raised the possibility of "a consortium solution" to the village's woes "that would unite the citizens of Las Trampas with Federal, State, and private agencies in voluntary association—an association whose goal would be renewal of village life, economically and socially, while attempting to preserve and interpret the outward forms that contribute so much to its distinctiveness" (NPS 1967a, i; see also Brown 1967, 10–11; Conron 1967b, 3; M. Grosvenor 1967). The NRGNHA (which covers not just a single village but three counties) provides precisely such a collaborative framework.

Unlike earlier efforts, however, the heritage area initiative builds upon a clearly articulated relationship between preservation and economic development. Embracing heritage tourism allows heritage area advocates to treat culture and economics as complementary rather than opposing interests. Nevertheless, heritage areas usually promote the continuance of cultural practices under radically *different* economic circumstances. They generally do not attempt to restore or revitalize the economic, social, and political conditions in which these practices originally developed (witness the mills converted into museums and cultural centers in northeastern heritage areas). In the name of heritage, "dying economies stage their own rebirth as displays of what they once were" (Kirshenblatt-Gimblett 1998, 151). Heritage area advocates tend to envision economies based on culture rather than cultures based on economies. This formal separation represents an important continuity between the NRGNHA and earlier preservation campaigns in New Mexico. According to the Northern Rio Grande National Heritage Area Act of 2006 (see appendix), one purpose of the heritage area is to "assist local communities and residents in preserving . . . cultural, historical and natural resources" (sec. 202). Yet six provisions detail private property protections, including prohibitions against requiring access to private land or modifying "any authority of Federal, State, or local governments to regulate land use" (sec. 207).

This legislative mandate — promote cultural traditions without interfering with land management — suggests that the NRGNHA may perpetuate the anti-politics of culture. However, many heritage area advocates I talked to insisted that historic and cultural preservation efforts must nurture people's relationship to land and water. "Hispanics revere land more than anything else, almost as much as their religion," said NRGNHA board member Orlando Romero (2003). He hoped that the NRGNHA would raise awareness about how important land is and why it needs protection. Ernest Ortega (2003) of the National Park Service emphasized the direct ties people have to land, regardless of ownership. Although the heritage area's management entity has no authority to manage land, it could represent communities in their negotiations with state and federal governments. For instance, the heritage area board could ask the supervisors of Carson and Santa Fe National Forests to modify policies to accommodate culturally significant practices such as firewood collection, grazing, and clay extraction. The next step would be to seek the aid of New Mexico's congressional delegates. To influence land management agencies in this way would be to practice politics with "a lower case p rather than an upper case P," Ortega explained. The NRGNHA board has pledged to "advocate for people's right to access to and appropriate use of public lands" (NRGNHA 2011). Forest Service representatives have expressed hope that the Northern Rio Grande National Heritage Area will help them in their work with communities surrounding the forests.[19]

What relationship will the heritage area have to the land grant movement? Pablo Sedillo (2003), a field representative from Senator Bingaman's office, observed that cultural preservation is central to both but that they are politically distinct. Romero and Ortega also recognized common ground but hoped the NRGNHA would not become entangled in contentious land politics, which often play out in the courts. Instead, they imagined the heritage area supporting historical research on land grants and helping to educate people about both land grants and acequias. The NRGNHA management plan thoroughly discusses the history of Spanish and Mexican land grants, their breakup after American colonization, and Nuevomexicano resistance since the early 1900s. It states that one of the heritage area's goals is to nurture sustainable agriculture and traditional land use. In this context it notes the significance of land grants and acequias and recommends ongoing collaboration with county, state, federal, and tribal land management authorities as well as land grant organizations (NRGNHA 2013). It remains to be seen what effect the NRGNHA will have on struggles over land and water in northern New Mexico.

Nonrecognition and the Counter-Ethnographic Present

Interest in preserving northern New Mexico's Hispano villages swelled in the 1930s, 1960s, and 1990s. But the final episode in the history of preservation in Las Trampas that I want to discuss came during the 1980s, before the heritage area initiative began. In fact, it was a moment in which the residents thwarted recognition and resisted the Park Service's bureaucratic desire to circumscribe the village. In the 1980s the NPS set out to clean up its National Historic Landmark files, and one designation that required attention was the village of Las Trampas. In the rush to designate the village an NHL in 1967 the Advisory Board recommended that the landmark's boundary "conform to the present visually evident village limits" (M. Grosvenor 1967). When the Park Service attempted to establish a more exact boundary, a temporal problem arose as well. According to the original designation, Las Trampas was important as a Spanish colonial settlement. Yet when the boundary review began, the NPS immediately found "that the church and surrounding field system are probably the only truly Spanish Colonial (pre-1821) features in Las Trampas" (Pepin-Donat 1982). Other structures in the village were much more recent, exhibiting nineteenth- and twentieth-century Anglo influences.[20] Settling the boundary issue would thus require more thorough documentation of the tangible Spanish colonial resources in the village. While all the National Park Service staff involved in the matter seemed supportive of the NHL designation and recognized the village's enduring importance, some did raise the possibility of reducing the landmark's coverage or even de-designating the village (B. Grosvenor 1986).

These concerns were purely bureaucratic, as was the National Park Service's response to them. In 1988 Patrick O'Brien, a Park Service historian, coordinated the effort to resolve the boundary issue. One of his principal goals was to establish the age of the buildings in Las Trampas to determine which fell into the time period reflected on the NHL nomination. After holding a public meeting in the village, O'Brien (1988a) wrote a letter to mayordoma Barbara Lopez explaining that the NPS wanted to map the village and the location of its historically significant buildings (as mayordoma Lopez would have supervised the upkeep of the church). "The NHL boundary study," he wrote, "involves an *intensive survey* of the exterior of all structures in the town and surrounding area and *their classification as contributing or noncontributing elements* to the Las Trampas NHL District. The survey includes photography, research, and detailed onsite work." It would take three or four days to complete. "This visual survey will be conducted so that *all the cultural resources of Las Trampas are inventoried and assessed* as to their historic significance and how they contribute to the NHL District. *Final boundary recommendations* will be based on this survey" (emphasis added). O'Brien apologized for the invasion of the community's privacy and asked Lopez for her help in notifying all the residents of the village of the forthcoming survey work.

Not surprisingly, the NHL files in the National Park Service archives in Santa Fe contain no response from Lopez to O'Brien. The "intensive survey" he proposed must have alarmed those Trampaseños who heard about it, perhaps reminding them of the surveys that facilitated the breakup of their land grant several decades earlier. In actuality, the NHL designation was mostly symbolic, imposing no restrictions or regulations on property owners and providing little financial support to residents wanting to maintain historic buildings. So the question of the extent of the historic district was relatively unimportant. Nevertheless, O'Brien (1988b) reported that the fifteen villagers attending the public meeting in Las Trampas had been "guarded but receptive" and that the meeting itself was "cordial but inconclusive." "The general tenor was one of suspicion, caution and a tendency to confuse National Park Service and National Forest Service functions," an understandable confusion that the NPS continues to combat in northern New Mexico. The attendees expressed "dissatisfaction with past information and a desire to know the exact location of the NHL boundaries." Some wanted to know why they had not been consulted when the designation was originally made and others if they could be removed from the district.

Moving ahead with the project, the NPS twice attempted to find a contractor to carry out the survey work in the village, but potential contractors expressed concern about their ability to complete the job given the residents' suspicion toward outsiders and the federal government. The Park Service finally concluded that it would be impossible to conduct a survey in Las Trampas and tabled the boundary study altogether (O'Brien 1988b; Caufield 1988).[21] The attempted resolution of the NHL boundary problem illustrates the federal government's interest in commemorating Las Trampas on the one hand and the villagers' desire to be left alone on the other. Outsiders' attempts to recognize the village have invariably entailed some form of objectification. The boundary issue, for instance, involved the abstract and rather meaningless task of drawing a line around the village to distinguish its historic and non-historic components. But the boundary study was neither the first nor the last time access to the village, physically or symbolically, was contested.[22]

The 1977 dedication of a commemorative highway sign and three bronze NHL plaques in front of the church was one such occasion. The event drew a number of preservationists from Santa Fe as well as a few locals. The outsiders were proud of the fact that the signs were bilingual, a first for the NHL program (Chauvenet 1985, 58–59; "Las Trampas Receives Historic Marker" 1977). But Dick Sellars, an NPS historian who attended the event, told me that he remembered someone loudly revving a car engine in the middle of the ceremony, apparently conveying the message that the outsiders were not welcome. The villagers also control access to the church. It is sometimes open to visitors on summer weekends, but at other times (as in the past) gaining entry requires finding a resident with the key, as I discovered personally.

More-private aspects of village life are off-limits to outsiders altogether. Architect John Gaw Meem learned this on his first trip to Las Trampas in the early 1920s. He and two friends traveled to the village during Holy Week in the hopes of witnessing a Penitente ceremony. The Penitentes are a brotherhood of lay religious leaders who fill in for priests in northern New Mexico and whose ritual practices have long fascinated Anglos. Two villagers served the visitors supper and entertained them while they waited for the rites to begin, but "they didn't seem to want to start, no doubt because we were there. But we hung on—we were quite shameless." When it was almost dawn and still nothing had begun, one of Meem's companions suggested that they not impose on their hosts any longer. The threesome got in their car to return home, and just as they reached the top of a hill outside the village they saw that people had gathered in the plaza and begun to chant. Beatrice Chauvenet notes that this "episode was characteristic of the village people. Misunderstood and often ridiculed, they politely but stubbornly refused to put on a show for outsiders. It was not until they came to know and trust Meem that he was able to be a sympathetic observer of a Penitente ceremony" (Chauvenet 1985, 45–46).[23] The visitors shamelessly sought a close-up view of what was probably the most private moment in the annual life of the village. The fact that the object of their quest appeared only as they were leaving (and only in their car's rearview mirror) added to its tantalizing appeal and confirmed its authenticity (cf. Povinelli 2002, 66–67).

Village Ethnography

As an anthropologist interested in Las Trampas, I was following in Meem's footsteps. Yet I was ambivalent about conducting ethnographic fieldwork there. I was mostly interested in how outsiders had represented the village. And there were good reasons *not* to do fieldwork in Las Trampas. The history of anthropology in the Southwest has been rocky. Anthropologists have invaded people's privacy, published information that should have remained secret, prioritized scientific documentation over community needs, and perpetuated exoticism and primitivism (e.g., Zumwalt 1992, 247–57). Burdened with a sense of professional guilt, I chose not to represent a single community in depth and focused on public matters. Staying in the archives in Santa Fe and writing about relatively powerful Anglos seemed like an ethical approach.

On the other hand, I was uneager to produce another text about Las Trampas that denied the villagers an opportunity to speak for themselves.[24] I therefore set out to talk to a few people who lived there. This made me nervous. I had neither the time, confidence, qualifications, nor tenacity of other writers who had taken up residence in Nuevomexicano villages and built trusting relationships with residents (e.g., deBuys and Harris 1990). I was an outsider who spoke Spanish poorly. In fact, had I known that Jake Kosek (2006, 2) was shot at the day he arrived in Truchas to begin ethnographic fieldwork, I may not have considered even long-distance research in Las Trampas![25]

Despite my ethical concerns and personal trepidation, though, my main problem turned out to be practical. On several occasions I drove up to Las Trampas, intent on asking people what they thought about the church, the village, preservation. But every time I went the church was locked and the dirt plaza was deserted. There are basically no public or tourist facilities in Las Trampas and no public officials to seek out. No one was to be found, and I could not muster the courage to begin knocking on doors. None of my acquaintances knew anyone who lived in Las Trampas, and I was hesitant to track down the few people the Park Service had worked with in years past. I therefore left New Mexico in 2004 without having talked to a single Trampaseño and with deep misgivings about writing about the village.

The Counter-Ethnographic Present

When I returned to New Mexico in 2005, I was determined to make another stab at engaging some Trampaseños in my work. This time my friend Sam Delgado, a member of the Northern Rio Grande National Heritage Area board and a proud son of the Española valley, offered to go with me to facilitate introductions. We met in Española at the Misión-Convento and drove together up to Trampas. The church was locked and the plaza empty when we arrived. It was a cool, sunny April day and I began taking some photographs while Sam walked over to the house of the man he thought was the mayordomo. No one was home, so he went from house to house around the plaza knocking on doors. I was utterly grateful he was doing this for me. Finally, he found someone at home who told us where the new mayordoma lived, and we got back in the car and drove up the road a ways to this woman's house. The village is tiny, consisting of only a few dirt roads splitting off the highway, so it did not take us long.

The first house we stopped at was not the right one, so we drove on a ways to a second house. All of this seemed rather adventurous to me. I never would have driven up to strangers' houses the way Sam did, but he seemed perfectly at home. He knocked on the door of the second house, and when a man answered he stepped inside and I could hear them conversing in Spanish. Feeling awkward and embarrassed, I hung back in the dirt yard and petted the dog. If I could only win over the dog, I thought, perhaps I could convince these people I was all right. Then Sam came out and said the woman had agreed to open the church for us, but only because I was writing a dissertation (a rather ironic entrée, I thought, given my anxieties about writing and representation). We drove back down to the church, and the woman followed us with the key.

The mayordoma, a woman in her sixties or seventies whom I will call Loretta Romero, was friendly and shook my hand, reiterating that the only reason she was letting us in was because I was a student. I thanked her. She let us into the church, and we walked around for about fifteen minutes. She and Sam talked the entire time, mostly in Spanish. She talked about how much of a burden it is on the community to maintain the church, how much the upkeep costs, and how neither the National Park Service nor any other agency has helped them much. As we walked around she pointed out notable features of the church and parts that needed attention. She was concerned about the church's future, since the village lacked the funds to maintain it. Furthermore, the parishioners did not always agree with the preservationists in Santa Fe on what was best for the church.

Finally, Sam asked if I had any questions, and I asked Mrs. Romero if it would be possible for me to return sometime later that week to talk to her some more. "Oh no, *mi hijo*," she said. "I'm a very busy person and don't have time." Sam asked if there was anyone else I could talk to about the history of the church and she said no, flatly. I thanked her profusely for her time and generosity. She shook my hand again and wished me luck. As we were leaving she asked where I was from and I answered Georgia. "This is a different world for you," she remarked. "Yes, a totally different world," I agreed. Then she said, "Well, I know what you probably think of us." Taken aback, I responded that it had been a privilege for me to be here and to work with New Mexicans. Her remark was understandable, considering how many outsiders like myself had described the residents of northern New Mexico's Hispanic villages as quaint, backward, superstitious, lazy, or primitive. She had no reason to trust me or expect anything of me. But my feelings were hurt nonetheless and I was sorry she misjudged me. I was a sympathetic and respectful visitor with only the best intentions, as far as I was concerned.

So this brought to a close my fieldwork in Las Trampas. Mrs. Romero had been friendly and accommodating but made it clear that it would be inappropriate for me to push any further. I was grateful for Sam's help in opening a door and knew that I could not have made it as far as I did without him. But now the door had been firmly shut, a gesture I respected. I was even relieved to have tried my best and knew immediately that I could recount this experience as evidence of my good faith effort to engage Trampaseños in my research. Nevertheless, my attempt to bring my account up to the ethnographic present (like Meem's attempt to witness the Penitente rite) was unsuccessful. Rather, I suggest that I have presented a counter-ethnographic present, a present that resists meaningful representation.

Silence, Representation, and Power

It occurs to me now that my misgivings about representing Las Trampas were naive and that the relationships between silence,

Las Trampas

representation, and power are more complex than I realized. Despite my concerns about my power as a writer, my inability to interact with Trampaseños—the foundation of anthropological inquiry—significantly undermined my authority to represent the village. Here the silence of Trampaseños is a powerful statement about the control they wield and the failure of an anthropologist to muster ethnographic expertise. I suspect that the residents of northern New Mexico's Hispanic villages (somewhat, but not exactly, like their Pueblo neighbors) have learned from a long history of exploitation, misrepresentation, and injustice that self-representation and silence can serve as alternative modes of resistance. My evidence, though, is too weak for me to characterize Mrs. Romero's behavior as resistance.

This story about my trip to Las Trampas does more than reveal my personal shortcomings as an anthropologist. It draws attention to a larger anthropological artifice. Long ago, Bronislaw Malinowski ([1922] 1984, 6–7, 25) insisted that the "proper conditions for ethnographic work" required "cutting oneself off from the company of other white men, and remaining in as close contact with the natives as possible, which really can only be achieved by camping right in their villages." He discouraged anthropologists from residing "in a white man's compound" and emerging "at fixed hours only to 'do the village.'" Malinowski believed that living with the natives would yield a better understanding of their society and help the anthropologist avoid European biases. The goal of anthropology, he wrote, is "to grasp the native's point of view."

Malinowski's vision of fieldwork remains influential to this day. The tactics he recommended have helped anthropologists distinguish their texts from other colonial genres and claim disciplinary legitimacy. Yet anthropology has deep colonial roots, as Malinowski's racialized recommendations suggest. Anthropologists have both challenged and reinforced colonial hierarchies. And while ethnographers have productively experimented with ways to convey other people's experiences, an outsider conveying an insider's perspective remains paradoxical. Dipesh Chakrabarty (1992, 19) is still basically correct that the subjects of ethnography "can only have a quoted existence in a larger statement that belongs to the anthropologist alone." My inability even to "do the village" makes it harder for me to distance myself from the other writers I have critiqued in this chapter. I am also unable to use the voices of Trampaseños to legitimize my own argument. Loretta Romero, whether she intended to or not, subverted a representational maneuver central to anthropology.

Many New Mexicans, including supporters of the Northern Rio Grande National Heritage Area, now claim the right to represent their own culture and history. This self-representation facilitates cultural recognition by objectifying heritage and conveying consent (self-representation directed at outsiders is automatically authorized). The case of Las Trampas, however, suggests that not consenting to this logic of representation and recognition may be a way to assert a meager amount of power when the scales seem so unevenly balanced. When it comes to representation and recognition, the people of Las Trampas cannot compete with wealthy and well-connected preservationists in Santa Fe, the National Park Service, the National Trust for Historic Preservation, the state Department of Tourism, the guidebook writers, the journalists, or the anthropologists. They are represented and they are recognized, almost always by others. Yet they are able to decline interviews, control access to their church, and limit tourist facilities around their plaza (see fig. 27). Perhaps ignoring and subverting the processes through which outsiders have demonstrated their dominance provides a way for the village to reclaim some of its autonomy. I admit that this conclusion is purely conjectural and that I have no ethnographic evidence to support it. And that is the point. Dear reader, I am an unreliable guide here.

Las Trampas

Fig. 27. Locked doors, San José de Gracia.

CHAPTER FIVE

Anthropology, Heritage, and Multicultural Justice

Anthropology and the heritage industry are closely related, especially in the American Southwest. The Southwest has been a preeminent "laboratory" for both archaeological and ethnographic research since the nineteenth century (Fowler 2000). This research was tied to tourism development, as the early history of the Museum of New Mexico illustrates. Archaeologists lobbied for the establishment of national parks around important Ancestral Puebloan ruins, and these parks became key sites for the public interpretation of both past and present Indian cultures (Fine 1988; Keller and Turek 1998, 30–42, 185–215; Rothman 1992, 56–83; Snead 2001). The Fred Harvey Company and the Santa Fe Railway worked together to market the Southwest to tourists and played a central role in its invention as an exotic American region. They hired anthropologists to develop ethnographic collections and publish brochures, catalogs, and books (Francaviglia 1994; Neumann 1999; Weigle and Babcock 1996). Anthropologists and the railroad collaborated on living ethnographic exhibitions at world's fairs, in Albuquerque's Indian Building, at the Grand Canyon, and elsewhere. Around 1915 anthropologist John P. Harrington commended the railroad for making "possible the exploiting and scientific study of the quaint peoples through whose ancient lands it runs. The rescuing of the customs of these Indians from oblivion will be an asset to the Santa Fe railroad as long as time lasts." These salvage efforts, he reasoned, would benefit tourists and scientists alike (Weigle and Babcock 1996, 68). Tourism advertisements continue to employ anthropological language in Santa Fe, "a city where one is confronted with a striking degree of popular enthusiasm for ideas and sensibilities historically associated with anthropology and anthropologists" (Mullin 2001, 1).

The overlap between anthropology and the heritage industry should come as no surprise, since heritage itself is a quasi-anthropological category. Richard Handler (1987, 137) encourages anthropologists to consider how the heritage industry's appropriation of the culture concept illustrates "some of the uses to which their own concepts and data have been or will be put." The liberal conception of heritage that is ascendant worldwide (everybody has heritage and everybody's heritage deserves recognition) owes much to the relativization and pluralization of culture in early-twentieth-century anthropology. American anthropologists challenged the Eurocentric equation of Culture with Civilization and described a world made up of many (equal) *cultures*. The recognition of heritage also relies on anthropological processes such as the investigation, documentation, interpretation, and representation of social life. Heritage area development requires cultivating an ethnographic gaze and recognizing "ethnographic landscapes" (Guthrie 2005, 62–82).

Despite this overlap between heritage development and anthropology, the heritage industry largely relies upon outdated anthropological concepts.[1] Edward Bruner (2005, 4, 7, 195) notes that "tourism is co-opting ethnography" but that it "performs outmoded anthropology" and chases "anthropology's discarded discourse, presenting cultures as functionally integrated homogenous entities outside of time, space, and history." Essentialist conceptions of race, culture, and identity in heritage productions not only produce inaccurate views of social life but also have dangerous political consequences.

I have argued that heritage interpretation and preservation in New Mexico perpetuate colonial hierarchies in three ways: by rendering subordinate groups more visible than dominant ones, by promoting an impossible standard of authenticity that binds Native Americans and Nuevomexicanos to the past, and by depoliticizing culture, identity, and the past. All of these tendencies have parallels in anthropology, but since the 1980s anthropologists have critiqued and moved away from them. Westerners were almost entirely absent from anthropological accounts through much of the twentieth century. Anthropologists even removed themselves from their ethnographies, assuming the role of invisible scientific observers. Recently, anthropologists have become more interested in Western societies and have recognized the importance of disclosing their own situated position as researchers and writers. Anthropologists have not only reproduced but also policed the notion of authenticity. Yet many anthropologists no longer consider authenticity a useful analytical concept. Finally, modernist anthropologists ignored colonial politics and advanced an apolitical conception of culture. In the past few decades, however, anthropologists have more explicitly addressed the politics of their field sites and their scholarship.

In this concluding chapter I propose integrating these more recent anthropological approaches into heritage interpretation and preservation. I begin with a discussion of objectification, a process common to both anthropology and heritage development. The objectification of heritage often raises concerns about authenticity, but I suggest that it is more important to examine its cultural and political context. The final sections of the chapter present concrete suggestions for nurturing multicultural justice in New Mexico.

Objectification and Authenticity

"Heritage" comes into existence when aspects of culture, identity, and the past are lifted out of everyday experience, held up for inspection, and labeled, at which point they become objects of consciousness. This process raises suspicion among some scholars. Christoph Brumann (2009, 277) notes that scholars often assume that the production of heritage leads to falsification (deviation from historical fact), petrification (freezing in time), decontextualization, and invigorated boundary maintenance. "Particularly outside anthropology, the tone [of scholarly texts about heritage] can . . . turn distinctly sour" (278). Brumann acknowledges that these assumptions "hold true for many empirical cases" (276) but provides two Japanese counterexamples (see also Handler 1987, 137–38). Disdain for tourism also led anthropologists to dismiss the study of heritage, since heritage production and tourism development often go together. "Cultural anthropologists may traditionally have shied away from sites of tourism because they felt they were somehow 'inauthentic' and that studying such sites thus jeopardized the authenticity of the anthropologist. Anthropologists were supposed to study the traditions presumably inaccessible to tourists" (Bender 2002, 9).

Modernist ethnographers typically sought to uncover the deep social structures that governed people's lives, although they were only vaguely aware of them. Consider, for example, a 1927 essay by Edward Sapir (1963, 548–49, 558–59) titled "The Unconscious Patterning of Behavior in Society," in which he evaluated the significance of cultural patterns that found expression in naive practice and were "more powerfully 'felt' or 'intuited' than consciously perceived." Sapir believed that "we act all the more securely for our unawareness of the patterns that control us" and that "a healthy unconsciousness of the forms of socialized behavior to which we are subject is as necessary to society as is the mind's ignorance, or better unawareness, of the workings of the viscera to the health of the body." He warned against dragging "all the forms of behavior into consciousness," since "any attempt to subject even the higher forms of social behavior to purely conscious control must result in disaster." Sapir distinguished the anthropologist from "the normal, naïve individual." "In the normal business of life it is useless and mischievous for the individual to carry the conscious analysis of his cultural patterns around with him. That should be left to the student whose business it is to understand those patterns." The anthropologist's special ability to perceive and interpret cultural patterns invisible to others—and often to render them visible in diagrams—was an important source of authority.

Anthropologists have come to acknowledge that the distinction between the naive native and the clairvoyant ethnographer has broken down (and was probably exaggerated to begin with), in no small part due to the growth of the heritage industry. Not only do the "natives" read and refer to the anthropological texts produced about them, but in documenting, interpreting, and representing their own culture and history they are also increasingly doing for themselves what anthropologists and other researchers did for them. Auto-ethnographic self-inscription (Dorst 1989), heritage productions, and tourism have become legitimate topics of anthropological investigation in and of themselves.

Compared to anthropologists, many heritage professionals remain more ambivalent about cultural self-consciousness and the relationship between heritage and tourism. On the one hand, they work to cultivate an ethnographic sensibility in order to raise people's consciousness about their heritage, which may need protecting. On the other hand, authenticity remains a concern in many heritage productions. For example, when a group of geographers met in 1992 to discuss strategies for protecting American heritage landscapes, they noted that local residents sometimes need help recognizing the ordinary cultural landscapes that surround them. But, warned one participant, "directing an area's 'self-reflection' away from damaging parody will be a problem." The danger of self-parody evidently emerges with tourism development. "Another threat to heritage landscapes is a loss of authenticity that can result from pandering to tourism. A wholesale shift in the economy from a traditional economic base to tourism or any attempts to fabricate 'heritage' resources may turn the landscape into a parody. Technical assistance could help communities avoid this threat" (NPS 1992, 11–12). According to this view, tradition bearers should become aware of their heritage without orienting their lives toward outsiders. Note that the heritage professionals' technical direction is an expression of authority and expertise (Handler 1987, 140).

Most heritage area advocates stress that protecting authentic heritage must come before tourism promotion. Jayne Daly (2003, 9–10) adds "a word of caution" to a National Trust for Historic Preservation report that more than twenty-five states have established heritage or cultural tourism programs since 1990, twenty of those since 1995. Heritage tourism represents a tremendous economic opportunity, but "it is important to differentiate between heritage areas that promote an integrated regional approach to resource protection and economic development and those that have begun to use the heritage area label simply to attract tourists," she writes. When theme parks and casinos build "heritage sites," or when heritage tourism programs lack careful analysis and planning, there is a risk of "inauthentic historic accounts or the 'commodification' of heritage — the reduction of heritage to the lowest common denominator to attract the largest paying crowd." Inadequate planning can also lead to community outrage and resource destruction. "The most successful heritage areas," Daly concludes, "are much more than tourist destinations." The conviction that heritage must precede tourism is ironic, since heritage and tourism development are complementary processes that both rely on and result in objectification.

The Social and Political Contexts of Objectification

The objectification of heritage always takes place within particular cultural and political contexts. Critically examining these contexts provides an opportunity for challenging the politics of authenticity, the politics of visibility, and the anti-politics of culture. For example, three adobe buildings I have analyzed in this book represent different kinds of heritage objects produced under different circumstances. The Museum of New Mexico monumentalized the Palace of the Governors by dissecting, excavating, labeling, interpreting, and exhibiting it. This process relegated Indians and Hispanos to the past while granting Anglo scientists purview over New Mexico's present and future.[2] In Española, the Misión-Convento is a re-created and relocated heritage object that anchors the city's claims to a Spanish colonial history. Like Santa Fe, Española has expunged its architectural heritage of Anglo influences, but in a predominantly Hispanic town this act is potentially subversive. The church of San José de Gracia in Las Trampas, unlike the other two buildings, still serves its original function and has not been hard plastered. Its social and environmental embeddedness lessens objectification, although preservationists have tried to turn the entire village into a bounded heritage object. They have faced significant resistance from villagers.

These three examples are not archetypes but simply demonstrate social variability. One last example should drive home how much ideas about objectification vary cross-culturally and the importance of political context. Rina Swentzell, an architectural and cultural historian from Santa Clara Pueblo, writes about adobe architecture and cultural objectification from a Pueblo perspective, although she by no means speaks for all Pueblo people.

Swentzell (1990b, 8–9) describes how Pueblo houses are culturally connected to one another and to the larger natural environment, including the earth, sky, and mountains. "They are not an end unto themselves but exist within the ordering of the cosmos. They do not call attention to themselves as separate entities or receive individualized focus, except for the role they play in the larger whole" (Swentzell 2001, 72; see also A. Ortiz 1969). She recalls her childhood at Santa Clara and the meaningful way in which houses were blessed, healed, fed, and otherwise treated as organic beings. They were even tasted, since each adobe structure had a different taste and texture (a literal manifestation of the different kind of heritage objects I discussed earlier). Swentzell (1990b, 11) remembers watching a crack grow in one particular house over several weeks. "I asked my great-grandmother why the people who lived in that house were doing nothing about fixing the crack. She shook her finger at me and said that it was not my business to be concerned about whether the house fell or not." It had had a good life, and the time had come "for it to go back into the earth." Houses were "given the ultimate respect of dying," Swentzell remarks (9). "I feel so sorry for those places that are set up as exhibit places—those house museums. . . . It's like keeping people on machines—keeping them alive artificially for a longer time than they should be kept alive. Places should be allowed to die" (quoted in Gillette 1992, 28).

This reluctance to preserve adobe structures, widespread

among the Pueblos, relates to a larger set of beliefs about objectifying culture. Swentzell (2001, 69) recalls how her great-grandmother chastised her for helping her schoolteacher learn Tewa: "No, we don't do that! We do not give our language to other people who will lay it on the table, cut it into pieces, and study it. When we, as a group of people, are ready to die, our language must go with us." Some (but not all) Pueblos today have decided not to create material records of their languages but to maintain them orally.

For Swentzell, self-consciously focusing on cultural objects leads to decontextualization and loss of meaning.[3] "I value tremendously the unselfconsciousness, and absence of aesthetic pretension, which led to doing everything straightforwardly yet which still considered the context and the connections so that practical and symbolic function were never lost" (Swentzell 1990b, 12). Swentzell prefers an unself-conscious way of making pots that is integrated into everyday life rather than focused on creating objects for sale in a tourist market ("The Butterfly Effect" 1989, 28–29). When I interviewed Swentzell in her home outside Santa Fe she put it to me this way: when people are living in a real way their lives are rooted in their relationship to the natural environment, which in turn influences their relationships with other beings. As the Pueblos have moved away from being self-sustaining communities, their cultures have been lifted "up out of that real essential plane of living to something that . . . doesn't have a directness to it, that doesn't have a realness about it." When you are truly connected to the place where you live and to your environment, she suggested, "you know what you're supposed to do from day to day, and you move through it in a more intuitive [way], because you know where those relationships are, and you know what your role is, and you know where things come from, not intellectually so much as just knowing them with your whole body" (Swentzell 2003b).[4]

Contact between groups generally promotes awareness of both self and others, and the increasing self-consciousness Swentzell laments is largely the result of New Mexico's double colonization.

Spanish and American colonialism brought about both deliberate and accidental social change among the Pueblos (see Swentzell 1990a and 1991). Assimilationist campaigns directly threatened indigenous ways of life and inspired a struggle for cultural survival that has lasted more than four hundred years. In the twentieth century, romanticized images of Indians, the commodification of cultural difference, and multicultural politics produced incentives for cultural preservation and performance. These contradictory forces, some of which threatened to eradicate Pueblo distinctiveness and others which promoted it, have resulted in many forms of cultural objectification. Pueblo communities have built cultural centers and museums, created written records of their languages, documented oral and visual traditions, recorded songs and stories, and so forth. I asked Swentzell (2003b) about this strategy of objectifying culture in order to preserve it, and she said she found it very sad. When people have to work so hard at learning the language or maintaining their traditions, when their efforts are so deliberate and self-conscious, their culture has been reduced to something intellectual and theoretical, she maintained.[5]

Cultural objectification is both a result of and response to colonialism, and it is vital to investigate this colonial context. But if anthropologists were more concerned about authenticity than colonial domination in the past, is it possible that we have become *too* focused on power now? When I sent Swentzell an earlier version of this chapter to read, she thanked me for taking her thoughts seriously but wrote: "I don't think that you understand the incredible philosophy of the Pueblos, as I understand it. First, I do not believe that our most fundamental problems are about power—or even inequality, which comes from a sense of insecurity." This perspective, she suggested, was Eurocentric. "My issue with the West is its mindset—its philosophical stance—characterized exactly by what you are proposing—to be mainly concerned with power and inequality in the human world. I believe that the more fundamental issue is our spiritual space—which is a universal concern." Swentzell (2007) reasoned that the violence in our world today stems from materialism and fights over who owns what, "which, from what I read in your paper, is what the whole heritage discussion is about."[6] Swentzell's comments helped me to see the irony of my suggestion that we need to focus more on power in order to unravel the pernicious effects of colonialism. My attempt to critique multicultural heritage productions from an anticolonial perspective reproduced a fundamental preoccupation of Western culture. Furthermore, I was using her ideas—twisting them, apparently—to make my own argument (something I was unable to do in my discussion of Las Trampas).

I find Swentzell's work revelatory. It opens up new possibilities for social action. But I also realize that my ability to represent her point of view is limited. I cannot speak for her; she has already spoken for herself. Perhaps the best I can do as an anthropologist is to expose the situatedness and partiality of my own argument. When we remain invisible as writers, producing authoritative, disembodied texts, we discredit all other voices. Paying more attention to the politics of visibility in our work by disclosing our own positions, seriously acknowledging perspectives that do not support our ideas, and rendering our texts more vulnerable to alternative readings may help to correct this ironic (and often accidental) colonial effect.[7]

Forgetting about Heritage

Swentzell (2007) is less concerned about heritage and its conservation than about whether people have compassion, integrity, and respect for one another and the natural world. "Pueblo thinking, from my point of view, is about relationships, assumed equalness and the cycles of life." I asked her what she would like Santa Clara Pueblo to be like in twenty-five years. She replied that she does not care what language people are speaking or what they are doing. "I would like to see a community that is really concerned about basic relationships, about the world and themselves. I would like to see a loving, caring community, and it's not there." What about dances, which have been an important part of Pueblo life for centuries? "Oh, I'd like to see dances that would just make the people happy and feel like they . . . are taking care of each other and taking care of the place. . . . I don't care what the dances look like, I don't care what the language sounds like. Those are all expressions of who we really are inside. When I hear that sound I like to just feel, I'm a part of this place, I'm a part of this group, isn't this wonderful. I'm in a safe, secure place" (Swentzell 2003b). When we met for breakfast in July 2010, I asked Swentzell if she was concerned about "culture," and she said no, not really. Deemphasizing culture in northern New Mexico would be a radical move.

Swentzell (2003b) also emphasizes the value of creativity and an orientation to the present rather than the past (in dances, for example), another departure from the heritage movement. Heritage productions in northern New Mexico highlight and celebrate people's relationship to the past. Yet this past orientation has disadvantages. Concerns about authenticity can constrain cultural expression and political action. The past may also prevent different groups from coming together in the present. For this reason I heard some supporters of the Northern Rio Grande National Heritage Area say they hoped to lay the past to rest, to move beyond the history of Spanish conquest in order to emphasize shared experiences and the importance of coexistence.[8]

Preoccupation with the past can even be psychologically and physically damaging. Angela Garcia (2008, 725), for instance, shows that drug use in the Española valley is linked in multiple ways to painful memories of the past. People in northern New Mexico say that "history is a wound" and that "heroin cures everything." "Thus, while elders worry that the younger generation is all too willing to forget the past, the young are just as likely to understand the heroin problem as a contemporary consequence of it, while still offering heroin as a remedy for the pain that accompanies the past." Garcia tells the story of Alma, a Nuevomexicana who left the village of Tierra Amarilla when she was a teenager "because she said she was choking on the memories of her elders, particularly her father's violent despair over the loss of ancestral lands. Her retreat from their memories, she said, was drugs" (732). Alma found solace in an evangelical Christian community in Española. The treatment she had received at a detoxification clinic "didn't work because its focus on the past made life unbearable." In contrast, Alma reported that the pastor at the Christian fellowship "talks about the future; he says that's what counts. The future—so you can be blessed and go to heaven" (737). Despite the discovery of this new future-oriented community, Alma was unable to overcome her addiction and died of an overdose when she was twenty-eight years old.

Other people Garcia (2010, 94) talked to, though, believed that remembering the past and struggling for land were necessary for a healthier future. Said one: "Our past[,] . . . our connection to the land and to our heritage *is* our future. The problem is young addicts are lost without it. That's why they use. They don't have a tie to their history." Another activist promoted agricultural revitalization as a way to fight the heroin epidemic. He wanted to help young Hispanos "get back to their roots" and to coax new life from a ruined landscape (101–2). One of the most hopeful developments Garcia describes is the creation of a community garden at a detoxification clinic. Gardening had therapeutic value for patients (especially women) who were able to draw on horticultural experience from their childhood (206–9).

Forgetting the past and focusing on the present is no panacea, and it may make it more difficult to address colonial injustices. Consider the depoliticizing potential of a Forest Service ranger's recommendation in 1999: "If these people [Hispanos] would let go of history a little they would get something done here. You cannot live in the past; you need to let go of the past to move forward. All people talk about is what they have lost; they cannot seem to get beyond this. It's sad. . . . It has become who they are" (quoted in Kosek 2006, 43). Moving forward here implies laying down legal struggles and land claims. Even if it were possible for Hispanos to "let go of history," certainly not all would want to, considering the significance of the past for their identities. Letting go of history would therefore eliminate both a motivation for political action and the possibility of cultural recognition. These radical moves away from culture, identity, and the past have both emancipatory and hegemonic potential. They deserve deeper consideration but are beyond the scope of this book. I turn now to a consideration of multicultural politics that revolve around heritage, not its abandonment, and to steps that would promote justice.

Multicultural Justice

The multicultural projects under way in twenty-first-century New Mexico, including the Northern Rio Grande National Heritage Area, are rooted in the romantic regional tradition that Chris Wilson masterfully analyzes in *The Myth of Santa Fe*. Wilson shows that ideas about culture, identity, and the past—ideas expressed in and reproduced by architectural movements, historic preservation efforts, public performances, visual art, historical monuments, urban planning, political projects and policies, and the crafting of individual and collective identities—have perpetuated inequality and injustice in New Mexico. He identifies three forms of denial in New Mexican public history: denial of cultural and racial mixing, the violence of Spanish and American conquest, and the effects of capitalist modernity in the region. "These three manifestations of historical amnesia . . . interfere with the public understanding of the origins of contemporary social, economic, and political structures." The invisibility of certain groups (such as Chicanos and the working class) in public discourse facilitates their political marginalization, and a romantic view of history "deprives people of an image of themselves as active agents for contemporary social change. Such a fictionalized reality also inhibits the hybridization of the traditional with the modern, the local with the international, which is necessary for the continued vitality and relevance of any local culture" (Wilson 1997, 312–13).

My research builds upon Wilson's. I have attempted to show that multicultural projects can reproduce colonial power relations by advancing a narrow and constraining view of cultural authenticity, rendering dominant groups less visible than subordinate ones, and diverting attention away from politics. While my research focuses squarely on northern New Mexico, these processes are typical of multicultural projects elsewhere. Social justice necessitates addressing each of these features of multiculturalism.

Authenticity is an impossible expectation that no group can ever fully meet. In New Mexico, the authenticity of Indians and Nuevomexicanos mostly depends upon their racial and cultural purity and the maintenance of "traditions" predating American colonization. A less restrictive multicultural politics therefore requires destigmatizing cultural exchange and miscegenation. In a discussion of "coyote consciousness," Wilson (1997, 170) recommends cultivating "an appreciation of complexity, the hybrid, and the creative flux of culture meeting culture. A realistic acknowledgement of cultural interaction and racial mixing can complement the positive aspects of ethnic identity and help hold the negative ones in check. Santa Fe (and other modern societies) might begin by giving equal standing in public symbols, rhetoric, and ideology to the cultural and racial hybrid." Celebrating syncretic cultural expressions, porous ethnic boundaries, and border crossings is vital (e.g., Gandert et al. 2000, esp. Gutiérrez's essay).

Evidence of racial and cultural mixing already erupts even where dominant discourses of authenticity are strongest. For example, in the 2007 "Young Guns of Northern New Mexico" art exhibit, held inside Española's Misión, Chicano imagery strikingly contrasted with the Spanish coats of arms hanging on the walls. In 2001 a group of teenagers took over the Española fiesta, a celebration of Juan de Oñate that had, like other public rituals in New Mexico (e.g., Horton 2001), excluded mestizos. The teenagers renamed the Fiesta Queen "La Señorita Valoria La Mestiza" to honor the valley's mixed heritage. This innovation provided a new opportunity for recognition. Said one organizer: "The name La Mestiza opened it up to a whole lot of different cultures. . . . Like myself. I'm mixed. I have Hispanic, Native American, everything in me, and it opens it up more. It kind of explains the person of our valley more" (quoted in Sharpe 2001). "We're all mixed," said the young woman who was crowned La Mestiza. A fiesta council member from San Juan Pueblo explained: "We are trying to set an example for our leaders. . . . We are trying to open closed doors between pueblo leaders and leaders of the Española Valley . . . in God's eyes we're all the same" (quoted in Stone 2001;

see also Trujillo 2009, 51–52). Acknowledging racial and cultural mixing does not simply lead to a more inclusive politics of recognition by expanding the catalog of legitimate identities in the region. In "opening up" identity, it also breaks down ethnic boundaries and facilitates new alliances based on shared experiences.

Equally important is the acknowledgment that Nuevomexicanos and Indians are modern people living in the twenty-first century. Cultural change and participation in a capitalist economy are frequently interpreted as indicators of loss and death (and thus grounds for denying political rights), but they could just as well demonstrate creativity, vitality, and adaptability. The portal market in front of the Palace of the Governors provides an opportunity for tourists to interact with Indians as modern-day people. Artists sometimes comply with but at other times challenge tourist expectations. Deirdre Evans-Pritchard (1990, 147), for example, describes a Cochiti silversmith who deliberately wore business suits to Santa Fe's annual Indian Market, and examples of Indians satirizing tourists and forcing them to acknowledge their own unrealistic assumptions about Indians abound. Opportunities for Native Americans and Nuevomexicanos to produce and sell contemporary art (art not described as "traditional") have expanded significantly in New Mexico. Their ongoing expansion will require encouraging tourists and art buyers to question the concept of cultural authenticity. The Museum of New Mexico could help lead this educational mission, perhaps as part of its new efforts to interpret the portal program (Palace of the Governors 2006, 7–8).

Deconstructing authenticity in New Mexico is risky, since Hispanos and Indians have used strategic essentialism to achieve a variety of goals, from securing exclusive use of the Palace portal to gaining allies in the fight for access to national forests. Identities are also built around notions of authenticity, even in the most private contexts. The point is not to deny authenticity but to ensure that subjective, social, and political legitimacy no longer hinges on it, opening up new possibilities for identity formation and political action. Images of Nuevomexicanos as villagers with deep ties to land *and* as migrant workers, soldiers, and wage laborers should no longer seem incongruous, nor should images of Indians as dancers, potters, casino operators, consumers of mass media, storytellers, and Christians (e.g., Kosek 2006, 103–5; Guthrie 2010a, 317).

The politics of authenticity in New Mexico has played a role in rendering groups that do not or cannot identify with "pure" Spanish or Native American heritage (including mestizos, Mexican immigrants, African and Asian Americans, and working-class people) much less visible in public spaces. Public recognition and political representation might reduce these groups' marginalization. Even Nuevomexicanos and Indians whose heritage receives positive public attention continue to find themselves excluded from other social arenas and burdened with demeaning stereotypes. More consistent, respectful recognition could improve their status and redress internalized racial inferiority. However, the invisibility of *dominant* groups is just as problematic as that of subordinate ones. Focusing attention on subalterns both provides new opportunities for discipline and deflects attention from people in power. As supposedly cultureless, modern people, Anglos enjoy the privilege of being normative. They rarely face doubts about their authenticity or citizenship due to the color of their skin, the language they speak, or their cultural identities.

Multicultural justice therefore requires bringing Anglo-American colonizers, settlers, capitalists, lawyers, prospectors, tourists, scientists, and anthropologists into view as culturally and historically particular actors.[9] This involves shifting "from a conception of injustice that focuses on its significance for those who suffer it, to one that focuses on its meaning for those who commit it" (Markell 2003, 35).[10] As I noted in chapter 1, the New Mexico History Museum, which opened behind the Palace of the Governors in 2009, makes a major contribution to the critical examination of Anglo-American dominance in New Mexico. The museum's permanent exhibition inverts the emphasis of historical interpretation in the Palace. It breezes through New Mexico's pre-American history while substantially and critically interpreting the Treaty of Guadalupe Hidalgo, U.S. Indian policy, the development of the atomic bomb, New Mexico's expanding tourism industry, and even the work and lives of anthropologists in New Mexico. Native Americans and Hispanics are clearly active participants in the twenty-first century. Unfortunately, the exhibit is not at all self-reflexive. There is no interpretation of interpretation, and visitors are never invited to question the museum's synthesizing narrative. As at the Palace of the Governors, the museum establishment remains invisible and unassailable. A more dialogical interpretive strategy and the installation of an exhibit at the Palace on the history of the Museum of New Mexico itself would help to expose one of New Mexico's most powerful colonial institutions to critique.

The absence of Anglos in New Mexican visual art, public pageantry, and historical monuments (Rodríguez 2001; Wilson 1997, 315) also presents an opportunity for creative commentary. The few remaining monuments to Anglo enterprise and dominance in New Mexico (including Kenneth Adams's tricultural mural at the University of New Mexico and the war memorial on the Santa Fe plaza) attract protest and invite critical interpretation (Horton 2010, 137–38; Rodríguez 2001, 199–201; Wilson 1997, 315–16; Wilson 2003, 27–29).[11] The National Park Service, which has done far more to preserve and interpret sites associated with Native American cultures and Spanish colonialism in the Southwest than with American colonialism and settlement, could also broaden its efforts.[12] Happily, historic preservationists have begun to show more interest in preserving sites associated with twentieth-century American history in New Mexico (particularly those more than fifty years old, a requirement for inclusion in the National Register of Historic Places).

Exposing powerful groups and institutions to critique is just a first step along the road to a more just society. Open political engagement is another. Promoting social justice in New Mexico must involve addressing wealth disparities, access to land and water, the negative impacts of development, and other material conditions. Heritage interpretation and preservation, while consistently drawing attention to Native American and Hispanic communities, has more often impeded than facilitated this process. Most heritage projects in New Mexico are not only apolitical; they deflect attention away from and actively depoliticize political and economic issues. In Las Trampas, preservationists have denied the link between cultural change and land loss, sometimes explicitly, converting evidence of poverty and marginalization into a reassuring sign of cultural survival. The National Park Service was even able to depoliticize the Spanish colonization of the Southwest in its 1991 study, making it safe for mass consumption and public recognition.

This anti-political effect is not inevitable, however. Culture, identity, and the past are shot through with power relations, and their interpretation can provide opportunities for political discourse and action. For example, early Anglo patrons of Native American art in New Mexico recognized the relationship between culture and politics and fought hard political battles for Indian land rights. The Indian art world remains a key but underutilized site for promoting tribal sovereignty. Ritual performance and political expression easily go together. For instance, the Matachines dance and other syncretic ritual dramas allow Indians and Hispanos to comment on and cope with interethnic relations and the history of conquest in northern New Mexico (Gandert et al. 2000; Rodríguez 1996). The performance of "traditional culture" has become a political tool for both Indians and Nuevomexicanos, and interweaving such performances with explicit political demands can be productive (see Kosek 2006, 129–38). I like the image of Hispano weavers, potters, woodworkers, and healers displaying their wares in the rotunda of the New Mexico state capitol in 1996 as part of a protest against restrictive national forest policies, a banner hanging on the wall declaring "Sin Tierra No Hay Justicia: Sin Justicia No Hay Paz" (Without Land There Is No Justice: Without Justice There Is No Peace) (Varela 2001, 169). It may be true "that, in this continual struggle, artistic expression alone will not safeguard ancestral land and water rights" (170), but linking heritage and politics can be powerful. Once again, engaging in the politics of culture without becoming ensnared in the politics of authenticity requires sensitivity and skill.

Repoliticizing New Mexico's double colonial past will also make it easier to draw attention to injustice and inequality in the present. Addressing colonial violence without glorifying it will be difficult and painful, as the cuarto centenario controversy revealed, but a soft, depoliticized discourse of multicultural coexistence has significant limits. Increasing opportunities for respectful dialogue about colonial legacies will be vital. Chris Wilson's (1997, 315–22) discussion of works of art and public performances that raise questions about Spanish conquest, Indian policy, and New Mexico's nuclear industry suggests the potential of artistic commentary on difficult issues. Museums, historic sites, and national parks are also well positioned to nurture this kind of public debate. For example, I would enjoy seeing an honest discussion of Frank Bond's manipulation of Nuevomexicano ranchers at his house overlooking the Española plaza.

The Prospects for a New Multiculturalism

Having argued that multicultural justice depends upon repoliticizing culture, rendering dominant groups more visible in heritage productions, and dismantling narrow views of authenticity, I would like to make two related clarifying points. First, not all the above suggestions will be popular. Apolitical cultural performances are pleasant, reassuring, and nonthreatening. Why sully them with politics? Indian and Nuevomexicano heritage is interesting and colorful, and it has been underappreciated in the past, so why turn away from it now? Native Americans wearing blue jeans and using computers and Hispanics working in offices and speaking English start to look like "ordinary" Americans. Would it not be better for them to maintain their cultural distinctiveness, especially if they receive special rights?

The reforms I have proposed will also be unpopular because they threaten the status quo, which is precisely the point. People and institutions who benefit from the current social and political order may have little incentive to pursue them and might directly oppose them. Federal agencies and state-run institutions have good reasons not to draw critical attention to their own present-day (or even past) policies and practices. Complicating matters further is that hegemonic multiculturalism is not simply practiced by those in power but also by those in subordinate positions, and the line between the two groups is blurry. Nuevomexicano elites, for instance, have reasons to support the interpretation of the Palace of the Governors as a site of Spanish glory, not of twentieth-century American control. If civic leaders in Española began to celebrate the valley's trailer parks, its casino architecture, or the social scene outside Wal-Mart (see L. Romero 2001), they would face losing not only local support but also national recognition.

Yet the uncertain popularity of these reforms is promising, not a deterrent. After all, a more just society depends upon social change and a transformation of power relations. Destabilizing the status quo is *bound* to be unpopular, at least for those who benefit from it. The acceptability of multiculturalism in general and celebrations of Native American and Hispanic heritage in particular is contingent upon their unthreatening nature. Promoting culinary traditions is safe; commemorating the massacre of Native Americans (or Spanish priests) is not. A more radical multiculturalism—a multiculturalism that challenges rather than perpetuates colonial hierarchies—cannot be unthreatening.

The second clarifying point has to do with the sources of anti-colonial multiculturalism. Multiculturalism is not a centralized, or even coherent, political project in New Mexico now, and I do not envision its becoming one. It is a loose collection of efforts more than a government policy. The creative, subversive projects already under way in New Mexico have diverse origins. Although some policy changes are in order (regarding the production and sale of "Indian art" or access to national forests, for instance), productive changes are as likely to come from artists, curators, teachers, ranchers, performers, writers, parishioners, preservationists, and activists as from government officials. Exhibits, cultural centers, panel discussions, films, preservation projects, public monuments, and publications have been and will continue to be key sites for the politics of multiculturalism. Powerful institutions and government agencies have an important role to play. The

Museum of New Mexico, for instance, could do much to open up discussions about authenticity. The National Park Service could facilitate public conversations about the politics of Spanish and American conquest. However, it is unlikely that sites of power will ever produce the most radical forms of social critique, which usually come from the margins.

Given this decentralized model of political action, the popularity of multicultural reforms becomes less of an issue. Reform does not depend upon convincing everybody about the validity of a political project, since in fact it consists of multiple projects with diverse origins. These projects need not be coordinated and may even be contradictory. Diverse interest groups might come together on some issues and not on others. For example, Indians and Hispanos might unite in a critique of American assimilationist policies but diverge sharply when it comes to commemorating Spanish colonization. Because the politics of recognition in New Mexico has been polarizing and essentializing, it has impeded coalition building. A new kind of multiculturalism that nurtures flexibility, improvisation, and creativity is both possible and practical.

Epilogue

Danza de los Antepasados

The Northern Rio Grande National Heritage Area has become an active organization. An executive director is working with an assistant from an office in Española. It has taken a long time to complete a management plan, but each new draft shows improvement.[1] Through a small grants program, the NRGNHA has distributed more than $90,000 to community groups for historic preservation projects, art and music programs, petroglyph recording, video projects, the construction of an earthen oven at the Española farmers' market, performances and festivals, agricultural revitalization at San Ildefonso Pueblo, language conservation at Santa Clara Pueblo, an acequia history project, tourism development, and educational projects, among other initiatives. It also commissioned a film that explores people's ongoing relationships to land and water in northern New Mexico, from farming and ranching to adobe making and skiing. Through personal narratives the film documents intergenerational experiences of both cultural continuity and painful social change (Lindblom, Gomez, and Valerio 2011).[2]

A NRGNHA open house and "Danza de los Antepasados" (Dance of the Ancestors) in June 2011 gave me the clearest indication of the heritage area's social and political potential. It took place on a Saturday afternoon at the Taos Agricultural Center in a building that looked like a warehouse. The venue, at the end of a gravel road on the south side of town, was well off the main tourist track. When I arrived, a diverse mix of locals was milling around and sitting at folding tables covered with colorful table cloths. A ten-dollar ticket purchased a raffle entry and a lunch of Frito pies (corn chips topped with chile, cheese, and onions). Representatives from several nonprofit organizations sat behind tables at the edge of the room.

The program began with the Rainer Family Dancers, all dressed in brilliant blue and white. The family was itself multicultural: the father was from Taos Pueblo, the mother from one of the plains tribes. They performed plains and Pueblo dances, accompanied by a drum. At one point they invited audience members to join them, creating an even more diverse ensemble.

Next, Ballet Folklórico Mis Sueños, a dance troupe from Española Valley High School, performed a variety of social dances from Mexico and New Mexico to recorded and live music. The dancers ranged from little children to teenagers and went through multiple costume changes. Their high heels and boots punctuated the rhythm of the music on a plywood dance floor. With roots in both Mexican nationalism and the Chicano movement, ballet folklórico is a genre with complex cultural politics (Nájera-Ramírez, Cantú, and Romero 2009). But the Mexican connection was unmistakable. The announcer indicated the origin of each dance: Veracruz, Nuevo León, Chiapas, Jalisco. I heard that some of the dancers were actually Mexican immigrants. Far from bypassing Mexico and celebrating Spanish purity, the performers built a bridge between Mexico and New Mexico. I recalled several early NRGNHA advocates telling me they hoped the heritage area would embrace Mexicans and others (Delgado 2002; O. Romero 2003).

In between the dances, David Garcia, an Española native and graduate student at the University of Texas, talked, played acoustic guitar, and sang in Spanish. Several songs celebrated the relationship between people and land. Garcia extolled ranchers, woodcutters, and acequias. He played "Nuevo México Lindo" ("Pretty New Mexico") as Ballet Folklórico danced. Garcia's performance of "Estado de Vergüenza" ("El Corrido de Arizona") by the California-based Chicano group Los Cenzontles was explicitly political. The song addresses Arizona's strict immigration policy passed in 2010, but Garcia introduced it by criticizing the state's contemporaneous ban of ethnic studies programs in public schools. He translated some of the song's lyrics into English before he began. The song describes Arizona as a shameful, fearful, racist state that has legalized discrimination, a national disgrace. It advocates immigration reform and denounces ignorance. The corrido ends by calling people to take pride in their contribution to the nation and to oppose discrimination using "voices, votes, and money." After the song Garcia declared that high school programs (like the Ballet Folklórico) are important because they help kids know who they are. His performance proved that the Northern Rio Grande National Heritage Area could provide a space for integrating culture and politics. The Danza de los Antepasados was neither apolitical nor bound to the past.

The final act of the day, a rock band from Taos named Suave, brought the danza to a close on an upbeat note. They sang in both English and Spanish and mentioned several times that they were available for weddings. When they broke into "Come On, Let's Go," Sam Delgado leaned over and told me he had seen Ritchie Valens perform in California in the 1950s. Here was another Mexican American connection. Later on a woman pulled me up to dance. Wearing cowboy boots, a cowboy hat, blue jeans skirt, and white blouse, she was dressed perfectly for the event. As we danced she told me she was a retired Pojoaque High School teacher.

Throughout the afternoon, heritage area board members announced raffle winners. Prizes included artwork and services from local businesses. I was delighted to win a twenty-five-dollar gift certificate to Tierra Wools, a wool-spinning, -dyeing, and -weaving cooperative in Los Ojos owned by the women who work there. I had known about Tierra Wools for years. It is an offshoot of Ganados del Valle, a community development initiative begun in the 1980s to revitalize the churro sheep industry in the Chama valley. Ganados was on the front lines of the battle between land grant heirs, environmentalists, and federal and state land managers in

Fig. 28. The Rio Grande near Taos.

northern New Mexico. Using tactics of civil disobedience, it has helped traditional land users maintain their ties to land and community (Pulido 1996, 125–90; Varela 2001). When I visited Tierra Wools' retail shop in Los Ojos a few days later, I toured the facilities and bought a weaving to take home with me.

After the danza was over I helped put away tables and chairs, then left. I had driven the High Road in the morning (the church in Las Trampas was locked), so I took the Low Road back to Santa Fe. I had forgotten how spectacular the drive is. The Rio Grande sparkled in the late afternoon sunlight (see fig. 28). I thought about how the NRGNHA might affect the politics of multiculturalism in northern New Mexico. One of the most promising features of the heritage area model is its looseness. The NRGNHA will never have the cohesiveness of the Palace of the Governors, where the Museum of New Mexico has been able to micromanage the semiotics of heritage. The scale of heritage areas prevents them from being totalizing frames, despite the fact that critics sometimes compare them to theme parks. Legislative restrictions on land management authority and the requirement that all federal funding be matched locally mean that the NRGNHA will have to partner with individuals, communities, organizations, and governments. Its management plan consistently emphasizes the value and importance of collaborative partnerships (NRGNHA 2013). The NRGNHA board pledges to "honor the values and experiences of all people" and to "accept a community's definition of its needs" (NRGNHA 2011).

Early advocates of the Northern Rio Grande National Heritage Area urged the federal government to recognize New Mexico's traditional Hispanic and Native American cultures, their four-hundred-year coexistence, and their place in the United States. Congress assented, and in 2006 it established and funded the heritage area.[3] Since then people do not talk about recognition as much. This shift has important political implications. Practicing the politics of recognition paid off in New Mexico, but it also had costs. An essentialist view of New Mexico's cultural difference severely limits the ability of New Mexicans to respond to social, economic, and environmental challenges in the twenty-first century. Celebrating the cultural authenticity of subaltern groups deflects attention away from the effects of American colonization. Well-founded suspicions toward the politics of recognition—the kind evident in Las Trampas—may have hindered public engagement with the initiative early on and may impede future progress.[4] Deviating from the politics of recognition leads to more promising political strategies. I saw this potential at the danza. Although recognition can have concrete benefits for marginalized groups, fundamentally challenging colonial injustices requires a different kind of multicultural politics.

Northern Rio Grande National Heritage Area Act

Title II(A) of the National Heritage Areas Act of 2006

Public Law 109-338

109th Congress

SEC. 201. SHORT TITLE.

This subtitle may be cited as the "Northern Rio Grande National Heritage Area Act."

SEC. 202. CONGRESSIONAL FINDINGS.

The Congress finds that—

(1) northern New Mexico encompasses a mosaic of cultures and history, including 8 Pueblos and the descendants of Spanish ancestors who settled in the area in 1598;

(2) the combination of cultures, languages, folk arts, customs, and architecture make northern New Mexico unique;

(3) the area includes spectacular natural, scenic, and recreational resources;

(4) there is broad support from local governments and interested individuals to establish a National Heritage Area to coordinate and assist in the preservation and interpretation of these resources;

(5) in 1991, the National Park Service study Alternative Concepts for Commemorating Spanish Colonization identified several alternatives consistent with the establishment of a National Heritage Area, including conducting a comprehensive archaeological and historical research program, coordinating a comprehensive interpretation program, and interpreting a cultural heritage scene; and

(6) establishment of a National Heritage Area in northern New Mexico would assist local communities and residents in preserving these unique cultural, historical and natural resources.

SEC. 203. DEFINITIONS.

As used in this subtitle—

(1) the term "heritage area" means the Northern Rio Grande Heritage Area; and

(2) the term "Secretary" means the Secretary of the Interior.

SEC. 204. NORTHERN RIO GRANDE NATIONAL HERITAGE AREA.

(a) ESTABLISHMENT.—There is hereby established the Northern Rio Grande National Heritage Area in the State of New Mexico.

(b) BOUNDARIES.—The heritage area shall include the counties of Santa Fe, Rio Arriba, and Taos.

(c) MANAGEMENT ENTITY. —

(1) The Northern Rio Grande National Heritage Area, Inc., a non-profit corporation chartered in the State of New Mexico, shall serve as the management entity for the heritage area.

(2) The Board of Directors for the management entity shall include representatives of the State of New Mexico, the counties of Santa Fe, Rio Arriba and Taos, tribes and pueblos within the heritage area, the cities of Santa Fe, Española and Taos, and members of the general public. The total number of Board members and the number of Directors representing State, local and tribal governments and interested communities shall be established to ensure that all parties have appropriate representation on the Board.

SEC. 205. AUTHORITY AND DUTIES OF THE MANAGEMENT ENTITY.

(a) MANAGEMENT PLAN.—

(1) Not later than 3 years after the date of enactment of this Act, the management entity shall develop and forward to the Secretary a management plan for the heritage area.

(2) The management entity shall develop and implement the management plan in cooperation with affected communities, tribal and local governments and shall provide for public involvement in the development and implementation of the management plan.

(3) The management plan shall, at a minimum—

(A) provide recommendations for the conservation, funding, management, and development of the resources of the heritage area;

(B) identify sources of funding;

(C) include an inventory of the cultural, historical, archaeological, natural, and recreational resources of the heritage area;

(D) provide recommendations for educational and interpretive programs to inform the public about the resources of the heritage area; and

(E) include an analysis of ways in which local, State, Federal, and tribal programs may best be coordinated to promote the purposes of this subtitle.

(4) If the management entity fails to submit a management plan to the Secretary as provided in paragraph (1), the heritage area shall no longer be eligible to receive Federal funding under this subtitle until such time as a plan is submitted to the Secretary.

(5) The Secretary shall approve or disapprove the management plan within 90 days after the date of submission. If the Secretary disapproves the management plan, the Secretary shall advise the management entity in writing of the reasons therefore and shall make recommendations for revisions to the plan.

(6) The management entity shall periodically review the management plan and submit to the Secretary any recommendations for proposed revisions to the management plan. Any major revisions to the management plan must be approved by the Secretary.

(b) AUTHORITY.—The management entity may make grants and provide technical assistance to tribal and local governments, and other public and private entities to carry out the management plan.

(c) DUTIES.—The management entity shall—

(1) give priority in implementing actions set forth in the management plan;

(2) encourage by appropriate means economic viability in the heritage area consistent with the goals of the management plan; and

(3) assist local and tribal governments and non-profit organizations in—

(A) establishing and maintaining interpretive exhibits in the heritage area;

(B) developing recreational resources in the heritage area;

(C) increasing public awareness of, and appreciation for, the cultural, historical, archaeological and natural resources and sites in the heritage area;

(D) the restoration of historic structures related to the heritage area; and

(E) carrying out other actions that the management entity determines appropriate to fulfill the purposes of this subtitle, consistent with the management plan.

(d) PROHIBITION ON ACQUIRING REAL PROPERTY. — The management entity may not use Federal funds received under this subtitle to acquire real property or an interest in real property.

(e) PUBLIC MEETINGS. — The management entity shall hold public meetings at least annually regarding the implementation of the management plan.

(f) ANNUAL REPORTS AND AUDITS. —

(1) For any year in which the management entity receives Federal funds under this subtitle, the management entity shall submit an annual report to the Secretary setting forth accomplishments, expenses and income, and each entity to which any grant was made by the management entity.

(2) The management entity shall make available to the Secretary for audit all records relating to the expenditure of Federal funds and any matching funds. The management entity shall also require, for all agreements authorizing expenditure of Federal funds by other organizations, that the receiving organization make available to the Secretary for audit all records concerning the expenditure of those funds.

SEC. 206. DUTIES OF THE SECRETARY.

(a) TECHNICAL AND FINANCIAL ASSISTANCE. — The Secretary may, upon request of the management entity, provide technical and financial assistance to develop and implement the management plan.

(b) PRIORITY. — In providing assistance under subsection (a), the Secretary shall give priority to actions that facilitate —

(1) the conservation of the significant natural, cultural, historical, archaeological, scenic, and recreational resources of the heritage area; and

(2) the provision of educational, interpretive, and recreational op-

portunities consistent with the resources and associated values of the heritage area.

SEC. 207. PRIVATE PROPERTY PROTECTIONS; SAVINGS PROVISIONS.

(a) PRIVATE PROPERTY PROTECTION.—

(1) NOTIFICATION AND CONSENT OF PROPERTY OWNERS REQUIRED.—No privately owned property shall be preserved, conserved, or promoted by the management plan for the Heritage Area until the owner of that private property has been notified in writing by the management entity and has given written consent for such preservation, conservation or promotion to the management entity.

(2) LANDOWNER WITHDRAWAL.—Any owner of private property included within the boundary of the heritage area, shall have their property immediately removed from within the boundary by submitting a written request to the management entity.

(3) ACCESS TO PRIVATE PROPERTY.—Nothing in this subtitle shall be construed to require any private property owner to permit public access (including Federal, State, or local government access) to such private property. Nothing in this subtitle shall be construed to modify any provision of Federal, State, or local law with regard to public access to or use of private lands.

(4) LIABILITY.—Designation of the heritage area shall not be considered to create any liability, or to have any effect on any liability under any other law, of any private property owner with respect to any persons injured on such private property.

(5) RECOGNITION OF AUTHORITY TO CONTROL LAND USE.—Nothing in this subtitle shall be construed to modify any authority of Federal, State, or local governments to regulate land use.

(6) PARTICIPATION OF PRIVATE PROPERTY OWNERS IN HERITAGE AREA.—Nothing in this subtitle shall be construed to require the owner of any private property located within the boundaries of the heritage area to participate in or be associated with the heritage area.

(b) EFFECT OF ESTABLISHMENT.—The boundaries designated for the heritage area represent the area within which Federal funds appropriated for the purpose of this subtitle shall be expended. The establishment of the heritage area and its boundaries shall not be construed to provide any nonexisting regulatory authority on land use within the heritage area or its viewshed by the Secretary, the National Park Service, or the management entity.

(c) TRIBAL LANDS. — Nothing in this subtitle shall restrict or limit a tribe from protecting cultural or religious sites on tribal lands.

(d) TRUST RESPONSIBILITIES. — Nothing in this subtitle shall diminish the Federal Government's trust responsibilities or government-to-government obligations to any federally recognized Indian tribe.

SEC. 208. SUNSET.

The authority of the Secretary to provide assistance under this subtitle terminates on the date that is 15 years after the date of enactment of this Act.

SEC. 209. AUTHORIZATION OF APPROPRIATIONS.

(a) IN GENERAL. — There are authorized to be appropriated to carry out this subtitle $10,000,000, of which not more than $1,000,000 may be authorized to be appropriated for any fiscal year.

(b) COST-SHARING REQUIREMENT. — The Federal share of the total cost of any activity assisted under this subtitle shall be not more than 50 percent.

Introduction

1. The heritage area also includes the Jicarilla Apache reservation. When the Spanish arrived in New Mexico they immediately distinguished "Pueblo" Indians, who lived in settled agricultural communities, from more nomadic groups such as Navajos and Apaches. Spanish colonial activity focused almost exclusively on Pueblo peoples, whom Spaniards considered more civilized. This Eurocentric hierarchy of indigenous economies and cultures endures to this day. Apaches have received much less attention than the Pueblos from tourists and heritage professionals in northern New Mexico. Because of their marginal place in Spanish colonial history and northern New Mexico's heritage industry, I will say little about Apaches in this book. The same applies to recent Mexican immigrants to northern New Mexico.

2. The fact that the legislative process took four years had more to do with congressional politics, a logjam of heritage area bills, and a general uncertainty about the national heritage area program than with issues relating specifically to New Mexico.

3. Molly Mullin (2001, 97) maintains that "the shift in emphasis, on the part of white activists in [New Mexican] Indian affairs, away from coercive assimilationism and towards a paternalistic version of multiculturalism was promoted by a number of factors, including the influence of early twentieth-century reform movements, the rise of American cultural nationalism, the increasingly popular influence of anthropology, and the expansion of tourism."

4. For example, in 2009 Larry Whitten, a Texan, bought a motel in Taos (a tourist town famous for its Hispanic and Native American heritage), prohibited his employees from speaking Spanish in his presence, and required some of them to Anglicize their names. Widespread public out-

rage in and beyond northern New Mexico revealed little public tolerance for policies many considered racist.

5. Many theorists warn against interpreting the "post" in "postcolonial" as meaning "after" or "past," as if independence completely erased colonialism and its effects. Stuart Hall (1996) conceives of postcolonialism as a reconfiguration (not transcendence) of colonial power relations. Likewise, multiculturalism represents a new configuration of power not necessarily opposed to colonialism.

6. For a variety of reasons, the development of the NRGNHA has been slow. Limited resources, suspicion toward the federal government, squabbles among board members, and tensions between communities have impeded progress. Coaxing people to attend public meetings and participate in a bureaucratic process that can seem culturally foreign has been difficult. This has been especially true of Native Americans. As sovereign nations, tribes are able to control resources and negotiate with the federal government in a way that Nuevomexicano communities cannot. Since the 1990s, casinos have also provided some tribes with an important new source of income. Indians therefore have less of an incentive to participate in the heritage area.

7. An early example of the politics of recognition in New Mexico is a debate around the turn of the twentieth century over the use of Spanish in public schools. English-only advocates viewed bilingualism as an impediment to full and loyal citizenship. Nuevomexicano state superintendents challenged this belief and argued that students had a right to speak and be taught in Spanish. In 1912 New Mexico became the only officially bilingual state in the union (Nieto-Phillips 2004, 197–205).

8. An important report on the future of the national park system published in 2001 by the National Park System Advisory Board is littered with references to our shared American heritage (a nationalistic mantra and classic NPS rhetoric), but the section on living cultures and heritage areas focuses on "indigenous and local people" and "diverse ethnic groups and nationalities" (NPSAB 2001, 22–23). This is the only section of the report where diversity and difference overshadow a unified national experience.

9. The production of heritage is not always (or even usually) a strategy for securing the recognition of others. It may well be internally oriented. In New Mexico, Indians and Hispanics sometimes express a desire for self-recognition. For instance, when the New Mexico state legislature celebrated Hispanic Culture Day in 2003, Senator Ben Altamirano (2003) noted that until 2002 the legislature had "overlooked the simple act of recognizing" the importance of Hispanic culture in New Mexico, perhaps

due to its "strength and pervasiveness." Yet each generation was losing some of the language and traditions, he warned. It was therefore important to "remind ourselves who we are," since "he who does not know his history is a foreigner in his own land."

10. Recognition and redistribution are not mutually exclusive strategies (see Fraser and Honneth 2003). Official recognition can lead to concrete political and economic gains for subaltern groups. However, the cultural logic of recognition (which addresses status hierarchies) can divert attention away from economic structures. This depoliticizing potential may be one reason why social justice movements are increasingly organized around culture and demands for recognition rather than class and demands for redistribution: they appear less threatening to the status quo. In New Mexico, the politics of recognition has gained more traction than the politics of redistribution (the NRGNHA exemplifies this fact). Politicians at the national level have been happy to endorse heritage interpretation and preservation projects, but large-scale attempts to address land grant politics have been inconclusive (e.g., General Accounting Office 2004).

11. Multicultural programs often give the impression that subordinate groups have more culture than dominant ones, reversing a colonial understanding of how culture and history are globally distributed. European colonizers often assumed that they had a monopoly on culture (i.e., Civilization) and history (the colonized were people without history). Yet once again this is only an apparent reversal. According to the logic of late modernism, *transcending* culture and history is the ultimate achievement, which only Europeans and Euro-Americans have been able to pull off.

12. I have focused on sites where New Mexicans are concerned about the relationships between culture, identity, and the past, whether or not they explicitly use the term "heritage." Since culture, identity, and the past are not distinct in people's lives, it makes sense for anthropologists to consider them together. And just as they are loosely configured in people's experience, so too can they be loosely configured in anthropological analysis. I am not particularly interested, in other words, in developing a theory of heritage per se (see Guthrie 2010a).

1. The Palace of the Governors

1. The building was called "el palacio" from the time of its construction, since it was an official government outpost of the Spanish empire. The Palace has never been palatial, though.

2. Still, one of the Palace's first claims to fame as a historical site was the fact that Lew Wallace had written part of his novel *Ben Hur* while

residing there as governor. Clearly associated with the Palace's recent American rather than older Spanish or Mexican history, the "Ben Hur Room" (where he supposedly wrote) attracted keen interest from tourists and local residents alike (e.g., Nusbaum 1978, 86).

3. The museum and the school were intimately related institutions, sharing Hewett as director, the same staff, and the same facilities. They formally separated in 1959.

4. The strategy proved successful, and increasing numbers of tourists poured in from all over the world to experience Santa Fe's distinctive atmosphere. In 1957 the city passed a stringent historic design ordinance for the downtown area to ensure that the city would maintain a uniform appearance (Wilson 1997, 252–59). Santa Fe–style architecture now completely dominates Santa Fe, from the adobe monuments around the plaza to countless fake adobe, concrete block buildings and big box stores elsewhere.

5. The fiesta and its cultural politics have changed significantly over time. Today it provides key opportunities for both multicultural celebration and the reassertion of Hispano nationalism (see DeBouzek and Reyna 1992; Grimes [1976] 1992; Horton 2010; Montgomery 2002, 128–57; Wilson 1997, 181–231).

6. The idea that the Palace *represents* or *symbolizes* something endures into the twenty-first century, and *what* it symbolizes remains just as ambiguous. For example, in a book published by the Museum of New Mexico Press, Emily Abbink suggests that the Palace "remains a powerful symbol of cultural influence, violence, and fusion"; represents "stability, identity, and creativity of spirit"; and symbolizes "our common heritage, both violent and peaceful" (2007, 114, 117). Indeed, in the coming century, "the Palace will represent *New Mexico*, highlighting its unique contributions to shaping the nation's identity" (119; emphasis added). Frances Levine (2008, 121) writes: "As a National Historic Landmark, the Palace stands beside other great symbols of U.S. history—Paul Revere's home, Mount Vernon, and Monticello. Each U.S. landmark reminds visitors of the events and people who played a role in developing this nation."

7. The museum considered the scientific study of the past to be not only a sign of civilization's progress but also a means to it. Noting the architectural "renaissance" exemplified by the New Mexico Building at the 1915 Panama-California Exposition in San Diego, the museum concluded, "We progress most rapidly when we take advantage of the lessons of the past, and to know archaeology and history is to save time otherwise lost in experimenting or working along lines that had been already followed

to their logical conclusion by our forefathers" ("Report of the Museum of New Mexico" 1914, 2). The San Diego exposition deliberately juxtaposed the primitive past and the industrial, Anglo-American present in order to demonstrate civilization's progress (Kropp 1996).

8. Anglo-Americans have frequently assumed the role of scientist or businessman in the rhetoric and imagery of triculturalism in New Mexico, just as Indians often appear as artists and Hispanics as conquistadores, farmers, and laborers (Nieto-Phillips 2004, 106–7, 122–24, 163–64; Rodríguez 2001, 199–201; Wilson 2003, 27–28). Their association with science affirms a progressivist view of southwestern history, in which Anglo-Americans usher in (and dominate) the modern age while other groups are relegated to the past. Ironically, academic anthropologists outside of the Southwest, including Franz Boas, considered Hewett unscientific (Tobias and Woodhouse 2001, 79–83).

9. Santa Fe has become a city of museums. Besides the units of the Museum of New Mexico, other museums include the stylish Georgia O'Keeffe Museum (opened in 1997) and the Museum of Spanish Colonial Art (2002), which houses the collections of the Spanish Colonial Arts Society in a Pueblo-Spanish Revival–style building designed by John Gaw Meem. The city boasts a number of other museums, including a couple devoted to Native American art, not to mention hundreds of art galleries.

10. A 1961 report discussed restoring to "the old Palace some of its own inherent exhibit value, unparalleled in the nation, which is so badly (although with the best intentions) mutilated in its 'restoration' for museum use in 1909, and which has since been completely ignored." Failure to exhibit the building's historic structure "is a colossal wastage of what could be one of the nation's outstanding historic monuments—an exhibit in itself ideally fashioned to frame and enhance its interior displays" (quoted in Conron and Woods Architects 2004, 144).

11. Other current exhibits include an overview of New Mexico history, a portrait gallery, a life-size diorama of a northern New Mexico church interior, the Segesser Hides (two large historical scenes painted on buffalo hides between 1693 and 1730), an exhibit of New Mexican devotional art, a print shop featuring mostly working historic printing and binding equipment, and temporary exhibit space. Recent temporary exhibits have covered topics such as Jews in New Mexico, private printing presses in the state, Jack Kerouac's life and writing, and the Old Spanish Trail. A hallway has been used to display historic photographs of Santa Fe and the Palace itself. Other public areas in the museum include a courtyard (used for outdoor programs) and a museum shop (which sells books, food

products, clothing, southwestern Indian art, and other gifts related to New Mexico). The exhibits are arranged in no particular order, and there is no single course through the museum. Visitors enter the museum on the plaza side of the building and usually complete a counterclockwise tour of the building. Although some twentieth-century exhibits implied American supremacy through periodization, linear progressivism, or systems of scientific classification, I focus narrowly on the display and interpretation of the Palace itself.

12. This heightened sensitivity to the Palace's historicity coincided with the professionalization of the historic preservation movement in the late 1960s and 1970s. During this period preservationists turned sharply away from historical revivalism and speculative restorations, espousing instead a modernist call for the honest use of materials and historical transparency. The codification of national preservation standards and the adoption of meticulous new procedures (such as the creation of historic structure reports) would have influenced the treatment of the Palace of the Governors at this time (Wilson 2004, 198).

13. The Prince Reception Room represents the Palace in 1893, when Bradford Prince was governor of New Mexico. Over the course of several decades Prince articulated a progressive view of Nuevomexicanos that highlighted their Spanishness, glorious conquistador past, and cultural rather than racial identity. This view was essential for the campaign for statehood. Like the view that Mexicans were racially inferior, it ultimately served Anglo interests by depoliticizing New Mexico's colonial history, downplaying entrenched inequality, denigrating miscegenation, and promoting static, essentialized views of Indians and Hispanics. Prince was not only an influential politician but also the long-term president of the New Mexico Historical Society and the founder of the Society for the Preservation of Spanish Antiquities (Gómez 2007, 64–69; Nieto-Phillips 2004, 74–75, 160–69). Multicultural politics and historic preservation similarly intersected in the work of the Museum of New Mexico, so memorializing Prince in the Palace of the Governors was fitting. The historical society and the museum, under the leadership of Prince and Hewett, respectively, were rivals in the early twentieth century, but the society eventually transferred its collections to the museum (Stevenson 2009, 252–55).

14. On other excavations in and around the Palace, see Conron and Woods Architects 2004, 30–98.

15. Frances Levine (2008, 121) writes that the 1970s restoration "took into account historical authenticity" and set a precedent for using "careful documentation and authentic materials and details."

16. I developed a survey consisting of twenty-five open-ended and multiple-choice questions that covered the respondents' basic visitor experience (how they heard about the Palace, why they came, what part of the Palace they liked best, etc.) and their understanding of the Palace's meaning, the Nusbaum Room, the portal market, and the significance of the Palace for Santa Fe and New Mexico. I sat at a table inside the museum with a sign inviting visitors to take a ten-minute survey in order to receive a coupon for the museum shop. All but one of the respondents were from out of state, and twenty had never been to the Palace before. Eleven had taken a docent tour before completing the survey. The small size and voluntary nature of the survey mean that it is not a representative sample, but the responses did reveal both a variety of perspectives and some clear patterns.

17. Historic preservation law in the United States does provide definitions of "historic" and standards of significance. The designation of the Palace as a National Historic Landmark reflects these standards. However, the laws are themselves made up, and most Americans are unaware of their specifics. The Palace is *historic* not simply because the law says it is but because of the social process I am describing.

18. The Palace was but one site for this subjective transformation that Tony Bennett (1988) has called the "exhibitionary complex." Mark Neumann (1999, 99–103), for example, describes efforts to tame crowds of spectators at the Grand Canyon and the deliberate cultivation of a scientific gaze in order to turn the canyon into an exhibit of itself.

19. I had walked down the portal many times before noticing these exposed sections of wall. Usually the Indian artists sitting with their backs against the wall and their work in front of them are the main attraction. With so much on display—jewelry, Indians, wall—it is easy to miss something.

20. Three other principles guided this work. First, the building cannot be restored to a single period but should represent a span of history. Second, all pre-1909 architectural features should be preserved and made visible to the public whenever possible. And finally, any restoration work must be based on sound documentation in order to avoid "replacing fantasy colonial details with fantasy Victorian ones" (Weber 1974, 41–42). Conron and Lent Architects, who worked with the museum to renovate the Palace in the 1970s, "fully agreed upon" these principles (Conron and Woods Architects 2004, 198).

21. Abbink's (2007) history of the Palace of the Governors, published by the Museum of New Mexico Press, extends further than Shishkin's.

Indeed, Abbink notes the 2009 opening of the new state history museum behind the Palace as if it had already happened (99). Her epilogue projects us far into the future, and she reminds us that "history is not a closed book" (118–19). Yet Abbink actually has little to say about the history of the Palace of the Governors *as a museum.*

22. Here we see evidence of two different ways in which historicization can reinforce power relations. For if relegating Indians and Hispanos to history means casting them from the present (and future), documenting the history of Anglos in the Southwest can be a way of justifying their regional presence.

23. In the Nusbaum Room, the pottery and other artifacts on display may be thought of as representations of the original artifacts on display in the Puye Room, just as the furniture in a period room serves as a representation of the room's original furniture. Whether the artifacts themselves are originals or reproductions is an important curatorial distinction (which could be disclosed to visitors) but does not greatly affect their representational function.

24. Visitors had to read exhibit signs carefully to experience the Nusbaum Room as a meta-exhibit. About half of the visitors in my survey thought the exhibit's focus was pottery. Some visitors were most interested in the room itself (including the murals), others in the pottery on display, and still others in the history of museum curation.

25. Consider, for example, an exhibit that ran from 2001 to 2002 at the Museum of Indian Arts and Culture in Santa Fe. Titled "Tourist Icons: Native American Kitsch, Camp & Fine Art Along Route 66," the exhibit presented a wide range of tourist souvenirs from the Southwest and encouraged visitors to think critically about their status and function. The exhibit deconstructed categories of visual culture and raised questions about the appropriation of religious images and the commodification of culture. The brochure that accompanied the exhibition stated, "Tourist Icons challenges viewers to reassess their underlying attitudes toward art and popular culture. It explores what these works reveal about both the makers and consumers of souvenirs." Yet although the brochure mentioned in passing the politics of contemporary museum practice, the exhibit was never explicitly self-critical (or even critical of museums in general), making it possible for visitors to leave feeling superior to earlier tourists. Its critical approach and its attempt to destabilize the categories of kitsch, camp, and fine art emphasized intellectualism and encouraged visitors to become metacritics: critics of earlier critics who may have dismissed tourist souvenirs too hastily. More than the Palace exhibits, the

Tourist Icons exhibit exposed recent history to critique, but it ultimately conveyed a sense of enlightenment. Drawing critical attention to the past, it never asked visitors to question the interpretive authority of the museum or *its* place within a tourist economy.

26. This is not to say that metatourism has displaced older touristic modes in New Mexico. Many tourists today still encounter Route 66 as their predecessors did, unironically, not metatouristically. They may recognize the kitsch, but their attitude toward Route 66 is not primarily critical, nor are they thinking much about the historical context of tourism. So, for example, the Route 66–themed casino on the Laguna Pueblo Reservation west of Albuquerque is chock full of nostalgia, but visitors are not encouraged to adopt a critical or ironic stance toward all the recycled imagery.

27. The cover of the 2001 New Mexico state vacation guide, which was organized around the theme of Route 66's diamond jubilee, featured a photograph of a man and woman driving on a scenic stretch of the highway, smiling and waving at the camera. The front license plate of their convertible reads "TOUR NM." A caption inside the guide reveals that both hail from Grants, New Mexico, and that the car, a 1970 Ford Mustang, belongs to the man. So here we have two New Mexicans gleefully touring New Mexico (note the license plate) probably with a healthy sense of nostalgia (note the Mustang). The message the photograph conveys is ambiguous, however. Vacation guides usually advertise what tourists can see and do when they visit. But are we, as potential vacationers, supposed to identify with these two tourists, to imagine taking their place? *That could be me—I could be there.* Or are we to assume that we might arrive in New Mexico only to find that the natives have become tourists themselves? Such a discovery could radically destabilize the structure of tourism as a social practice.

28. The Segesser Hides were moved to the Nusbaum Room because the room in which they had been displayed was closed during the construction.

29. The Museum of New Mexico recognized this parallel. In November 2003 it published an eight-page "re-creation" of part of the first edition of its journal, *El Palacio*, from November 1913, which included an article about Nusbaum's restoration of the portal. Interspersed with the old articles were new articles that detailed the work of the museum in 2003, including articles on current exhibits and the new museum. The format of the publication, with old and new articles intermingled, was somewhat confusing, but as an explanatory note put it, "what is old is new again," evoking the language of the 1913 New-Old Santa Fe exhibit.

30. The simulation resulted from a collaboration between the New Mexico Highlands University media arts department and the New Mexico Department of Cultural Affairs. According to a project statement, it "is the first step in building a description and visualization of the past for public viewing and as a tool for continuing dialogue among professionals and other interested parties." The statement concluded enigmatically: "The results presented here are not meant as fact or truth, but as a means for examining the many facts, truths, interpretations that exist in documents, below the ground, and that have yet to be discovered."

31. The subtlety of these power plays may help explain why the Palace has not become a focus of protest and resistance in New Mexico. Indeed, the Palace itself (in contrast to the portal program, which I discuss in the next chapter) has always been a relatively uncontroversial historic site. The presence of Native Americans under the Palace portal has softened the building's status as a symbol of Spanish rule (unlike several sites I discuss in chapter 3). Nor does the Palace appear as a symbol of American dominance or oppression.

2. The Palace Portal

1. Lucy Lippard (1999, 63) describes this as "the strangest sight" in all of Santa Fe. The tourists lined up under the portal, facing the seated Indian artists, "are shoulder to shoulder, heads bowed in homage, as though performing some strange ritual contra dance."

2. Note that MacCannell's use of "sight" instead of "site" emphasizes the visual construction of tourist attractions through sightseeing.

3. Mark Neumann (1999, 167) has studied tourism at the Grand Canyon. Agreeing with Percy, he acknowledges that "people cannot but help have an image of the canyon before they arrive." Yet Neumann's research suggests that tourists do not necessarily consider this a problem. "The tourists I met along the rim and who wrote me about their trips suggest that these images are not necessarily an obstacle to their experience of the canyon; they provide a frame that helps them to see and appreciate the canyon" (see also Guthrie 2005, 88–89).

4. Besides getting off the beaten track, another strategy for seeing sights in and of themselves is to seek unexpected or unauthorized views of them or to take advantage of jarring circumstances—a typhus outbreak, bomb explosion, or manhunt for an escaped convict at the Grand Canyon, for example (Neumann 1999, 291–338; Percy [1954] 1975, 49–50, 60–61).

5. MacCannell overstates tourists' desire to get backstage. Many tourists care more about seeing a good show than learning about actors' lives

(Bruner 2005, 6). Edward Bruner (18–19) also conceives of tourism in terms of performance but suggests that tourists are involved in a "coproduction." He "sees tourism as improvisational theater with the stage located in the borderzone, where both tourists and locals are actors."

6. Percy ([1954] 1975, 51–56) argues that tourists have surrendered their sovereign ability to see the world to experts who can authenticate their experiences. "Kwakiutls are surrendered to Franz Boas; decaying Southern mansions are surrendered to Faulkner and Tennessee Williams" (55).

7. The portal case pitted the cultural and economic protection of Indian peoples against the protection of civil rights. Deirdre Evans-Pritchard (1987, 290, 293; 1990, 76–77) reports that some lawyers think the Livingstons' argument was technically stronger than the museum's but that the case had a more important *moral* dimension. She proposes that public opinion was instrumental in deciding the case and that the decision hinged on the powerful association of tradition and morality.

8. Others disputed how "traditional" the exclusive use of the Palace grounds by Indians was (e.g., Joyce 1978), but the district court in the Livingston case downplayed the significance of the space's multicultural use (*Livingston v. Ewing* 1978, 832).

9. Several pieces of legislation now support the district court's conclusion about the relationship between artworks and their makers. The New Mexico Indian Arts and Crafts Sales Act of 1978 and the federal Indian Arts and Crafts Act of 1990 both define Indian art as art made by Indians and prohibit false marketing.

10. I did not conduct further interviews with portal artists myself because I did not want to duplicate this research, did not have the time to build the deep relationships with portal artists that Hoerig and Laughlin had, and wanted to avoid subjecting program participants to more anthropological investigation when I did not feel it was necessary. I am therefore indebted to Hoerig and his careful ethnographic work.

11. Interestingly, Paul Livingston was an outspoken critic of this living exhibit rhetoric as he was battling for a place under the portal. "As a humanist, I find that totally degrading and humiliating, for Indians to be considered part of a building owned by the state," he said, calling the portal market "a public, racially segregated display of people" (Myers 1978; see also Frederick 1978; Puente 1979).

12. In his study of postmodern consumption in Chadds Ford, Pennsylvania, John Dorst (1989, 65, 157–60, 166–68) shows that artisanal, preindustrial production techniques are thought to suit the suburb's image. A heritage festival that promotes symbolic exchange and a traditional social

order masks the actual exchange of money for goods. "An important part of what gets produced and endlessly reproduced in the advanced capitalist economic, social, and moral order of Chadds Ford are the simulacra of an *archaic* economic, social, and moral order. Subsistence, self-reliance and making by hand are its touchstones." The crafts fair he describes thus combines the characteristics of marketplace and spectacle, casting visitors as both clientele and audience.

13. Describing a similar case, Timothy Mitchell (1988, 10) notes the realism of the Egyptian bazaar at the 1867 Exposition Universelle in Paris, where visitors spent real money: "The commercialism of the donkey rides, the bazaar stalls and the dancing girls was no different from the commercialism of the world outside. This was the real thing, in the sense that what commercialism offers is always the real thing. The commercialism of the world exhibitions was no accident, but a consequence of the scale of representation they attempted and of the modern, consumer economy that required such entertainment."

14. In response to artist protests, the museum eventually loosened this rule. The director of the Palace, "recognizing the sometimes complex nature of kinship," can approve minor exceptions for specific vendors, especially those who were participating in the program prior to 1987 (Hoerig 2003, 206, 213–15 [Rules 1F, 7A, and 71]). Evans-Pritchard (1990, 89–90) observes that this grandfather clause permitted custom and usage to override the museum's official guidelines in much the same way that custom had been used to justify its Indians-only policy. So, for example, although one artist was selling things that did not conform to the museum's standards of authenticity, "the fact that she had sold at the portal since she was a child made her, herself, a traditional attribute of the portal."

15. "That has to do something to you, to have to always be so accommodating," remarked Rina Swentzell, a scholar and former potter from Santa Clara Pueblo, of tourist expectations. "Your whole activity is directed by others." Swentzell saw a lack of integrity in the production of "art for art's sake" (quoted in Sagel 1987). Anthropologist Margaret Bender (2002, 10–11), on the other hand, acknowledges that Native American artists must take buyer expectations into consideration but notes that "the artifacts and practices produced for tourists can never be only a reflection of the desires and demands of the non-native consumers because the context in which they are produced differs from that in which the tourists formulate their desires." Furthermore, desires do not always develop within a single culture and may be shaped by the artists themselves.

16. The vendors' annual meeting combines elements of Euro-American parliamentary democracy and Puebloan cultural values and norms (Hoerig 2003, 147–52).

17. The contrast between written regulations and authentic "tradition" evokes the old (and incorrect) anthropological assumption that the subjects of anthropological inquiry are completely unconscious of the rules governing their behavior. Bronislaw Malinowski ([1922] 1984, 11) urged ethnographers to document the unwritten rules of tribal life. The natives themselves cannot articulate the rules. They "obey the forces and commands of the tribal code, but they do not comprehend them; exactly as they obey their instincts and their impulses, but could not lay down a single law of psychology." The fact that tribal laws are unconscious validates their authenticity and justifies the work of the anthropologist, who makes what was once unconscious conscious and converts what was oral into writing.

18. Implicit in Hoerig's argument is the fact that *every* part of Native Americans' lives is real for them (this clarification helps us avoid the trap of considering some settings more real than others).

19. Evans-Pritchard's characterization of the restrictions inside the frame of the portal program as "external" suggests that she considers the portal to be outside of the world of tacit, authentic Indian culture.

20. To be fair, Evans-Pritchard's dissertation is a focused critique of how the American legal system handles the concept of tradition, not a critique of the concept itself, and in the former she is astute. It is unfortunate, though, that she does not direct more critical attention to the single concept around which her analysis revolves.

21. Hoerig and Evans-Pritchard both highlight the agency of participants in the portal program, who "retain significant control over the forces of tourism, deciding what elements of their culture and how much of themselves to open up to the tourist gaze" (Hoerig 2003, 17). Yet while Hoerig emphasizes the cooperative working relationship between the artists and the Museum of New Mexico, Evans-Pritchard (1987, 1990) paints a more antagonistic picture, documenting instances in which the artists subvert tourist expectations and resist policies imposed by the museum. This interpretation allows her to maintain the image of Indians as true tradition bearers constrained by outside forces and to avoid theorizing the artists' active participation at the level of policy.

22. I am not sure the subjectivity of the Indians selling their artwork under the Palace portal is being commodified. Molly Mullin (2001, 166), writing about Santa Fe's annual Indian Market, cautions against assum-

ing that people interested in buying Indian art are also attempting to buy Indianness. The structure of Rodríguez's argument is illuminating nonetheless.

23. Rina Swentzell (2003a, 68, 71), who is from Santa Clara Pueblo but lived in Taos in the 1950s, recalls the ubiquity of images of Indians around Taos at that time: "The wealthy Anglos really did set the tone for the place. As we looked at those images of who we were supposed to be . . . we felt idealized, yet unworthy of that adoration. There was always the feeling that we were not good enough or could not measure up to how we were represented." Swentzell acknowledges that Hispanics felt left out because they were not considered as special as Indians by Anglos. "But really, in the end, who are the more fortunate people? Those who can move and grow more with their own rhythm or those who do not know their own rhythm anymore because of overpowering outside impositions and expectations?"

24. Measuring actual Aborigines against an abstract notion of Aboriginality resembles the tourist's comparison of a sight to its markers. "It looks just like the postcards!" Or, "It's not as big as I expected it to be." Walker Percy ([1954] 1975, 58–59) suggests that tourists suffer because of their inability to see sights in and of themselves but that treating individuals as specimens or avatars inflicts an additional violence. "As Kierkegaard said, once a person is seen as a specimen of a race or a species, at that very moment he ceases to be an individual." Percy gives the example of a dogfish awaiting dissection in a biology lab. As a specimen, "the dogfish itself is seen as a rather shabby expression of an ideal reality, the species *Squalus acanthias*. The result is the radical devaluation of the individual dogfish." It is a short step from biology to anthropology and the politics of recognition. Human beings are subject to the same fate as the dogfish.

3. The Española Valley

1. "Española was designed for commerce, not postcards," according to the Lonely Planet guide to Santa Fe and Taos. Its setting is beautiful, "but the city itself feels absolutely no need to gussy itself up for sightseers." The comparison to Santa Fe is meant as a compliment: in Española "the adobes are all real, restaurants are authentic and inexpensive, and masterpieces [i.e., lowrider cars] by the city's world-famous artisans are on exhibit at Sonic drive-ins rather than museums" (Penland 2004, 122). Peterson 1984 also celebrates Española's lowrider scene as an indicator of its cultural authenticity.

2. Molly Mullin (2001, 124) has shown that in New Mexico "culture" and lower-class status are often considered mutually exclusive: "in their patronage of specific visions of 'cultural' difference, Indian art patrons implicitly crusaded against other forms of difference, differences which to them were more threatening than any they would attribute to 'culture.'" This assumption about culture and class is clearly evident in Española.

3. This does not mean that there is consensus in the Española valley about what counts as "culture" or that civic identities are uncontested. Cultural production in this region is always embedded in structures of race, class, and ethnicity. Despite this contentious field of cultural politics, though, powerful constituencies do have the ability to spotlight certain cultural forms through public projects and to marginalize others. Still other features of the cultural landscape never contend for "cultural" status. No one in the Española valley, for instance, seems eager to establish a museum dedicated to the culture of casinos or chain stores (where local people actually spend a lot of time working, shopping, and hanging out).

4. Michael Trujillo (2009, 96–126) productively compares two sets of anthropologists who have conducted fieldwork in the Española valley. The first set (Paul Kutsche, John R. Van Ness, and Charles Briggs) focused on Hispanic villages, their cultural traditions, and their struggles over land. The second set (Joseph W. Whitecotton, Richard Stewart Ellis, and Alfredo Jiménez Núñez) worked in and around the city of Española itself. With their different anthropological interests and theoretical perspectives, these authors produced wildly different accounts of the same region. The geographic scale of the first set of ethnographies is smaller than that of the second, less-well-known set. An analysis of Hispanics living in and around Española requires a broader consideration of assimilation and acculturation within a social and political system dominated by Anglo-Americans.

5. In 1880 the Denver and Rio Grande Railway Company literally stopped in its tracks after reaching Española, having conceded not to complete the line to Santa Fe as part of an agreement that divvied up rail development rights in the West. Española thus became the unlikely terminus of the railroad until the Santa Fe connection was completed by a new company in 1886.

6. For example, a highway sign read "Welcome to the City of Española . . . Founded 1598." The sign was evidently installed in association with the American bicentennial in 1976 and included the slogan "New Mexico A Cultural Mosaic" along with Puebloan iconography and the stylized silhouette of a conquistador (see Masco 2006, 163).

7. Consider also a print advertisement planned by the Española Valley Chamber of Commerce in the 1980s: a conquistador eyes a lowrider and its driver and says, "The natives seem friendly enough but they do ride strange mounts" (Peterson 1984).

8. Some scholars believe that the Spanish first moved into Okhay Owingeh, on the east side of the Rio Grande, before moving across the river to Yunque Owingeh. Others believe they settled at Yunque from the beginning. Florence Hawley Ellis (1987, 14–18; 1989, 11–14) suggests that the confusion may arise from the fact that the two Tewa villages were closely related and were both referred to as "San Juan Pueblo" by the Spanish.

9. According to Ellis (1987, 12), the events leading up to the excavation constituted a "tale of archaeology-to-the-rescue." During the 1940s and 1950s archaeologists from the Museum of New Mexico rushed to San Juan Pueblo on several occasions after receiving word of adobe-making projects that threatened the site. "Nothing produces better adobes than the walls of old ruins in which adobe has been used." Ellis (1987, 12–13; 1989, 18–22) also credited several men at San Juan with discovering important artifacts at the site, which eventually reached experts in Santa Fe and Washington DC. The Museum of New Mexico appealed to the governor of San Juan and to the United Pueblos Agency in Albuquerque, but it was not until 1959 that the Pueblo invited the University of New Mexico to conduct a full-scale excavation.

10. Articles on each of the Pueblos in the *Eight Northern Indian Pueblos 2007–08 Official Guide* emphasize the connections between political sovereignty, economic development, and cultural survival, although the guide's subtitle (which singles out art and culture) and the majority of images inside appeal to a narrower discourse of cultural tradition.

11. In an article on lowrider culture in the Española valley, Brenda Bright (1998, 587) remarks, "Most area residents come to Española for shopping, making Riverside Drive the central place in a town that has no real center." This lack of a center was a crucial motivation for creating the Española plaza, which has never become the "central place" designers envisioned.

12. In 2011 a controversy erupted when the Archdiocese of Santa Fe proposed building a retreat center next to the santuario. The two sides in the debate disagree about the value of "development," but both advocate preservation. The Northern Rio Grande National Heritage Area has become involved, supporting community planning efforts.

13. This materialist argument is less prominent in the chapter on drug use in Trujillo's 2009 book than in his 2006 article.

14. In addition to workers commuting from Chimayó to Los Alamos and scientist/tourists reversing the journey, Chimayó and Los Alamos have also been ceremonially linked. Beginning in 1983, a Pilgrimage for Peace combining Nuevomexicano and Pueblo ritual practices has carried healing soil from the santuario to Ashley Pond in Los Alamos (Masco 2006, 173–74).

15. In the 1980s one Española resident reported buying an almanac only to discover that the map of New Mexico included the tiny villages of Hernandez and Abiquiú (made famous by Ansel Adams and Georgia O'Keeffe, respectively) but not the city of Española (Peterson 1984).

16. Richard Lucero, Española's former mayor, commented that "we've always been in the shadow of some other New Mexico city," whether it be Santa Fe, Los Alamos, or Taos. "But we have the oldest missions in the U.S. that have been used and worshipped in for more than 300 years. We still have the matachines and penitente rituals. We are still living in the ways of our ancestors—not our grandfathers, not our great-grandfathers, but our great-great-grandfathers. We have to make sure that what happened in the last 400 years doesn't get lost" (quoted in Ooms 1993, 3). Note the geographical slippage in Lucero's statement. The first "we" here seems to refer to the city of Española, but the second "we" apparently includes the entire Española valley (with its four-hundred-year history). Lucero's comment about "living in the way of our ancestors" is highly selective.

17. The city rejected offers by corporations to develop the plaza. Lucero expressed disinterest in out-of-state commercial investment in the plaza, explaining, "We don't want another shopping center" (Roy 1990b).

18. New Mexico's arid climate and years of drought have meant that there was little or no vegetation on the plaza (I was surprised to return to Española in 2009 to find trees and green grass around the gazebo). While traditional New Mexican plazas usually lack heavy vegetation, plans for the Española plaza suggest the city imagined the space having a more park-like environment, promising "gardens, flowers, trees, lawns and greenery" (Plaza de Española Foundation 1992).

19. The city's logo, developed in concert with the plaza project, combines images of a Pueblo pot, conquistador's helmet, and locomotive to represent Española's tricultural identity. The plaza logo itself, however, reimagines and updates New Mexico's traditional racial pantheon by featuring four highly stylized human figures (one of which is shaded) in a geometric design (see Guthrie 2005, 227). Most of the people I talked to in Española were not sure what the plaza logo symbolized. One explanation I found (Bird 1988) stated that the fourth figure represented a tourist,

whose recognition as one of northern New Mexico's archetypical figures is surely overdue. Mayor Lucero (2003) told me the figure could represent any newcomer to the Española valley, be it a tourist, Muslim, or Sikh. The valley's residents have welcomed these new cultures, he said. Lucero's comments suggest that the plaza project may have at least tentatively embraced a new *multi*culturalism (a discourse with a wider, national currency), but the plaza plan itself is firmly rooted in the regional logic of triculturalism.

20. The first major exhibit, a traveling photography exhibit from the Smithsonian Institution titled "Americanos: Latino Life in the United States/La Vida de los Latinos en los Estados Unidos," opened in 2003 and garnered positive press for the city.

21. Other early descriptions of the Misión, including the one in the plaza proposal, gave a more generic explanation of the building, stating that it would be a composite of sixteenth- and seventeenth-century Spanish colonial churches in New Mexico, or that it would be built in the style of those churches. By the time it was built, however, the Misión was clearly supposed to be a re-creation of one particular (and particularly important) church: San Miguel.

22. The ceremonial brick making proved premature. Construction on the Misión-Convento did not begin for another six years, and ground-breaking ceremonies for that building would be held again in 1996.

23. Religion frequently tests the limits of recognition in northern New Mexico. The ACLU also challenged the public expression of religion at the Cross of the Martyrs in Santa Fe (Guthrie 2010a, 311). And one member of the Northern Rio Grande National Heritage Area board told me about a project to teach Spanish colonial woodworking in public schools. After he was told "we have to keep religion out of it," he decided not to get involved. "I will not compromise religion for anybody, especially when it's teaching our history, because you cannot teach our history without getting religion involved; it was so important. You know, they don't have to practice it, but they have to know about it, because that's how it was."

24. The distinction between church and replica (like that between the sacred and the secular) seems to have been legally relevant but not culturally meaningful in northern New Mexico. Just because a building is a representation or part of an exhibit does not mean that it cannot have religious significance. For example, I was once inside the chapel at El Rancho de las Golondrinas, a living history museum southwest of Santa Fe that features a range of Spanish colonial building types, when a tourist entered, approached the altar, kneeled, and crossed herself. From my

perspective we were inside an exhibit, but for her, apparently, a cross is a cross regardless of its location. Similarly, Fran Levine told me that some of the guards at the Palace of the Governors pray every morning in the New Mexican chapel that was constructed as an exhibit within the museum, not as a place of worship. In Española, people regularly use the Misión, which is not a consecrated church, for weddings and anniversary masses as well as for public meetings (Weideman 2005). Lou Baker (2003), the director of the Española plaza, thought the Misión could have religious significance for people "because religion is heavily entrenched in our culture here, and they take it very seriously. . . . You couldn't be sacrilegious with it at all, because you would offend a lot of people." It would be inappropriate, she said, to have parties or dancing in the Misión.

25. Villa is an accomplished artist who specializes in Spanish colonial-style painting and woodwork. Her husband, José, served as the vice-chairman and then the executive director of the Northern Rio Grande National Heritage Area before he retired. Clare Villa became well known in the valley after working with the Española Valley Arts Festival for ten years and renovating the interior of her church in Alcalde in the Spanish colonial style. She contributed to the Misión project not only artistically but also by navigating city politics and enlisting the support of two dozen other artists.

26. Culture, too, is treated reverently in the Misión. Catholic clergy have expressed concern about the same "folk" practices that tourists and anthropologists have admired in northern New Mexico. For example, Sylvia Rodríguez (2006, 99) reports a conversation with a nun in Ranchos de Taos who "wondered privately whether in Ranchos, people's 'culture was really their religion.'" Catholic New Mexicans, of course, would vehemently deny this assertion. Rodríguez analyzes Nuevomexicanos' reverent, self-conscious, and oftentimes conservative attitude toward culture within the context of rapid social change, conflict over land and water, and the threat of Anglo-American hegemony.

27. When I asked Mayor Lucero why Española would want to send people (including tourists) elsewhere instead of keeping them within the city limits, he gave an economic answer: "Where do the people from Chimayó come to shop? Española. Where do the people from Truchas come to shop? In Española. Where do the people from Alcalde come to shop? In Española. Where do the people from El Rito come to shop? In Española. So should we promote them like they promote us? Yes. . . . I believe so strongly in regionalization" (R. Lucero 2003). This conviction made him a strong supporter of the Northern Rio Grande National Heritage Area.

28. In 1994 these concerns came to a head when Ross Chavez defeated incumbent Richard Lucero in the mayoral race. Chavez campaigned in favor of backing off the plaza project in order to provide better basic services, which he felt had been neglected under Lucero's administration (Roy 1994). His coup was short-lived, though, as Lucero, a consummate and well-connected politician, reclaimed his post in 1998. Nevertheless, Chavez's successful campaign signaled a broader uncertainty about the plaza project and its financing, slowed progress, and put the brakes on Lucero's political momentum, at least temporarily.

29. Fears of becoming another Santa Fe, where locals were displaced and alienated from their city center, were stoked by an effort to designate the area around the new plaza a historic district and institute a set of architectural regulations and zoning restrictions. In 1993 the city council implemented a plan to preserve mercantile-era architecture around the plaza and give the area "a more harmonious appearance" (Roy 1990a, 1993b). The plan was somewhat vague in terms of architectural style, and today no part of Española has anywhere near the architectural unity of downtown Santa Fe, which instituted its own historic design regulations in 1957.

30. The Historic Preservation Act requires that any development receiving federal funding must be reviewed at the state level to determine if it has a negative impact on historic resources. The Española Plaza Project would seemingly have undergone such a review, but I have been unable to find any record or discussion of it, either at the New Mexico Historic Preservation Division or State Archives.

31. Promotional material I picked up on the plaza in 2011 advertised the plaza as "authentic New Mexico." A brochure promoted the Bond House ("former home of a successful mercantile family"), Misión-Convento ("replica of 1598 Spanish Church" featuring "traditional church decoration of the last four centuries"), and veterans' memorial together, promising "a glimpse of authentic Northern New Mexico" and inviting visitors to enjoy "a relaxing afternoon by the fountains" (which are often dry) in a "family atmosphere."

32. In 1990, 17 percent of Española's residents identified themselves as "Mexican, Mexican-American, or Chicano," while 67 percent identified themselves as "other Spanish/Hispanic." In 2000 these percentages were 14 and 71, and in 2010 they were 30 and 56. While "other" Hispanics remained the majority over this twenty-year period, the increase in people identifying as Mexican in 2010 is notable.

33. This reassertion of racial and ethnic divisions reversed a liberal

Mexican policy that advanced the legal equality of Spaniards and Indians (Nieto-Phillips 2004, 37–40).

34. Gómez (2007) concludes that claims to whiteness empowered elite Nuevomexicanos but came at a price: co-optation by American colonizers. Hispanics' efforts to distance themselves from non-white groups facilitated American colonization and helped to reproduce an American racial hierarchy in the Southwest.

35. The sexual politics of New Mexico's double colonial history meant that campaigns for recognition and counter-recognition were also gendered. As Sarah Horton (2010, 139) argues with respect to Nuevomexicanos portraying Diego de Vargas as a virile conquistador in the Santa Fe fiesta, the "assertion of a militarized masculinity—an attempt to counter the impotency implied by Anglo domination—is accomplished only through a symbolic emasculation of Pueblo Indians."

36. The report did note that some of the sites were still in use and had important significance for living people. It also recognized more generally a cultural connection between the Spanish colonization of New Mexico and contemporary New Mexican communities. The study stressed the need to consult with Hispanic and American Indian communities before proceeding with commemorative activities (NPS 1991, 2–3, 43). Yet even when acknowledging the enduring social meaning and cultural legacy of Spanish colonization, the "Alternative Concepts" report never addressed the political dimensions of contemporary Pueblo and Nuevomexicano folklife. Ongoing traditional practices are often shot through with unresolved issues of power, domination, and resistance.

37. The report did acknowledge that the imposition of an Anglo legal system in New Mexico "resulted in conflicts, especially in the areas of water management and land tenure, where the practices of Anglo and Spanish cultures strongly differ" (NPS 1991, 13), but it did not elaborate any further on these conflicts.

38. In 1992 and 1993 New Mexico's congressional delegation introduced legislation that would have enacted some of these recommendations through public-private partnerships. The three bills, S. 2544 (102nd Congress) and S. 294 and H.R. 1561 (103rd Congress), were all titled "Colonial New Mexico Commemorative Act." Both Senate bills passed the Senate but died in the House.

39. The various names used for the plaza reflect the themes guiding its development. Newspaper articles and other documents from the 1980s and 1990s referred to the plaza as the "Northern New Mexico Commemorative Plaza," "Spanish Commemorative Plaza," "Tri-Cultural

Plaza," "Multicultural Plaza," and "Christopher Columbus Quincentenary Plaza," among other variations. None of these names lasted as long as the more general "Plaza de Española" (or its English equivalent), which prevails today.

40. Eliu Martinez (2001), a former president of the Española fiesta council, strongly objected to demilitarizing Oñate: "Mexican/Spanish history has been badly suppressed by Anglo/American historians. . . . Now I find it hard to believe we Mexican/Spanish Americans are suppressing our own history (good or bad)." Michael Trujillo (2009, 70–72) describes an even more radical reconceptualization of Oñate in the 2004 fiesta, when a float sponsored by the Española Christian Center included (in addition to an evangelical preacher and a man representing the crucified Christ) a man wearing shorts, basketball shoes, a conquistador's helmet, and a Spanish-style smock. Over his shoulder he bore a giant hypodermic needle as if it were a cross. He was followed by a woman dressed as a devil, who whipped him. "Thus, Christ's suffering and crucifixion and New Mexico's founder were brought together in what can only be described as Oñate's Passion." The hypodermic needle added another level of meaning to this already complex imagery, as Christ, Oñate, and the drug addict were fused into one.

41. If the Plaza de Española was Richard Lucero's pet project, the Oñate Center was political boss Emilio Naranjo's. For a discussion of politics in Rio Arriba County and the enduring legacy of the *patrón* system evident in these competing projects, see Cabral 1991.

42. An anonymous letter to the *Santa Fe Reporter* claimed that the foot was amputated on December 29, 1997 ("Proud Actions" 1998).

43. A few days after the amputation, the *Rio Grande Sun* published a satirical interview with the "funloving foot filchers," who were using the statue's foot as a flowerpot. The article lampooned Arellano's theory: "The director out there says the Gringos did it and everyone knows no Gringo is going to get out of a warm bed to saw the foot off a statue of someone he never heard of" (Trapp 1998). Two years later, a critically acclaimed memoir included an account of the caper (Nasdijj 2000, 140–56), but its author was later exposed as a fraud who had created a fictitious life.

44. The *Albuquerque Journal* reported that two Los Alamos seventh graders studying Oñate also opposed replacing the foot. Said one: "I think they should leave the foot off the statue and put a plaque there telling about his treatment of Native Americans. . . . I also think, if we can't celebrate the United States coming into Santa Fe because it would offend

the Hispanics, we shouldn't be able to celebrate the Spanish conquest of NM, because that certainly offends lots of people." Another wrote: "I believe that whoever cut off Oñate's foot was doing the right thing. Oñate did this to many people. They suffered and it only seems right that this statue should also be punished. I also think that the foot should not be reattached. When the Acomans had their feet cut off, they could not have them reattached so neither should the Oñate statue" (Calloway 1998). Los Alamos ("the hill") provided a privileged position from which these students could observe and comment on events in the Española valley.

45. Baker (2003) recognized the brutality of Spanish colonization but disliked the idea of trying not to offend anyone. Hispanos "don't tell the Native Americans what they can't celebrate and what they can, so I feel it's inappropriate for them to tell us what we can't celebrate and what we can. I mean, we can't even bring Oñate to our fiestas anymore, because some people feel offended about it." Instead, she advocated acknowledging the violent history in order to avoid repeating it.

46. Early plans for the plaza called for monuments to both Oñate and Po'pay, although neither has been installed (Hagan 1988; Plaza de Española Foundation 1995). A sculpture that includes stylized figures of two conquistadores did end up on the Española plaza, but it is less than monumental. Still, one woman from Santa Clara Pueblo told me that she found the sculpture hurtful and had asked the mayor to remove it on several occasions to no avail.

47. Laura Gómez (2007, 82) identifies similar dynamics in the early twentieth century. In his *Concise History of New Mexico*, published in 1912, Bradford Prince foregrounded conflict between Pueblo Indians and Hispanics, removing "Euro-Americans from the zone of racial conflict." He also emphasized Spanish conquest while downplaying American conquest. "This mythmaking shored up Euro-Americans' position at the center of the racial order by positioning them as mediators between Mexicans and Pueblo Indians." This helped to erase the history of alliances between Indians and Nuevomexicanos against Americans and to impede future alliances.

48. Before the stamp went into production, Christmas decorations in the photo were removed and "1598" and "USPS" were added in microprinting (a security measure) above the two front windows in the photograph (Amick 1999, 181).

49. In 1996 and 1997 Clare Villa, who later coordinated the reredo project inside the Misión, produced two posters, each featuring a pane of four mock 32-cent U.S. postage stamps. The first pane bore the title

"Capillas del Valle [Chapels of the Valley]: Private Places of Worship in Northern New Mexico." The second, which advertised the 1997 Española Valley Arts Festival, was titled "Capillas Escondidas [Hidden Chapels]: Community Worship in Northern New Mexico." Each imaginary pane of stamps (complete with perforations and a fake USPS copyright) included paintings of four chapels, similar to those that wound up inside the Misión. What is remarkable about these posters is that Villa imagined, before the release of the actual Spanish settlement stamp, the Postal Service featuring images of private, Christian places of worship on postage stamps with Spanish titles. Villa told me that she chose the stamp format because she thought it would be cool, but the posters provide another example of a subversive presentation of New Mexico's Christian/Hispanic heritage within a framework of American nationalism. In 2011, I found prints of the make-believe stamps for sale in two gifts shops in the Española Convento.

50. Consider the impact of LANL on the surrounding Pueblos. LANL threatens Pueblo nations through the appropriation of land, contamination of natural resources, destruction of sacred sites, and multimillennial requirements of nuclear waste management. However, in other ways the lab has created new opportunities for the articulation of Pueblo sovereignty. For example, a series of federal laws passed in the 1990s gave the Pueblos new standing in their negotiations with the lab, which must now deal with them on a government-to-government basis (Masco 2006, 114–15). In the mid-1990s Pojoaque Pueblo announced plans to pursue storage of U.S. nuclear waste as a lucrative but dangerous form of economic development. The announcement was in part a political tactic to win government approval of the Pueblo's casino plans. The ploy was "both an example of the high-stakes international politics that have taken place around nuclear materials in New Mexico since 1943, and a new political strategy in which plutonium is one necessary tool of statecraft" (155).

51. Orlando Romero (2003) told me a story about when he used to work at the state library in Santa Fe, which was near the bus station downtown. A man came in speaking broken English: "I don't know where he thought he was, but he kept telling me 'Banco? You know where Banco is? Banco, so I can trade dollars, dollars to Banco?' And I said 'Banco downtown,' I told him, 'Banco downtown, but why are you speaking to me this way?' 'Oh you speak English?' He'd just gotten off the bus, walked up the street to the state library. Here's the big 'State Library' sign out front, and I couldn't believe it! This was in the seventies! 'Banco?' I never forgot it. 'Banco, dollars?' This is an American traveling in his

own country!" Romero, who was on the Northern Rio Grande National Heritage Area board, concluded: "We need this recognition badly . . . , to make sure that Americans understand that the presence of these cultures here are very valid American realities."

52. Members of New Mexico's National Guard made up a significant number of the soldiers who suffered through the Bataan Death March during World War II, and northern New Mexicans have lived with nuclear anxieties since the establishment of Los Alamos National Laboratory in 1943. Many northern New Mexicans perceive military service as a good way to escape poverty, and even as the wall was dedicated in Española, new enlistees were preparing to leave home to help fight the war in Iraq.

53. At a 2005 symposium at the University of New Mexico, Elena Ortiz-Junes went so far as to suggest that Po'pay "acted on principles later articulated in the Declaration of Independence and the Emancipation Proclamation." Pueblo peoples lived by "American ideals like life, liberty, and the pursuit of happiness" (Archuleta 2007, 334). Elizabeth Archuleta herself (337) compares Po'pay not only to George Washington but also to Thomas Jefferson and Abraham Lincoln.

54. When the National Park Service first began talking to people in northern New Mexico about the possibility of establishing a heritage area, it held two public meetings in 1999 and 2000 at the Misión-Convento, which became the movement's home base. The heritage area's interim board began meeting at the Convento and at the Bond House.

4. Las Trampas

1. One exception was the revitalization of "Spanish colonial" arts in the 1930s. Anglo patrons realized that arts programs could serve both cultural conservation and economic development (Montgomery 2002, 160).

2. Most of the preservationists I met in New Mexico were interested in preserving both the built environment and cultural practices. One member of the Northern Rio Grande National Heritage Area board, though, was less optimistic about (and interested in) sustaining old ways of life. He told me that urbanization, the decline of New Mexico's agricultural economy, and the increasing importance of formal education made it difficult to keep agricultural traditions alive. Although he was committed to preserving adobe architecture (especially churches), he emphasized people's ability to adapt to changing circumstances. His disinterest in intangible heritage made him exceptional.

3. Jake Kosek (2006, 109–10) shows that U.S. Forest Service policies, too, reveal a contradictory understanding of the relationship between His-

panos and the forests of northern New Mexico. While the Forest Service recognized the importance of this relationship and expressed a desire to protect Hispano culture, it significantly limited Nuevomexicanos' ability to extract resources from the forest.

4. According to local tradition, the church, built under mythic circumstances, dates to the 1580s, before Oñate had even colonized New Mexico (e.g., Leyba 1933). One of the first descriptions of the plaza-centered village and church was that of Fray Francisco Atanasio Dominguez (1956, 99), who passed through Las Trampas in 1776. He described the villagers as "a ragged lot" who "are as festive as they are poor, and very merry. Accordingly, most of them are low class, and there are very few of good, or even moderately good, blood. Almost all are their own masters and servants."

5. Acequias, which continue to be used today, have been a crucial feature of Nuevomexicano communities since Spanish colonization. Not only do they function as irrigation ditches, but they represent the focus of community labor and identity. The farmers who use a given acequia, called *parciantes*, elect a *mayordomo* who oversees the distribution of water and the annual spring cleaning of the ditch (a cooperative community event). Acequia organizations have been recognized as political subdivisions by the state of New Mexico and thus play an important role in contemporary water politics. Acequias also have an ecological impact on the landscape, recharging the aquifer, circulating nutrients, and providing habitat for plants and animals (see Crawford 1988; Rivera 1998; Rodríguez 2006; Wilson and Kammer 1989; 41–56).

6. Americans were also fascinated by the strange, mysterious, and macabre elements of Hispano culture in northern New Mexico, particularly when it came to the Penitente religious order and their secret rites. An American traveling through Las Trampas in 1881 was drawn to the "picturesque medievalism" of the village and described in mysterious tones the carved skeletal figure of death, seated in a cart, that he found inside the church. Such figures of "*la Muerte*" were a common nineteenth-century folk art form used in Penitente rituals (Kessell 1980, 102). John Gaw Meem, who was involved in the restoration of San José de Gracia in the 1930s, described his first visit to the chapel in similarly gothic terms. He was fascinated to discover that tombs lay beneath the floor, although he refrained from digging them up since "that would have been desecration." Also intriguing were the indecipherable "hieroglyphic" designs painted on the ceiling. "But the most fascinating place was" a room whose walls "were splattered with blood," evidence that Penitente rites had been performed there (Chauvenet 1985, 46; see also Calvin 1948).

7. As Jake Kosek (2006, 21) puts it, from land grant politics and forest exploitation to the atomic bomb and the heroin trade, "northern New Mexico and its forest politics have never existed in isolation from the international circuits of extraction and knowledge that have radically transformed the western United States over the last century."

8. Horton's analysis of diasporic Hispanos reflects recent anthropological interest in transnationalism and cultural identities sustained through migration (Horton 2010, 184, 198–99). Ann Fienup-Riordan (2000, 152) has made a similar argument about Yup'ik Eskimos migrating to Anchorage, Alaska. Some writers have interpreted out-migration from Yup'ik villages and the influx of American goods, technologies, and values as an indication of the villages' deterioration. Yet Fienup-Riordan maintains that "Yup'ik communities are not disintegrating, their lifeblood gradually seeping away. Many can be seen as actually expanding and recreating themselves in unprecedented ways until today, when they are as strong and vital as at any time in their 2,500-year history." She urges us "to take a broader view of community, defined not simply by residence but by kinship and exchange relations," and she documents a geographically far-reaching system of travel and sharing that links urban Yupiit with their village kin. As in New Mexico, this expanded Yup'ik community has facilitated the perpetuation of traditional practices, albeit in a new context. Not only do these practices help to maintain villages, but they have also led to the "Yup'ification" of Anchorage (160).

9. Sylvia Rodríguez (2006, 29–30) cites census data that suggest similar trends—and significant gentrification—through the end of the century. Between 1990 and 1999, 13,000 people moved into Taos County and 11,000 people moved out. "Whereas out-migrants tend to be young, Hispanic, and comparatively poor, most in-migrants are older, wealthier, more educated, and Anglo." Between 1970 and 2000 the county's population went from 86.3 to 57.9 percent Hispanic, from 6.9 to 42.1 percent Anglo, and from 6.8 to 6.6 percent American Indian. "In sum, whereas the American Indian proportion has remained stable during the past 30 years, the Anglo (or non-Hispanic white) proportion has increased sixfold, and the Hispanic proportion has decreased by a third."

10. The report suggested that better community planning could enhance the unique character of the villages. "In Trampas, for example, the objective would be to strengthen the plaza oriented character of the village by encouraging any new development to adhere to this character rather than stringing out along the highway" (ICADP and NMSPO 1963, 124).

11. The list of agency staff participating in the study includes few

Spanish surnames, although a list of "interested citizens" in the area includes thirteen Trampaseños and twice as many residents of Peñasco.

12. The agreement specified the width of the roadway and the material that would be used to construct fences and two bridges. The nineteenth-century schoolhouse would remain in place. Other details were aimed at ensuring that the improved road blended in with the village landscape as much as possible (Conron 1968, 31).

13. Owings had a personal and professional interest in the church of San José de Gracia, which reminded him of the modern architecture of Bertram Grosvenor Goodhue: "I would do what I could to help preserve that which meant so much to me spiritually and professionally. It *was* the American aesthetic!" (Owings 1970, 30). Owings's autobiography includes a chapter on his and his wife's experience in the Southwest presented in highly romantic and exoticizing terms. The first half deals with the Hopi kachina cult and snake dance and the second half with Las Trampas (Owings 1973, 213–28).

14. Owings was not the last to praise women for their contributions to the restoration of San José de Gracia. The craft of *enjarrando*, or work with adobe, in which women traditionally play a more prominent role than men, has become especially attractive to preservationists interested in recognizing the work of women and minorities. In 1988 Jack Neckels, the director of the Rocky Mountain Region of the National Park Service, successfully nominated the community of Las Trampas for a National Trust for Historic Preservation award for their work in restoring the church. Neckels suggested that recognizing the community's efforts would be a way to acknowledge the contributions of Hispanics and women to American history, which was especially appropriate considering the upcoming Columbian quincentennial (Neckels 1988; Adelo 1988; see also Gillette 1992, 86; Sweeney 1988, 15).

15. Preservationists imagined Las Trampas as a sort of living history museum. Most of these open-air museums (such as Virginia's Colonial Williamsburg or Rancho de las Golondrinas, which opened in 1972 southwest of Santa Fe) import historic buildings to a park-like environment and employ costumed actors to demonstrate preindustrial work, crafts, and pastimes. Las Trampas, on the other hand, would have required neither reconstruction nor reenactors, since real live Spanish Americans still lived there. And, as we have seen, the preservationists believed this exotic population still more or less lived in the eighteenth century—or at least could resuscitate a traditional lifestyle under the proper conditions (e.g., Jones 1967, 5). On Rancho de las Golondrinas, see Lippard 1999, 68–70; on the

connection between New Mexico and Colonial Williamsburg, see Wilson 1997, 252.

16. Copies of the 1967 report are kept on file in the National Park Service's Santa Fe office and National Historic Landmark program archives in Washington DC. Most of the report has also been republished (Sax 1986).

17. The report suggested bringing some urban amenities, employment opportunities, and night life to a town such as Peñasco in order to encourage young people to stay in the region (so long as the new regional center did not have to pay "the urban price of over-crowding, anonymity, defiled air, and cultural or social friction"). "The village as a way of life thus could become viable in the 20th century as a species of garden suburb" (ICADP and NMSPO 1963, 134, 137).

18. Great Smoky Mountains National Park, Canyon de Chelley National Monument, and Cape Cod National Seashore are early examples of park units that accommodated living communities in various ways. Nontraditional parks created in the 1970s include Pinelands National Reserve in New Jersey, Lowell National Historical Park in Massachusetts, Santa Monica Mountains National Recreation Area outside of Los Angeles, Ebey's Landing National Historical Reserve in Washington State, and Jean Lafitte National Historical Park and Preserve in Louisiana. New partnership parks include Michigan's Keweenaw National Historical Park, Boston Harbor Islands National Recreation Area, and New Bedford Whaling National Historical Park in Massachusetts. For an interesting account of NPS efforts in the 1970s and 1980s to accommodate, and then to nurture, a farming community that existed within the Buffalo National River Preserve in Arkansas (efforts that went almost as far as the Las Trampas proposal but emphasized the settlement's physical features over intangible culture), see Sax 1985.

19. In his examination of forest politics in northern New Mexico, Jake Kosek (2006) documents a long history of both individual and institutional racism toward Hispanos. However, since at least the 1960s the Forest Service has also endorsed cultural conservation as part of its community outreach (deBuys 1985, 263–67; Kosek 2006, 96–97). This dimension of the relationship between Nuevomexicanos and the Forest Service deserves further study.

20. One NPS staffer noted that the 1967 report that led to the NHL designation emphasized the village's ambience over specific structures of historical significance, omitted details about alterations, and acknowledged that the defensive wall that originally surrounded the village was gone and

that most buildings retained little of their Spanish colonial character (B. Grosvenor 1986).

21. The Park Service had better luck assessing the church of San José de Gracia itself (e.g., Janus Associates 1986).

22. In 1998 the NPS returned to the issue of the still-vague NHL boundary with a more collaborative approach, enlisting the help of New Mexico State University's Public History Program. A team from the university worked with a group of Trampaseños to document the historic structures in the village, recording the physical condition of the buildings and the valley's social history. The report they produced (Hunner et al. 1999) emphasized their respectful and productive collaboration. It included NHL surveys for sixteen structures in the village, including the church. This new documentation enhanced the NHL file, and the NPS, now focusing on other priorities, has not returned to the issue of the historic district's boundary since then.

23. Some outsiders have also attempted to protect Las Trampas from overexposure, if only to keep the village to themselves. Ross Calvin (1948, 18) began an article on the village with some reluctance: "one almost hesitates to write of it for fear of diverting the tourist trade down its winding road and thus marring its charm. Few photographers and still fewer writers and painters have discovered Trampas, and it's a place which no visitor should be permitted to enter without passing a suitable examination."

24. I also felt compelled as an anthropologist to do ethnographic fieldwork, and given the extent to which I had already uncovered preservationist perspectives, the obvious object of such fieldwork was the village itself. It was easy to imagine Las Trampas—a small, localized, subaltern community—as a site of ethnographic research (cf. Bruner 2005, 231–52).

25. At first Kosek (2006, 2) thought the man shooting at him had made a mistake, but then he shot again. "Yelling at the top of his lungs in Spanish he suggested that I had better 'fucking get [my] mother-fucking white ass off the grant and out of [his sight]' or he was going to put 'a fucking hole in [my] head.'" Despite this terrifying introduction to Truchas (and thanks to a few more supportive neighbors), Kosek stuck it out.

5. Multicultural Justice

1. Patchen Markell (2003, 168–71) argues that the adoption of outmoded anthropological concepts in liberal theories of multiculturalism accommodates a desire for sovereign agency and allays concerns that the number of groups seeking recognition might be unlimited.

2. An entirely different set of ideas about objectification is evident *out-*

side the Palace of the Governors. Some critics interpret the restrictive rules governing the portal market and the artists' self-conscious conformity to tourist expectations as evidence of the fossilization of Native American tradition. If the objectification of the building as a historic structure appears to be the result of the scientific preservation of heritage, the objectification of Native American tradition threatens indigenous authenticity.

3. Swentzell admits that her own attempts to figure out Pueblo culture and social change are "a very non-Pueblo thing." Beliefs are not the same once they have been formalized, and formalization is a sign of assimilation. "I'm wondering where people like myself are now" ("The Butterfly Effect" 1989, 27–28). In a thoughtful article on Swentzell, Jane Brown Gillette (1992, 28–29) observes that "to be on the edge—half in, half out of the unconscious beliefs of your forefathers—is an illuminating, but not necessarily comfortable, place to be."

4. In an article on Swentzell, Jane Brown Gillette (1992, 84–86) shows that these issues are gendered: "If the Pueblo world, for Swentzell, is feminine, unconscious, inclusive, relative, and active, the Western world is male, conscious, exclusive, absolute, and static." Western culture has suppressed feminine characteristics. "Our consciousness is not going to save us," Swentzell states. "But underneath it all are qualities that all human beings have, the unconscious qualities. I think the power is there. We are always looking for the balance." Swentzell told me in 2010 that she saw Pueblo communities becoming more masculine as they became more Westernized, especially in their governance.

5. Colonized people sometimes blame themselves for culture loss (e.g., Povinelli 1999, 35–36). This self-doubt is one of the most insidious and subtle effects of colonization.

6. Swentzell's critique of power relates to her reflections on self-consciousness. She observed that some cultures "are more aware of definitions/boundaries and identity and I believe that these become a greater issue/focus when the culture as a whole is about ownership, possessiveness and power. No culture is ever free of these—but, there are degrees to this focus." Citing the example of Chaco Canyon, an Ancestral Puebloan site in northwest New Mexico, Swentzell noted that "there are degrees of intellectualism. . . . Chaco was different than Mesa Verde and surrounding regions in terms of explicit hierarchy, formalism and possibly power. I do believe that the majority of people—even those out of Chaco—made a decision in the late 1200s to resume life in a more subdued, less power-oriented manner" (Swentzell 2007; see also Swentzell 2004, 50).

7. Akhil Gupta's (1998, 30) attempt to make his ethnography of agri-

culture and postcolonial development projects in India "'vulnerable' to reinterpretation and rethinking," to produce "a text that *invites* rethinking and reanalysis," and to convey incommensurable perspectives without synthesizing them into a new narrative represents an interesting experiment in ethnographic modesty. The result is intelligent and productive, but the book sometimes seems fragmentary, and while Gupta convincingly documents incommensurability, his analysis still comes across as masterful.

8. One NRGNHA board member put it this way: "let's not use that history to be divisive, let's use that history to celebrate our common roots and where we've been but more importantly where we are and where we want our children to be." Others were more interested in educating people about and preserving the past itself. Orlando Romero (2003) took a middle position: "I think that if people truly know their history, the beauty as well as the warts, that's the first step. Because once you get that out of the way, the accusations stop. 'Well, you killed my people', then 'No, no, well you killed my people,' then blah, blah, blah, blah. I think once you get that over with and go beyond that—and I think that's what the heritage area would do—go beyond that first step of recrimination." Romero went on to say that he thought the recriminations would come more from present-day actions (he was particularly concerned about environmentally insensitive development) than from the past. There is no question that the history of Spanish colonialism is the foundation of the NRGNHA, but its relevance and meaning are not fixed.

9. Nancy Fraser's (2003, 47) analysis of recognition and its relationship to redistribution is nuanced and pragmatic. Fraser argues that context determines what misrecognized groups need. Some may need to be unburdened of demeaning stereotypes and recognized for their humanity. Others may need their distinctiveness acknowledged. "In still other cases, they may need to shift the focus onto dominant or advantaged groups, outing the latter's distinctiveness, which has been falsely parading as universal. Alternatively, they may need to deconstruct the very terms in which attributed differences are currently elaborated." I can think of instances in which New Mexicans could benefit from each of these approaches, but the third strategy (shifting the focus to dominant groups) has been used the least and may have the most potential to advance social justice in New Mexico.

10. Markell (2003, 6) challenges the view that "the politics of recognition [is] practiced exclusively by those people and groups who are already socially marked as 'particular.' On this view, the politics of recognition is a matter of how much or what kind of recognition *we*—speaking, in the

voice of universality, for the 'larger society'—ought to extend to *them*."
However, "it takes at least two to struggle." Markell deliberately focuses
attention on "actors who are not ordinarily represented as being engaged
in the politics of recognition . . . precisely because these are often the actors who make politics into a matter of recognition in the first place."

11. One marble panel on the Santa Fe monument reads: "To the heroes who have fallen in the various battles with Indians in the territory of
New Mexico." Until the 1970s, the word "savage" modified "Indians."
A plaque now appropriately interprets the memorial: "Monument texts
reflect the character of the times in which they are written and the temper
of those who wrote them. This monument was dedicated in 1868 near
the close of a period of intense strife which pitted northerner against
southerner, Indian against white, Indian against Indian. Thus, we see on
this monument, as in other records, the use of such terms as 'savage' and
'rebel.' Attitudes change and prejudices hopefully dissolve."

12. Of the thirteen national parks and monuments in New Mexico,
seven interpret pre-Columbian archaeological sites or the Spanish colonial period, four preserve nature, and two interpret U.S. history. One of
those two sites (El Morro National Monument) renders twentieth-century
American activity much less visible than earlier historical periods (Guthrie
2010b). The other (Fort Union National Monument) preserves a U.S. military site but mostly interprets life at the fort. Both could become key sites
for the interpretation of American colonization in New Mexico.

Epilogue

1. The National Park Service criticized the first drafts of the management plan on several grounds. It found that the historical overview in
the first draft (submitted in February 2010) was unbalanced and lacked
tribal perspectives. "As a consequence, the history presents a relatively
'sanitized' interpretation of the conquest and colonization of the northern
Rio Grande River region by the Spanish and does not convey the dramatic and tragic consequences experienced by the numerous Pueblo and
Native American populations and their associated cultural traditions."
The NPS required "an integrated, accurate," and completely revised historical overview (Billings 2010, 2). It did not mention that the historical
narrative barely mentioned *American* colonization at all. For the second
draft of the management plan, submitted a year later, the NRGNHA hired
former state historian Robert Tórrez to write a new historical overview.
This new narrative was significantly longer and more critical. It included
multiple perspectives on interethnic conflict and delved into both Spanish

and American colonization. The NPS regional office in Denver has since required the NRGNHA to revise other parts of the plan. Writing multiple drafts and responding to NPS feedback has taken time and caused frustration. The NRGNHA legislation stipulated that the secretary of the interior receive the plan by 2009. As of March 2013, the management plan is still being revised and awaits regional approval.

2. The speakers in the film include Pueblo Indians, an Apache woman, two genízaro brothers (genízaros were detribalized Indians), Nuevomexicanos, and Anglos. Many share ecological knowledge gained from multigenerational land use. Several poignantly discuss assimilationist policies. I attended the Santa Fe premier of the film (*Land Water People Time*) in June 2012. The event, held at El Museo Cultural, attracted almost two hundred people and provided an opportunity to promote the NRGNHA and the work of grantees. Several speakers emphasized the heritage area's reliance on partnerships and the importance of agricultural revitalization.

3. The heritage area proposal came as much from the National Park Service as from citizens, although it required citizen involvement. The NPS worked with New Mexico's congressional delegates to draft the legislation. The call for recognition thus partially originated in the executive branch of the federal government, and two branches set its terms. All of this followed the collaboration between Congress and the NPS in the early 1990s to commemorate Spanish colonialism in New Mexico. This substantial governmental involvement already raises doubts about the counterhegemonic potential of recognizing New Mexico.

4. The NRGNHA has not entirely abandoned the politics of recognition and the politics of authenticity. Authenticity is a theme of its management plan (NRGNHA 2013). And in 2013 the NRGNHA supported a state resolution "recognizing Northern Rio Grande weaving as an important tradition unique to Northern New Mexico and highlighting the importance of preserving the tradition by establishing standards of authenticity." House Memorial 11, introduced by Debbie Rodella of Española, required the state's regulation and licensing department to work with Northern New Mexico College and the NRGNHA to establish standards of authenticity for procedures, designs, and materials. Fakes from outside New Mexico are a major concern, but so too is traditionalism. This initiative, which harkens back to efforts in the twentieth century to ensure the authenticity of Native American and Hispanic art, received some criticism from artists ("Better Design Needed for Weaving Proposal" 2013; Roberts 2013). The resolution unanimously passed the New Mexico House of Representatives in February 2013.

Abbink, Emily. 2007. *New Mexico's Palace of the Governors: History of an American Treasure*. Santa Fe: Museum of New Mexico Press.

Adelo, A. Samuel. 1988. "Las Trampas Honored in Cincinnati." *Santa Fe New Mexican*, Nov. 27, A7.

Altamirano, Ben. 2003. Hispanic Culture Day. Transcript of Feb. 11 speech to New Mexico state legislature. Acquired by T. Guthrie from Senator Altamirano's office.

Amick, George. 1999. "32¢ Spanish Settlement of the Southwest." In *Linn's U.S. Stamp Yearbook 1998*, 175–82. Sidney OH: Linn's Stamp News.

Archuleta, Elizabeth. 2007. "History Carved in Stone: Memorializing Po'Pay and Oñate, or Recasting Racialized Regimes of Representation?" *New Mexico Historical Review* 82 (3): 317–42.

Armijo, Patrick. 1998. "NM Puts Imprint on New Stamp." *Albuquerque Journal*, Mar. 19, D3.

"Artisan Disputes Ruling on Portal Bias Charge." 1978. *Santa Fe New Mexican*, July 2, D6.

Babcock, Barbara A. 1997. "Mudwomen and Whitemen: A Meditation on Pueblo Potteries and the Politics of Representation." In *The Material Culture of Gender, The Gender of Material Culture*, ed. Katharine Martinez and Kenneth L. Ames, 253–80. Winterthur DE: Henry Francis du Pont Winterthur Museum.

Baker, Lou. 2003. Interview by the author. Dec. 17. Española, New Mexico.

"Bakke and Portal." 1978. Editorial. *Santa Fe New Mexican*, July 9.

Baldauf, Scott. 1998. "New Mexico's Year of Fiestas Dampened by a Divisive Past." *Christian Science Monitor*, May 27, 3.

Barrett, Brenda. 2003. "Roots for the National Heritage Area Family Tree." *George Wright Forum* 20 (2): 41–49.

Batson, Robert N. 1998. "The Art of San José de Gracia." *Tradición Revista* 3 (1): 39–44.

Bender, Margaret. 2002. *Signs of Cherokee Culture: Sequoyah's Syllabary in Eastern Cherokee Life*. Chapel Hill: University of North Carolina Press.

Bennett, Tony. 1988. "The Exhibitionary Complex." *New Formations* 4:73–102.

"Better Design Needed for Weaving Proposal." 2013. Editorial. *Albuquerque Journal*, Feb. 13, Santa Fe/North sec. 3.

Billings, Kathy. 2010. Letter from Pecos NM, to José Villa, Española NM, Mar. 24. Copy given to T. Guthrie by Glenna Dean, 2011.

Bird, Kay. 1988. "Wraps Come Off Plaza de Española." *Santa Fe New Mexican*, Nov. 19, A3.

Bodine, John J. 1968. "A Tri-Ethnic Trap: The Spanish Americans in Taos." In *Spanish-Speaking People in the United States: Proceedings of the 1968 Annual Spring Meeting of the American Ethnological Society*, ed. June Helm, 145–53. Seattle: University of Washington Press.

Boettcher, Carlotta. 2003. Interview by the author. Dec. 30. Santa Fe, New Mexico.

Bottoroff, Leslie. 1966. "Trampas Residents Want Road Improved." *Santa Fe New Mexican*, Dec. 18, B1.

Brandtner de Martinez, Irene. 1998. "History's Context." Letter to the editor. *Santa Fe New Mexican*, Apr. 12, F5.

Briggs, Charles L., and John R. Van Ness, eds. 1987. *Land, Water, and Culture: New Perspectives on Hispanic Land Grants*. Albuquerque: University of New Mexico Press.

Bright, Brenda. 1998. "'Heart Like a Car': Hispano/Chicano Culture in Northern New Mexico." *American Ethnologist* 25 (4): 583–609.

Brooke, James. 1998. "Conquistador Statue Stirs Hispanic Pride and Indian Rage." *New York Times*, Feb. 9, A10.

Brown, William E. 1963. "National Survey of Historic Sites and Buildings Form for Las Trampas NM." "NHLS—New Mexico—Las Trampas Historic District—Taos Co." file, National Park Service archives, Santa Fe.

———. 1967. "Significance of Las Trampas, Suitability-Feasibility Critique, Alternate Proposal." In *Las Trampas: A Special Report for the Advisory Board [on National Parks, Historic Sites, Buildings, and Monuments]*. Santa Fe: Southwest Regional Office, National Park Service.

Brumann, Christoph. 2009. "Outside the Glass Case: The Social Life of Urban Heritage in Kyoto." *American Ethnologist* 36 (2): 276–99.

Bruner, Edward M. 2005. *Culture on Tour: Ethnographies of Travel*. Chicago: University of Chicago Press.

Bunting, Bainbridge. 1961. "San Jose de Gracia Church, Trampas, Taos County. Written Historical and Descriptive Data, Historic American Buildings Survey." HABS No. NM-61. San Francisco: National Park Service.

———. 1964. *Taos Adobes: Spanish Colonial and Territorial Architecture of the Taos Valley*. Fort Burgwin Research Center pub. no. 2. Santa Fe: Museum of New Mexico Press.

———. 1970. "Las Trampas." *New Mexico Architecture* 12 (9–10): 37–46.

"The Butterfly Effect: A Conversation with Rina Swentzell." 1989. *El Palacio* 95 (1): 24–9.

Cabral, Darien. 1991. "Española Man on a Horse." *Santa Fe Reporter*, Apr. 10, 7.

Calloway, Larry. 1996a. "Inflated Claims of Tax Cuts." *Albuquerque Journal North*, Aug. 22, 1.

———. 1996b. "The Eggnog Factor in New Mexico History." *Albuquerque Journal North*, Aug. 6, 1.

———. 1998. "Little Sympathy for Oñate Out There." *Albuquerque Journal*, Jan. 13, 1.

Calvin, Ross. 1948. "The Church of the Apostles." *New Mexico* 26 (2): 18, 31.

Casper, Monica J., and Lisa Jean Moore. 2009. *Missing Bodies: The Politics of Visibility*. New York: New York University Press.

Cattelino, Jessica R. 2004. "High Stakes: Seminole Sovereignty in the Casino Era." PhD dissertation, New York University.

———. 2008. *High Stakes: Florida Seminole Gaming and Sovereignty*. Durham NC: Duke University Press.

Caufield, James A. 1988. Letter from Albuquerque NM, to Gloria K. Vallier, Denver CO, May 26. "NHLs—New Mexico—Las Trampas Historic District—Taos Co." file, National Park Service archives, Santa Fe.

Chakrabarty, Dipesh. 1992. "Postcoloniality and the Artifice of History: Who Speaks for 'Indian' Pasts?" *Representations* 37:1–26.

Chauvenet, Beatrice. 1985. *John Gaw Meem: Pioneer in Historic Preservation*. Santa Fe: Historic Santa Fe Foundation/Museum of New Mexico Press.

Chávez, John R. 1984. *The Lost Land: The Chicano Image of the Southwest*. Albuquerque: University of New Mexico Press.

Chávez, Tom. 1998. "Legacy from New Mexico's Past, Lessons for the Future." *Santa Fe New Mexican*, Apr. 19, spec. sec. 5.

Comaroff, Jean, and John Comaroff. 1995. *Of Revelation and Revolution.* Vol. 1, *Christianity, Colonialism, and Consciousness in South Africa.* Chicago: University of Chicago Press.

"Commendation for the Citizens of Las Trampas." 1969. *Santa Fe New Mexican,* Aug. 24, Pasatiempo mag. sec. 4.

Conklin, Beth A. 1997. "Body Paint, Feathers, and VCRs: Aesthetics and Authenticity in Amazonian Activism." *American Ethnologist* 24 (4): 711–37.

Conron, John P. 1967a. "Las Trampas: A Proposal for a National Monument in New Mexico." In *Las Trampas: A Special Report for the Advisory Board [on National Parks, Historic Sites, Buildings, and Monuments].* Santa Fe: Southwest Regional Office, National Park Service.

———. 1967b. "Refinement of AIA Proposal." In *Las Trampas: A Special Report for the Advisory Board [on National Parks, Historic Sites, Buildings, and Monuments].* Santa Fe: Southwest Regional Office, National Park Service.

———. 1968. "The Treaty of Santa Fe." *Historic Preservation* 20 (1): 26–31.

———. 1986. Letter from Santa Fe NM, to Joseph L. Sax, Berkeley CA, Apr. 1. Copy in National Park Service files, Santa Fe.

Conron and Woods Architects. 2004. *Historic Structure Report: Palace of the Governors.* 2 vols. Santa Fe: Conron and Woods Architects. Fray Angélico Chavéz History Library, New Mexico History Museum, Santa Fe.

Cordova, Gilberto Benito. 1990. *The 3 1/2 Cultures of Española.* Albuquerque: El Norte Publications/Academia.

Crawford, Stanley G. 1988. *Mayordomo: Chronicle of an Acequia in Northern New Mexico.* Albuquerque: University of New Mexico Press.

Crick, Malcolm. 1989. "Representations of International Tourism in the Social Sciences: Sun, Sex, Sights, Savings, and Servility." *Annual Review of Anthropology* 18:307–44.

Crocchiola, Stanley. 1947. "Tourist's Query on Las Trampas Recalls Vibrant History of Site." *Santa Fe Register,* May 9, 1.

Culler, Jonathan. 1981. "Semiotics of Tourism." *American Journal of Semiotics* 1 (1–2): 127–40.

Dahl, Duane. 1989. "Villagers Apply New Skin Layer to Adobe Church." *Santa Fe New Mexican,* June 25, B1.

Daly, Jayne. 2003. "Heritage Areas: Connecting People to Their Place and History." *Forum Journal* 17 (4): 5–12.

Darko, Debra. 2003. "Palace Watch." *El Palacio* 108 (4): 28.

DeBouzek, Jeanette, dir., and Diane Reyna, videography. 1992. *Gathering Up Again: Fiesta in Santa Fe.* Albuquerque NM: Quotidian Independent Documentary Research.

deBuys, William. 1985. *Enchantment and Exploitation: The Life and Hard Times of a New Mexico Mountain Range.* Albuquerque: University of New Mexico Press.

deBuys, William, and Alex Harris. 1990. *River of Traps: A Village Life.* [Albuquerque]: University of New Mexico Press.

Dejevsky, Mary. 1998. "Hispanics Put Their Stamp on U.S. History." *The Independent* [London], July 13, 12.

Delgado, Samuel. 1998. "Divisiveness Threatens 400 Years of Cultural Heritage." Letter to the editor. *Rio Grande Sun*, Jan. 29, A6.

———. 2002. Interview by the author. Dec. 19. Santa Fe, New Mexico.

———. 2004. "Popé Isn't Proper Occupant of Statuary Hall." *Santa Fe New Mexican*, Feb. 7, A3.

Deutsch, Sarah. 1987. *No Separate Refuge: Culture, Class, and Gender on an Anglo-Hispanic Frontier in the American Southwest, 1880–1940.* New York: Oxford University Press.

Diaz, Elvia. 1998. "Damage Won't Hamper Events." *Albuquerque Journal*, Jan. 9, 1.

Dominguez, Fray Francisco Atanasio. 1956. *The Missions of New Mexico, 1776.* Trans. Eleanor B. Adams and Fray Angelico Chavez. Albuquerque: University of New Mexico Press.

Dorst, John D. 1989. *The Written Suburb: An American Site, an Ethnographic Dilemma.* Philadelphia: University of Pennsylvania Press.

———. 1999. *Looking West.* Philadelphia: University of Pennsylvania Press.

Ebright, Malcolm. 1994. *Land Grants and Lawsuits in Northern New Mexico.* Albuquerque: University of New Mexico Press.

Eichstaedt, Peter. 1990. "500 Residents Share Mayor's Plaza Dream." *Santa Fe New Mexican*, May 21, A3.

Elliott, Melinda. 1991. *Exploring Human Worlds: A History of the School of American Research.* Santa Fe: School of American Research.

Ellis, Florence Hawley. 1987. "The Long Lost 'City' of San Gabriel Del Yungue, Second Oldest European Settlement in the United States." In *When Cultures Meet: Remembering San Gabriel Del Yunge Oweenge*, 10–38. Santa Fe: Sunstone Press.

——— 1989. *San Gabriel del Yungue as Seen by an Archaeologist.* Santa Fe: Sunstone Press.

Española MainStreet. n.d. "Española MainStreet" [brochure]. Española
     NM: Española MainStreet.
"Española Project Downtown Savior." 1996. *Albuquerque Journal North*,
     Aug. 24, 4.
Española Valley Chamber of Commerce. 2004. *Española Valley Visitors
     Guide 2004/05*. Santa Fe: Valentine & Tate.
————. 2009. *Española Valley Visitors Guide 2009*. Española NM: Espa-
     ñola Valley Chamber of Commerce.
Eugster, J. Glenn. 2003. "Evolution of the Heritage Area Movement."
     Forum Journal 17 (4): 13–21.
Evans-Pritchard, Deirdre. 1987. "The Portal Case: Authenticity, Tourism,
     Traditions, and the Law." *Journal of American Folklore* 100 (397):
     287–96.
————. 1989. "How 'They' See 'Us': Native American Images of Tourists."
     Annals of Tourism Research 16 (1): 89–105.
————. 1990. "Tradition on Trial: How the American Legal System
     Handles the Concept of Tradition." PhD dissertation, University of
     California, Los Angeles.
Fanon, Frantz. 1967. *Black Skin, White Masks*. Trans. Charles Lam Mark-
     mann. New York: Grove Press.
Ferguson, James. 1994. *The Anti-Politics Machine: "Development,"
     Depoliticization, and Bureaucratic Power in Lesotho*. Minneapolis:
     University of Minnesota Press.
Field, Bill. 1978. "Vendor Policy." Letter to the editor. *Santa Fe New Mexi-
     can*, Mar. 4.
Fienup-Riordan, Ann. 2000. *Hunting Tradition in a Changing World: Yup'ik
     Lives in Alaska Today*. New Brunswick NJ: Rutgers University Press.
Fine, Kathleen. 1988. "The Politics of 'Interpretation' at Mesa Verde Na-
     tional Park." *Anthropological Quarterly* 61 (4): 177–86.
Fish, Stanley. 1997. "Boutique Multiculturalism, or Why Liberals Are
     Incapable of Thinking about Hate Speech." *Critical Inquiry* 23 (2):
     378–95.
"For Our Beloved Docents." 1985. Memorandum, July 8. "Palace of the
     Governors — Miscellaneous" vertical file, Fray Angélico Chávez His-
     tory Library, New Mexico History Museum, Santa Fe.
Forrest, Suzanne. 1998. *The Preservation of the Village: New Mexico's
     Hispanics and the New Deal*. Albuquerque: University of New Mexico
     Press.
Foucault, Michel. (1975) 1995. *Discipline and Punish: The Birth of the
     Prison*. Trans. Alan Sheridan. New York: Vintage Books.

Fowler, Don D. 2000. *A Laboratory for Anthropology: Science and Romanticism in the American Southwest, 1846–1930*. Albuquerque: University of New Mexico Press.

Francaviglia, Richard. 1994. "Elusive Land: Changing Geographic Images of the Southwest." In *Essays on the Changing Images of the Southwest*, ed. Richard Francaviglia and David Narrett, 8–39. College Station: Texas A&M University Press.

Fraser, Nancy. 2003. "Social Justice in the Age of Identity Politics: Redistribution, Recognition, and Participation." In *Redistribution or Recognition? A Political-Philosophical Exchange*, by Nancy Fraser and Axel Honneth, 7–109. London: Verso.

Fraser, Nancy, and Axel Honneth. 2003. *Redistribution or Recognition? A Political-Philosophical Exchange*. Trans. Joel Golb, James Ingram, and Christine Wilke. London: Verso.

Frederick, Don. 1978. "Portal Dispute Exciting for Livingston." *Santa Fe New Mexican*, June 25, B1.

Frei, Mary. 1982. "Las Trampas Villagers Assert Right to Forest." *Albuquerque Journal North*, Mar. 31, E5.

Freise, Kathy. 2007. "Contesting Oñate: Sculpting the Shape of Memory." In *Expressing New Mexico: Nuevomexicano Creativity, Ritual, and Memory*, ed. Phillip B. Gonzales, 233–52. Tucson: University of Arizona Press.

Frow, John. 1991. "Tourism and the Semiotics of Nostalgia." *October* 57: 123–51.

Gaines, Judith. 1983. "Islands in the Storm." *RuralAmerica* 8 (1): 28.

Gallegos, Flavio. 1966. "Trampas Needs Road." Letter to the editor. *Santa Fe New Mexican*, Nov. 8, A4.

Gandert, Miguel, et al. 2000. *Nuevo México Profundo: Rituals of an Indo-Hispano Homeland*. Santa Fe: Museum of New Mexico Press.

Garcia, Angela. 2008. "The Elegiac Addict: History, Chronicity, and the Melancholic Subject." *Cultural Anthropology* 23 (4): 718–46.

———. 2010. *The Pastoral Clinic: Addiction and Dispossession along the Rio Grande*. Berkeley: University of California Press.

Geertz, Clifford. 1983. "'From the Native's Point of View': On the Nature of Anthropological Understanding." In *Local Knowledge: Further Essays in Interpretive Anthropology*, 55–70. N.p.: Basic Books.

General Accounting Office. 2004. *Treaty of Guadalupe Hidalgo: Findings and Possible Options Regarding Long-standing Community Land Grant Claims in New Mexico*. GAO-04-59. Washington DC: U.S. General Accounting Office.

Geyer, Georgie Anne. 1998. "War of Statues." *Dallas Morning News*, Aug. 3, 13A.

Gillette, Jane Brown. 1992. "On Her Own Terms." *Historic Preservation* 44 (6): 26–33, 84–86.

Gins, Patricia. 1975. "Museum of New Mexico Shows Remodeled Palace Sections." *Albuquerque Tribune*, Mar. 13, B1.

Glendinning, Chellis. 2005. *Chiva: A Village Takes on the Global Heroin Trade*. Gabriola Island, Canada: New Society Publishers.

Gómez, Laura E. 2005. "Off-White in an Age of White Supremacy: Mexican Elites and the Rights of Indians and Blacks in Nineteenth-Century New Mexico." *Chicano-Latino Law Review* 25:9–59.

———. 2007. *Manifest Destinies: The Making of the Mexican American Race*. New York: New York University Press.

Gonzales, Phillip B. 2007. "'History Hits the Heart': Albuquerque's Great Cuartocentenario Controversy, 1997–2005." In *Expressing New Mexico: Nuevomexicano Creativity, Ritual, and Memory*, ed. Phillip B. Gonzales, 207–32. Tucson: University of Arizona Press.

"Good Work Well Done." 1913. *El Palacio* 1 (1): 1–2.

Grimes, Ronald L. (1976) 1992. *Symbol and Conquest: Public Ritual and Drama in Santa Fe*. Albuquerque: University of New Mexico Press.

Grosvenor, Beth. 1986. "Las Trampas NHL." Report on NHL boundary review, June 30; "NHLS — New Mexico — Las Trampas Historic District — Taos Co." file, National Park Service archives, Santa Fe.

Grosvenor, Melville B. 1967. Memorandum to Secretary of the Interior regarding Las Trampas NM, Apr. 19. "Advisory Board Press Releases" file, Records of the National Parks Advisory Board, National Register of Historic Places and National Landmarks Division, National Park Service, Washington DC.

"Group: We Have Oñate's Foot." 1998. *Albuquerque Journal*, Jan. 14, 1.

Gupta, Akhil. 1998. *Postcolonial Developments: Agriculture in the Making of Modern India*. Durham NC: Duke University Press.

Guthrie, Thomas H. 2005. "Recognizing New Mexico: Heritage Development and Cultural Politics in the Land of Enchantment." PhD dissertation, University of Chicago.

———. 2010a. "Dealing with Difference: Heritage, Commensurability and Public Formation in Northern New Mexico." *International Journal of Heritage Studies* 16 (4): 305–21.

———. 2010b. "History, Preservation, and Power at El Morro National Monument: Toward a Self-Reflexive Interpretive Practice." *CRM: The Journal of Heritage Stewardship* 7 (1): 46–67.

Gutiérrez, Ramón A. 1991. *When Jesus Came, the Corn Mothers Went Away: Marriage, Sexuality, and Power in New Mexico, 1500–1846*. Stanford: Stanford University Press.

———. 2002. "Charles Fletcher Lummis and the Orientalization of New Mexico." In *Nuevomexicano Cultural Legacy: Forms, Agencies, and Discourse*, ed. Francisco A. Lomelí, Víctor A. Sorell, and Genaro M. Padilla, 11–27. Albuquerque: University of New Mexico Press.

Hagan, Bob. 1988. "Española Thinks Big." *Albuquerque Journal*, Mar. 13, D1.

Hall, Douglas Kent. 1995. *New Mexico: Voices in an Ancient Landscape*. New York: Henry Holt.

Hall, Stuart. 1996. "When Was 'The Post-Colonial'? Thinking at the Limit." In *The Post-Colonial Question: Common Skies, Divided Horizons*, ed. Iain Chambers and Lidia Curti, 242–60. London: Routledge.

Handler, Richard. 1987. "Heritage and Hegemony: Recent Works on Historic Preservation and Interpretation." Review of *The Challenge to Our Cultural Heritage*, ed. Yudhishthir Raj Isar, and *Past Meets Present: Essays about Historic Interpretation and Public Audiences*, ed. Jo Blatti. *Anthropological Quarterly* 60 (3): 137–41.

———. 1988. *Nationalism and the Politics of Culture in Quebec*. Madison: University of Wisconsin Press.

Handler, Richard, and Jocelyn Linnekin. 1984. "Tradition, Genuine or Spurious." *Journal of American Folklore* 97 (385): 273–90.

Harrison, Birge. 1885. "Española and Its Environs." *Harper's New Monthly Magazine* 70 (May): 825–35.

Hillerman, Tony. 1970. "Las Trampas: They Survived the Trap." *New Mexico* 48 (7–8): 20–23.

"History Ignored?" 1999. Editorial. *Rio Grande Sun*, Aug. 26, A6.

Hobbs, Hulda R. 1946a. "The Story of the Archaeological Society I: Prologue: The Awakening of Interest." *El Palacio* 53 (4): 79–88.

———. 1946b. "The Story of the Archaeological Society II: The First Thirteen Years." *El Palacio* 53 (7): 175–86.

———. 1946c. "The Story of the Archaeological Society II: The First Thirteen Years (Concluded)." *El Palacio* 53 (8): 203–11.

Hobsbawm, Eric, and Terence Ranger, eds. 1983. *The Invention of Tradition*. Cambridge: Cambridge University Press.

Hoerig, Karl A. 2003. *Under the Palace Portal: Native American Artists in Santa Fe*. Albuquerque: University of New Mexico Press.

Hooker, Juliet. 2005. "Indigenous Inclusion/Black Exclusion: Race, Ethnicity and Multicultural Citizenship in Latin America." *Journal of Latin American Studies* 37 (2): 285–310.

Hooker, Van Dorn. 1977. "To Hand Plaster or Not??" *New Mexico Architecture* 19 (5): 11–16.

Horton, Sarah. 2001. "Where Is the 'Mexican' in 'New Mexican'? Enacting History, Enacting Dominance in the Santa Fe Fiesta." *Public Historian* 23 (4): 41–54.

———. 2002. "New Mexico's Cuarto Centenario and Spanish American Nationalism: Collapsing Past Conquests and Present Dispossession." *Journal of the Southwest* 44 (1): 49–60.

———. 2010. *The Santa Fe Fiesta, Reinvented: Staking Ethno-Nationalist Claims to a Disappearing Homeland*. Santa Fe: School for Advanced Research Press.

Hummels, Mark. 1998. "Made Whole Again: New Foot Attached to Oñate Statue." *Albuquerque Journal*, Jan. 17, A1.

Hunner, Jon, et al. 1999. "A Survey of the Historic District of Las Trampas NM." "NHLS—New Mexico—Las Trampas Historic District—Taos Co." file, National Park Service archives, Santa Fe.

ICADP and NMSPO (Interagency Council for Area Development Planning, and New Mexico State Planning Office). [1963]. *Embudo: A Pilot Planning Project for the Embudo Watershed of New Mexico*. N.p.

Janus Associates. 1986. "National Historic Landmark Condition Assessment Report: San Jose de Gracia Church, Las Trampas, New Mexico." "Condition assessment report—San José de Gracia church—Las Trampas, New Mexico" file, National Park Service archives, Santa Fe.

Johnson, Jeannie. 1998. "History Lesson on Sale." *Albuquerque Journal North*, July 12, 1.

Jones, David J. 1967. "Justification for a National Historic Site at Las Trampas." In *Las Trampas: A Special Report for the Advisory Board [on National Parks, Historic Sites, Buildings, and Monuments]*. Santa Fe: Southwest Regional Office, National Park Service.

Joyce, Brian. 1978. "Vendor Explains Actions." Letter to the editor. *Santa Fe New Mexican*, Feb. 22, A12.

Keller, Robert H., and Michael F. Turek. 1998. *American Indians and National Parks*. Tucson: University of Arizona Press.

Kessell, John L. 1980. *The Missions of New Mexico since 1776*. Albuquerque: University of New Mexico Press.

Kirshenblatt-Gimblett, Barbara. 1998. *Destination Culture: Tourism, Museums, and Heritage*. Berkeley: University of California Press.

Kosek, Jake. 2006. *Understories: The Political Life of Forests in Northern New Mexico*. Durham NC: Duke University Press.

Kropp, Phoebe S. 1996. "'There Is a Little Sermon in That': Constructing the Native Southwest at the San Diego Panama-California Exposition of 1915." In *The Great Southwest of the Fred Harvey Company and the Santa Fe Railway*, ed. Marta Weigle and Barbara A. Babcock, 36–46. Phoenix: The Heard Museum.

Kymlicka, Will. 1995. *Multicultural Citizenship: A Liberal Theory of Minority Rights*. Oxford: Oxford University Press.

"Las Trampas, New Mexico—A National Historic Landmark." 1967. *New Mexico Architecture* 9 (7–8): 9.

"Las Trampas Receives Historic Marker and Plaques." 1977. *New Mexico Architecture* 19 (4): 9, 17.

Lentz, Andrew. 1998. "Who Has Oñate's Missing Foot??" *Rio Grande Sun*, Jan. 15, A1.

Levine, Frances. 2003. Interview by the author. Nov. 12. Santa Fe, New Mexico.

———. 2008. "The Palace of the Governors: A Witness to History." In *Santa Fe: History of an Ancient City*, ed. David Grant Noble, 109–21. Rev. and expanded ed. Santa Fe: School for Advanced Research Press.

Leyba, Ely. 1933. "The Church of the Twelve Apostles." *New Mexico* 11 (6): 19–21, 47–52.

Lindblom, David, dir., Cynthia Jeannette Gomez, prod., and Daniel Valerio, prod. 2011. *Land Water People Time*. N.p.: Water in Motion.

"Links Historic Past with Living Present." 1913. *El Palacio* 2 (1): 1, 6.

Lippard, Lucy R. 1999. *On the Beaten Track: Tourism, Art, and Place*. New York: New Press.

Livingston v. Ewing. 1978. No. 77-192-M Civil. 455 F. Supp. 825; 1978 U.S. Dist. LEXIS 16561.

———. 1979. No. 78-1683. 601 F.2d 1110; 1979 U.S. App. LEXIS 14001; 19 Fair Empl. Prac. Cas. (BNA) 1716; 20 Empl. Prac. Dec. (CCH) P30,002.

Loewen, James W. 1999. *Lies across America: What Our Historic Sites Get Wrong*. New York: New Press.

López, Antonio. 1998a. "A Spanish View of History: Spain's Legacy Is Not an Issue of Race." *Santa Fe New Mexican*, Apr. 19, spec. sec. 9.

———. 1998b. "Joe Sando: An American Indian's View of New Mexico History." *Santa Fe New Mexican*, Apr. 19, spec. sec. 7.

Lopez, Ruth. 1999. "Pomp and Circumstances." *Santa Fe New Mexican*, Feb. 12, Pasatiempo mag. sec. 6.

Lovato, Andrew Leo. 2004. *Santa Fe Hispanic Culture: Preserving Identity in a Tourist Town*. Albuquerque: University of New Mexico Press.

Lowe, Jonathan, dir. 1997. *Culture as a Cure: La Cultura Cura*. Española NM: Hands Across Cultures Corporation.

Lucero, Alice D., and Marilyn Reeves. 1990. *City of Espanola Takes Pride: 1986–1990 and Beyond: Accomplishments, Current Projects, Future Plans*. Supplement to *Rio Grande Sun* Feb. 1.

Lucero, Richard. 2003. Interview by the author. Dec. 12. Española, New Mexico.

MacCannell, Dean. (1976) 1999. *The Tourist: A New Theory of the Leisure Class*. New York: Schocken Books.

———. 1992. *Empty Meeting Grounds: The Tourist Papers*. London: Routledge.

MacGregor, John. 1966. "NM Heritage Faces Destruction." *Santa Fe New Mexican*, Oct. 2, Pasatiempo mag. sec. 5–10.

———. 1967. "Las Trampas Church Given New Coating of Soft Plaster." *Santa Fe New Mexican*, Aug. 6, D6.

Malinowski, Bronislaw. (1922) 1984. *Argonauts of the Western Pacific*. Prospect Heights IL: Waveland Press.

Markell, Patchen. 2003. *Bound by Recognition*. Princeton NJ: Princeton University Press.

Martinez, Eliu. 2001. "Española Fiesta: Suppressing Our Own History?" Letter to the editor. *Santa Fe New Mexican*, July 26, A7.

Masco, Joseph. 2006. *The Nuclear Borderlands: The Manhattan Project in Post–Cold War New Mexico*. Princeton NJ: Princeton University Press.

May, Glenn. 1998. "Sharing Cultures Part of Mission Opening." *Rio Grande Sun*, Feb. 12, A21.

McCalmont, Tom. 1990. "Española Preservation Is Really Demolition." Letter to the editor. *Albuquerque Journal North*, Nov. 3, 4.

McDonald, Mike. 1978. "Proposes Portal Solution." Letter to the editor. *Santa Fe New Mexican*, June 3.

McGuire, Ginger. 2000. "History of the Valley." *Santa Fe New Mexican*, July 11, B1.

Memmi, Albert. (1957) 1991. *The Colonizer and the Colonized*. Trans. Howard Greenfeld. Expanded ed. Boston: Beacon Press.

Mitchell, Pablo. 2005. *Coyote Nation: Sexuality, Race, and Conquest in Modernizing New Mexico, 1880–1920*. Chicago: University of Chicago Press.

Mitchell, Timothy. 1988. *Colonising Egypt*. Berkeley: University of California Press.

Montgomery, Charles H. 2002. *The Spanish Redemption: Heritage, Power, and Loss on New Mexico's Upper Rio Grande*. Berkeley: University of California Press.

Mullin, Molly H. 2001. *Culture in the Marketplace: Gender, Art, and Value in the American Southwest.* Durham NC: Duke University Press.

Museum of New Mexico. 1912. *First Annual Report of the Museum of New Mexico.* Santa Fe: New Mexican Printing Company.

———. n.d. "FAQS about the New Mexico History Museum." Available at http://media.museumofnewmexico.org/nmhm/pdf/faq.pdf. Accessed June 5, 2009.

"The Museum of New Mexico." 1919. *El Palacio* 7 (4): 74–7, 83–91.

"Must Pay for Privilege." 1966. Editorial. *Santa Fe New Mexican,* Nov. 18, A4.

Myers, Michael. 1978. "Selling at Portal Developing into NM Version of Bakke Case." *Santa Fe New Mexican,* Apr. 9, B2.

Nájera-Ramírez, Olga, Norma E. Cantú, and Brenda M. Romero, eds. 2009. *Dancing across Borders: Danzas y Bailes Mexicanos.* Urbana: University of Illinois Press.

Nasdijj. 2000. *The Blood Runs Like a River through My Dreams: A Memoir.* New York: Houghton Mifflin.

Navarro, Bruno J. 1997. "Historic Building May Get New Life." *Santa Fe New Mexican,* Nov. 28, B1.

Neckels, Jack W. 1988. Letter to Bridget Hartman, Washington DC, May 19. "NHLS—New Mexico—Las Trampas Historic District—Taos Co." file, National Park Service archives, Santa Fe.

Neumann, Mark. 1999. *On the Rim: Looking for the Grand Canyon.* Minneapolis: University of Minnesota Press.

"New Lease on Life for the Church at Las Trampas NM." 1967. *New Mexico Architecture* 9 (9–10): 9–11.

Nieto-Phillips, John M. 2004. *The Language of Blood: The Making of Spanish-American Identity in New Mexico, 1880s–1930s.* Albuquerque: University of New Mexico Press.

NMHCPL (New Mexican Hispanic Culture Preservation League). 2010. "New Mexican Hispanic Culture Preservation League." Available at http://www.nmhcpl.org. Accessed Jan. 23, 2010.

NPS (National Park Service). 1967a. *Las Trampas: A Special Report for the Advisory Board [on National Parks, Historic Sites, Buildings, and Monuments].* Santa Fe: Southwest Regional Office, National Park Service.

———. 1967b. "National Parks Advisory Board Recommends Seven Sites as Historic Landmarks." Press release, May 28; "56th Advisory Board Meeting, April 17–19, 1967" file, Records of the National Parks Advisory Board, National Register of Historic Places and National Landmarks Division, National Park Service, Washington DC.

———. 1991. "Alternative Concepts for Commemorating Spanish Colonization." Denver: GPO.

———. 1992. "American Heritage Landscapes: The Geographers' Perspective." Report on Heritage Landscape Workshop, January 6–8, 1992.
Denver: National Park Service.

———. 2005. "Critical Steps and Criteria for Becoming a National Heritage Area." Available at http://www.cr.nps.gov/heritageareas/REP/
criteria.pdf. Accessed Sept. 30, 2005.

———. 2012. "What Are National Heritage Areas?" Available at http://
www.nps.gov/history/heritageareas/FAQ. Accessed June 1, 2012.

NPSAB (National Park System Advisory Board). 2001. *Rethinking the National Parks for the 21st Century*. Annual report of the National Park
System Advisory Board, John Hope Franklin, Chairman. N.p.

NRGNHA (Northern Rio Grande National Heritage Area, Inc.). 2007.
"Northern Rio Grande National Heritage Area" [brochure]. Mar. rev.

———. 2011. "Mission and Vision." Available at http://www.riograndenha
.com/mission-and-vision.html. Accessed March 3, 2013.

———. 2013. "The Northern Río Grande National Heritage Area Management Plan" [Feb. draft]. Copy given to T. Guthrie by Thomas
Romero, 2013.

Nusbaum, Rosemary. 1978. *The City Different and the Palace: The Palace of
the Governors: Its Role in Santa Fe History*. Santa Fe: Sunstone Press.

O'Brien, William Patrick. 1988a. Letter to Barbara Lopez, Las Trampas
NM, Mar. 3. "NHLS—New Mexico—Las Trampas Historic District—Taos Co." file, National Park Service archives, Santa Fe.

———. 1988b. Memorandum to Senior Historian, Cultural Affairs [Na-
tional Park Service], regarding Las Trampas NHL, June 20, with accompanying documents. "NHLS—New Mexico—Las Trampas Historic
District—Taos Co." file, National Park Service archives, Santa Fe.

"100 Years Ago." 1990. *Santa Fe New Mexican*, Oct. 26, B2.

Ooms, Sally MacDonald. 1993. "Espanola Is Building Fourth Plaza in Four
Centuries." *New Mexico Progress: Monthly Business and Economic
Report Published by Sunwest Bank*, Nov., 2–3.

Ortega, Ernest. 2003. Interview by the author. Dec. 18 and 19. Santa Fe,
New Mexico.

Ortiz, Alfonso. 1969. *The Tewa World: Space, Time, Being, and Becoming
in a Pueblo Society*. Chicago: University of Chicago Press.

Ortiz, Roxanne Dunbar. 1980. *Roots of Resistance: Land Tenure in New
Mexico, 1680–1980*. Los Angeles: Chicano Studies Research Center
and American Indian Studies Center, University of California.

Owings, Nathaniel Alexander. 1966. "Site Should Be Preserved." Letter to the editor. *Santa Fe New Mexican*, Oct. 2, A4.

———. 1970. "Las Trampas: A Past Resurrected." *New Mexico* 48 (7–8): 30–35.

———. 1973. *The Spaces in Between: An Architect's Journey*. Boston: Houghton Mifflin.

Palace of the Governors. 1997. "The Palace of the Governors: Native American Vendors Program" [brochure]. N.p.: Palace of the Governors.

———. 2006. *The New Mexico History Museum*. [Concept book] Available at http://www.palaceofthegovernors.org/conceptbook/nmhm.pdf. Accessed June 13, 2008.

Parsons, Jack, Carmella Padilla, and Juan Estevan Arellano. 1999. *Low 'n Slow: Lowriding in New Mexico*. Santa Fe: Museum of New Mexico Press.

Penland, Paige R. 2004. *Santa Fe and Taos*. Footscray, Australia: Lonely Planet Publications.

Pepin-Donat, Margaret. 1982. Memorandum to Acting Chief, National Register Division, Washington DC, regarding National Historic Landmark boundary reviews. "NHLs—New Mexico—Las Trampas Historic District—Taos Co." file, National Park Service archives, Santa Fe.

Percy, Walker. (1954) 1975. *The Message in the Bottle: How Queer Man Is, How Queer Language Is, and What One Has to Do with the Other*. New York: Farrar, Straus and Giroux.

Peterson, Iver. 1984. "Espanola NM Embraces Espanola Jokes and Laughs Last." *New York Times*, May 22, A14.

Phillips, Adrian. 2003. "Turning Ideas on Their Head: The New Paradigm for Protected Areas." *George Wright Forum* 20 (2): 8–32.

Plaza de Española Foundation. [1992]. Española plaza proposal. Copy given to T. Guthrie by Lou Baker, 2003.

———. [1995]. "Plaza de Española" [brochure]. Española NM: Plaza de Española Foundation.

Post, Stephen S. 2003. "Archaeology behind the Palace of the Governors: A New Look at History and Cartography." *El Palacio* 108 (3): 6–11.

———. 2006. "Buildings Lost and Found: Eighteenth-Century Foundations of a New Museum." *El Palacio* 111 (4): 38–41, 90.

Povinelli, Elizabeth A. 1999. "Settler Modernity and the Quest for Indigenous Traditions." *Public Culture* 11 (1): 19–47.

———. 2002. *The Cunning of Recognition: Indigenous Alterities and the Making of Australian Multiculturalism*. Durham NC: Duke University Press.

Pratt, Boyd C., and Robin Farwell Gavin. 1991. "Las Trampas." In *The Architecture and Cultural Landscape of North Central New Mexico*, ed. Boyd C. Pratt and Chris Wilson, 57–71. N.p.: New Mexico Endowment for the Humanities.

"Preservation Law Saves Historic Town." 1967. *History News* 22 (7): 144.

"Proud Actions." 1998. *Santa Fe Reporter*, Sept. 9–15, 5.

Puente, Maria. 1979. "Livingston Pledges to Appeal Portal Policy to High Court." *Santa Fe New Mexican*, June 18, A1.

Pulido, Laura. 1996. *Environmentalism and Economic Justice: Two Chicano Struggles in the Southwest*. Tucson: University of Arizona Press.

Ragan, Tom. 1996a. "A Mission to Attract Tourists." *Albuquerque Journal North*, Aug. 6, 1.

———. 1996b. "Dream of Plaza Mission Takes Shape in Española." *Albuquerque Journal North*, Mar. 29, 5.

"Report of the Museum of New Mexico." 1914. *El Palacio* 2 (3): 1–8.

"Restoration of the Palace." 1913. *El Palacio* 1 (1): 5.

Reyna, Diane, dir. 1992. *Surviving Columbus: The Story of the Pueblo People*. Albuquerque NM: KNME-TV. Distributed by PBS Video.

Rivera, José A. 1998. *Acequia Culture: Water, Land, and Community in the Southwest*. Albuquerque: University of New Mexico Press.

Roberts, Kathaleen. 2013. "Resolution Would Protect Textile Traditions." *Albuquerque Journal*, Feb. 18, Business Outlook sec. 5.

Rodríguez, Sylvia. 1987. "Land, Water, and Ethnic Identity in Taos." In *Land, Water, and Culture: New Perspectives on Hispanic Land Grants*, ed. Charles L. Briggs and John R. Van Ness, 313–403. Albuquerque: University of New Mexico Press.

———. 1989. "Art, Tourism, and Race Relations in Taos: Toward a Sociology of the Art Colony." *Journal of Anthropological Research* 45 (1): 77–100.

———. 1990. "Ethnic Reconstruction in Contemporary Taos." *Journal of the Southwest* 32 (4): 541–55.

———. 1992. "The Hispano Homeland Debate Revised." *Perspectives in Mexican American Studies* 3:95–114.

———. 1994. "The Tourist Gaze, Gentrification, and the Commodification of Subjectivity in Taos." In *Essays on the Changing Images of the Southwest*, ed. Richard Francaviglia and David Narrett, 105–26. College Station: Texas A&M University Press.

———. 1996. *The Matachines Dance: Ritual Symbolism and Interethnic Relations in the Upper Río Grande Valley*. Albuquerque: University of New Mexico Press.

———. 2001. "Tourism, Whiteness, and the Vanishing Anglo." In *Seeing and Being Seen: Tourism in the American West*, ed. David M. Wrobel and Patrick T. Long, 194–210. Lawrence: University Press of Kansas.

———. 2006. *Acequia: Water Sharing, Sanctity, and Place*. Santa Fe: School for Advanced Research Press.

Rolwing, Rebecca. 1998. "NM Plans to Mark 1598 Arrival of Conquistador Opens Wounds." *Dallas Morning News*, May 1, 28A.

Romero, Levi. 2001. "La Nueva Resolana." *New Mexico* 79 (5): 26–31.

Romero, Orlando. 1987. "San Gabriel Revisited, 1598–1984." In *When Cultures Meet: Remembering San Gabriel Del Yunge Oweenge*, 7–9. Santa Fe: Sunstone Press.

———. 1990. "Watch Out, Española!" *Santa Fe Reporter*, Sept. 19–25, 7.

———. 2003. Interview by the author. Dec. 20. Nambe, New Mexico.

Romero, Tony J. 1998. Letter to the editor. *Albuquerque Journal*, Apr. 5, B3.

Rosaldo, Renato. 1993. *Culture and Truth: The Remaking of Social Analysis*. Boston: Beacon Press.

Rothman, Hal K. 1992. *On Rims and Ridges: The Los Alamos Area since 1880*. Lincoln: University of Nebraska Press.

Roy, Donna. 1990a. "City Sees History in New Plaza." *Santa Fe New Mexican*, Sept. 28, B3.

———. 1990b. "Federal Officials Impressed with Effort on Plaza Plan." *Santa Fe New Mexican*, Feb. 28, B1.

———. 1990c. "Seven Flags Over Espanola Part of Project Dedication." *Santa Fe New Mexican*, May 19, B4.

———. 1992a. "Lawyer Protests Planned Mission." *Santa Fe New Mexican*, July 17, B1.

———. 1992b. "Shovels Ready for Espanola Plaza." *Santa Fe New Mexican*, Apr. 27, A4.

———. 1993a. "ACLU Won't Oppose Española's Plaza Chapel." *Santa Fe New Mexican*, Dec. 25, B1.

———. 1993b. "Española Plaza Will Preserve History." *Santa Fe New Mexican*, July 4, B1.

———. 1994. "Chavez Puts Española First, Plaza Second." *Santa Fe New Mexican*, Mar. 25, B3.

Sagel, Jim. 1987. "Architect Sees Pueblos Losing Focus." *Albuquerque Journal North*, Mar. 11, 1.

Said, Edward W. 1978. *Orientalism*. New York: Vintage Books.

Sánchez, Joseph P. 1990. *The Spanish Black Legend/La Leyenda Negra Española: Origins of Anti-Hispanic Stereotypes/Orígenes de los Estereo-*

tipos Antihispánicos. Albuquerque NM: National Park Service, Spanish Colonial Research Center.

Sando, Joe E., and Herman Agoyo, eds. 2005. *Po'pay: Leader of the First American Revolution*. Santa Fe: Clear Light Publishing.

Sandoval, Steve. 1985. "Antique Facade Discovered on Palace of the Governors." *Albuquerque Journal North*, Sept. 12, D1.

Santillanes, Millie. 1998. "Oñate Issue 'Clarification' Muddied Water Further." Letter to the editor. *Albuquerque Journal*, June 25, A15.

Sapir, Edward. (1927) 1963. "The Unconscious Patterning of Behavior in Society." In *Selected Writings of Edward Sapir in Language, Culture and Personality*, ed. David G. Mandelbaum, 544–59. Berkeley: University of California Press.

Sax, Joseph L. 1985. "The Almost Tragic Tale of Boxley Valley: A Case History in the Management of the National Parks." *Law Quadrangle Notes* 29 (2): 30–6.

———. 1986. "The Trampas File." *Michigan Law Review* 84 (7): 1388–1414.

Schuchart, Gunhild. 1978. "Indian Trade under the Portal of the Palace of the Governors in Santa Fe." Class paper; "Palace of the Governors—Portal Vendors" vertical file, Fray Angélico Chavéz History Library, New Mexico History Museum, Santa Fe.

Scott, Wayne S. 1966. "Las Trampas Gets Paved Road." *Albuquerque Journal*, Oct. 27, D4.

Sedillo, Pablo. 2003. Interview by the author. Nov. 25. Santa Fe, New Mexico.

Sharpe, Tom. 1991. "Richardson Hopes for Unity in Española Center." *Albuquerque Journal North*, Oct. 3, 1.

———. 1992. "Rio Arriba Projects Get Boost." *Albuquerque Journal North*, Mar. 12, 1.

———. 2001. "No Sword for Oñate at Fiesta This Year." *Santa Fe New Mexican*, July 1, B1.

Shishkin, J. K. 1972. *The Palace of the Governors*. [Santa Fe]: Museum of New Mexico Press.

Shockley, Linda. 1986. "The Organizational Man." *Santa Fe New Mexican*, July 10, spec. sec. 7.

Simmons, Marc. 1991. *The Last Conquistador: Juan de Oñate and the Settling of the Far Southwest*. Norman: University of Oklahoma Press.

———. 2003. "Another Look at Governor Juan de Oñate." *Santa Fe New Mexican*, May 10, B1.

Snead, James Elliott. 2001. *Ruins and Rivals: The Making of Southwest Archaeology*. Tucson: University of Arizona Press.

Snow, Cordelia Thomas. 1974. "A Brief History of the Palace of the Governors and a Preliminary Report on the 1974 Excavation." *El Palacio* 80 (3): 1–22.

Spicer, Edward H. 1972. "Plural Society in the Southwest." In *Plural Society in the Southwest*, ed. Edward H. Spicer and Raymond H. Thompson, 21–76. New York: Interbook.

Stevenson, Michael. 2009. "The Museum and Collections of the Historical Society of New Mexico, 1859–1977." In *Telling New Mexico: A New History*, ed. Marta Weigle, 247–55. Santa Fe: Museum of New Mexico Press.

Stingley, Steven. 1979. "Portal Racial Issue Rule Due." *Santa Fe New Mexican*, May 24, B1.

Stone, Marissa. 2001. "Changing of the Guard: Española Crowns La Mestiza." *Santa Fe New Mexican*, July 9, A1.

———. 2003. "Oñate Statue Moved." *Santa Fe New Mexican*, Apr. 30, A1.

Sweeney, Thomas W. 1988. "The Adobe Art of Anita Rodriguez." *Preservation News*, Mar., 15, 17.

Sweet, Jill D. 1989. "Burlesquing 'the Other' in Pueblo Performance." *Annals of Tourism Research* 16 (1): 62–75.

Swentzell, Rina. 1990a. "Conflicting Landscape Values: The Santa Clara Pueblo and Day School." *Places* 7 (1): 19–27.

———. 1990b. "Remembering Tewa Pueblo Houses and Spaces." *Native Peoples* 3 (2): 6–12.

———. 1991. "Santa Clara Pueblo: A Changing Community." In *The Architecture and Cultural Landscape of North Central New Mexico*, ed. Boyd C. Pratt and Chris Wilson, 13–20. N.p.: New Mexico Endowment for the Humanities.

———. 2001. "Pueblo Structures and Worldview." In *Recording a Vanishing Legacy: The Historic American Buildings Survey in New Mexico, 1933–Today*, ed. Sally Hyer, 69–73. Santa Fe: Museum of New Mexico Press.

———. 2003a. "Anglo Artists and the Creation of Pueblo Worlds." In *The Culture of Tourism, the Tourism of Culture: Selling the Past to the Present in the American Southwest*, ed. Hal K. Rothman, 66–71. Albuquerque: University of New Mexico Press.

———. 2003b. Interview by the author. Dec. 19. Santa Fe, New Mexico.

———. 2004. "A Pueblo Woman's Perspective on Chaco Canyon." In *In Search of Chaco: New Approaches to an Archaeological Enigma*, ed.

David Grant Noble, 49–53. Santa Fe: School of American Research Press.

———. 2007. Electronic message to the author. June 10.

Taylor, Charles. 1994. "The Politics of Recognition." In *Multiculturalism: Examining the Politics of Recognition*, ed. Amy Gutmann, 25–73. Princeton NJ: Princeton University Press.

"A Threat to Las Trampas." 1966. Editorial. *Santa Fe New Mexican*, Oct. 2, A4.

Tobias, Henry J., and Charles E. Woodhouse. 2001. *Santa Fe: A Modern History, 1880–1990*. Albuquerque: University of New Mexico Press.

Tollefson, Jeff. 2002. "History in the Making." *Santa Fe New Mexican*, June 1, B1.

Trapp, Robert. 1998. "SUN Gets Exclusive on Funloving Foot Filchers." *Rio Grande Sun*, Jan. 22, A7.

Trujillo, Michael Leon. 2005. "The Land of Disenchantment: Transformation, Continuity, and Negation in the Greater Española Valley, New Mexico." PhD dissertation, University of Texas, Austin.

———. 2006. "A Northern New Mexican 'Fix': Shooting Up and Coming Down in the Greater Española Valley, New Mexico." *Cultural Dynamics* 18 (1): 89–112.

———. 2009. *Land of Disenchantment: Latina/o Identities and Transformations in Northern New Mexico*. Albuquerque: University of New Mexico Press.

Usner, Don J. 1995. *Sabino's Map: Life in Chimayó's Old Plaza*. Santa Fe: Museum of New Mexico Press.

van Dresser, Peter. 1972. *Development on a Human Scale: Potentials for Ecologically Guided Growth in Northern New Mexico*. New York: Praeger.

Varela, Maria. 2001. "Collaborative Conservation: Peace or Pacification? The View from Los Ojos." In *Native Peoples of the Southwest: Negotiating Land, Water, and Ethnicity*, ed. Laurie Weinstein, 169–77. Westport CT: Bergin & Garvey.

Velasquez, Beth. 1991. "Fiesta! Oñate Commemoration Began Here in 1940s." *Rio Grande Sun*, July 11, A1.

Villa, Clare. 2003a. Interview by the author. Dec. 8. Española, New Mexico.

———. 2003b. Interview by the author. Dec. 11. Alcalde, New Mexico.

Weber, Michael F. 1974. "The Problems of Preservation." *El Palacio* 80 (3): 37–45.

Weideman, Paul. 2005. "Española Vibrates with Times Past." *Santa Fe New Mexican* Real Estate Guide, Oct. 2, 24.

Weigle, Marta, ed. 1975. *Hispanic Villages of Northern New Mexico: A Reprint of Volume II of the 1935 Tewa Basin Study, with Supplementary Materials.* Santa Fe: Lightning Tree.

———. 2010. *Alluring New Mexico: Engineered Enchantment, 1821–2001.* Santa Fe: Museum of New Mexico Press.

Weigle, Marta, and Barbara A. Babcock, eds. 1996. *The Great Southwest of the Fred Harvey Company and the Santa Fe Railway.* Phoenix: The Heard Museum.

Weyermann, D. 2000. "The Curse of Chimayó." *Dallas Morning News,* Apr. 17, A1.

Whitecotton, Joseph W. 1996. "Ethnic Groups and Ethnicity in Southern Mexico and Northern New Mexico: An Historical Comparison of the Valley of Oaxaca and the Española Valley." In *The Politics of Ethnicity in Southern Mexico,* ed. Howard Campbell, 1–32. Vanderbilt University Publications in Anthropology 50. Series ed. John D. Monaghan. Nashville TN: Vanderbilt University Press.

Wilson, Chris. 1997. *The Myth of Santa Fe: Creating a Modern Regional Tradition.* Albuquerque: University of New Mexico Press.

———. 1998. "Authentic Relic Passed Over for Stamp Image." *Albuquerque Journal,* Apr. 12, B3.

———. 2003. "Ethnic/Sexual Personas in Tricultural New Mexico." In *The Culture of Tourism, the Tourism of Culture: Selling the Past to the Present in the American Southwest,* ed. Hal K. Rothman, 12–37. Albuquerque: University of New Mexico Press.

———. 2004. "Place Over Time: Restoration and Revivalism in Santa Fe." In *Giving Preservation a History: Histories of Historic Preservation in the United States,* ed. Max Page and Randall Mason, 185–206. New York: Routledge.

Wilson, Chris, and David Kammer. 1989. *La Tierra Amarilla: Its History, Architecture, and Cultural Landscape.* Santa Fe: Museum of New Mexico Press.

Wilson, Chris, and Stefanos Polyzoides, eds. 2011. *The Plazas of New Mexico.* San Antonio TX: Trinity University Press.

Wood, Nancy. 1998. "Whose Land?" Letter to the editor. *Santa Fe New Mexican,* Apr. 1, A7.

Woods, Annie. 1990. "Dignitaries Pack Mud for Plaza Chapel." *Santa Fe New Mexican,* Aug. 13, A1.

WPA (Work Projects Administration). (1940) 1989. *The WPA Guide to 1930s New Mexico*. Tucson: University of Arizona Press. Orig. pub. as *New Mexico: A Guide to the Colorful State*.

Zoretich, Frank. 1999. "Baca Vetoes City Council Resolution on Oñate." *Albuquerque Tribune*, Mar. 17, A1.

Zumwalt, Rosemary Lévy. 1992. *Wealth and Rebellion: Elsie Clews Parsons, Anthropologist and Folklorist*. Urbana: University of Illinois Press.

INDEX

tion and, 170–71, 175–77; portal
market and, 62; repoliticization of,
236; of San Gabriel, 102–3. *See also*
commemoration of colonization
Colonial New Mexico Commemorative
Act, 271n38
commemoration of colonization: and
Americanness of New Mexico, 159–
64; commemorative stamp and, 156–
59, 273n49; and differing understandings of past, 149–53; Ernest Ortega
on, 165–66; Española plaza project as,
144–45; Hispanic identity and politics
of recognition and, 135–39; Juan de
Oñate and, 145–49; National Park
Service study on, 141–44; opposition
to, 99; by United States, 153–56
Commemorative Spanish Colonization
Center, 121, 144–45
commercialism, portal market and aversion to, 76–78
conquest, 142–43
Conron, John: on Highway 76 project,
192; on Las Trampas, 189, 200–201;
and Las Trampas Foundation, 194,
195; on Las Trampas residents, 204;
and Palace of the Governors renovation, 39
convivencia, 145
Córdova, Kathy, 10, 17, 35
critique: exposing normativity to, 61;
metatourism and limits of, 51–55
cuarto centenario celebrations. *See* commemoration of colonization
Culler, Jonathan, 51, 65, 66
cultural disintegration and adaptability,
202–3
cultural mixing, 231–32
cultural revitalization: as form of decolonization, 108; land grant activism
and, 109; and heroin epidemic, 229
culture: Anglos' treatment of economics
and, 176–77; class and, 265n2; in Espa-

ñola valley, 101–13; essentialist conceptions of, 9, 219; forgetting about, 228;
and liberal conception of heritage, 219;
in Misión-Convento, 269n26; politics
and, 235; production of, 265n3; religion as part of, 268n24; remembering,
227–30; transcending, 253n11. *See also*
anti-politics of culture; heritage
culture loss, 6, 106–9, 175, 281n5

Daly, Jayne, 222–23
dance(s), 119, 158, 161, 227–28,
240–41
Danza de los Antepasados, 239–44
decolonization, cultural revitalization
as, 108
Delgado, Samuel: assisting in fieldwork, 212–14; on colonization of
New Mexico, 155; defending Juan de
Oñate, 146; on identity, 140–41; on
NRGNHA tour, 131, 172; on Spanish
American identity, 137
Denver and Rio Grande Railway Company, 265n5
depoliticization: "Alternative Concepts
for Commemorating Spanish Colonization" and, 142–43; culture and,
11; through economic development,
174; heritage projects and, 235; and
letting go of past, 229; social justice
movements and, 253n10; of Spanish
colonialism, 98, 235. *See also* anti-
politics of culture
Deutsch, Sarah, 180, 181
de Vargas, Diego, 29, 32, 271n35
Domenici, Pete, 18, 35–36, 113, 157–58
Dominguez, Fray Francisco Atanasio,
276n4
Dorst, John, 261n12
drug abuse, 106–7, 108, 109, 228–29

Ebright, Malcolm, 182
economics, Anglos' treatment of culture
and, 176–77

Ellis, Florence Hawley, 103, 266n8, 266n9

El Palacio, 259n29

elsewhere, authentic, 79–81, 87, 92, 93–94

Embudo watershed report, 189–91, 204

enjarrando, 278n14

The Environment (Naranjo-Morse), 152–53

Española: cultural geography surrounding, 101–13; drug abuse in, 228–29; identity and, 162–63; overview of, 97–98; and problems of recognition, 98–101; self-identification of residents of, 270n32

Española fiesta, 145, 231

Española Main Street program, 133–34

Española plaza project. *See* Plaza de Española

Eustace, Mary, 72

Evans-Pritchard, Deirdre: on agency in portal market, 263n21; on authenticity of portal market, 80, 81, 83; on *Livingston v. Ewing*, 70, 261n7; on portal as staged authenticity, 87–88; on portal program's grandfather clause, 262n14; on production of art under Palace portal, 83–84

Evolution of the Palace exhibit, 37–44, 47

Ewing, George, 39

Faks, James, 72–73

federal government: Chimayó's drug problem and, 106; and commemoration of colonization, 99; and Hispanic New Deal, 186; as land manager, 2, 183; Las Trampas land grant and, 183; Northern Rio Grande National Heritage Area and, 1–3, 165, 243; as number-one employer in New Mexico, 109–10; recognition by, of multinational claims, 163–64; suspicion toward, 210. *See also* United States

Ferguson, James, 174

Fienup-Riordan, Ann, 277n8

Fletcher, Julianne, 35

Forest Service, 183, 275n3

Forrest, Suzanne, 187–88

Fraser, Nancy, 282n9

Fred Harvey Company, 218

Freise, Kathy, 153

Frow, John, 67

Garcia, Angela, 108, 228–29

Garcia, David, 240–41

Garcia, Michael, 141

Gillette, Jane Brown, 281n3, 281n4

Gomez, Donovan, 79

Gómez, Laura, 136

Grand Canyon, 65–66, 218, 257n18

Great Depression, 185–89

Gupta, Akhil, 96, 281n7

Hall, Douglas Kent, 138

Hall, Stuart, 252n5

Handler, Richard, 85–86, 88, 219

Harrington, John P., 218

heritage: anthropology and, 218–20; defined, 44; development of, 6–7; as global concern, 14; multicultural justice and, 230–36; politics and, 235; production of, 252n9; recognition of, 8–10; remembering and forgetting, 227–30. *See also* culture; objectification of heritage

heritage areas. *See* national heritage area(s); Northern Rio Grande National Heritage Area

Hewett, Edgar Lee, 26–27, 31, 68

Highway 76 project, 191–95

Hillerman, Tony, 179

Hispanic New Deal, 185–88

Hispanics/Hispanos/Nuevomexicanos: ambiguous position of, 98–99; and American colonization of New Mexico, 154–56; art of, 232; associated with past, 48–49; and colonization of New Mexico, 136; as colonizers and colonized, 98–99; diasporic, 181, 277n8; Hispanic New Deal and, 185–89; identity of, 136–39; as marked by heritage, 11–12; political rights of, 12; removed from portal market, 33–34, 69–71; represented in Española plaza project, 117–21; as servicemen and veterans, 161–62, 275n52

historicity: of Palace of the Governors, 44, 45–49, 256n12, 257n17; requirements for, 43–44

historic preservation. *See* politics of preservation

Historic Preservation Act, 194, 270n30

historic preservation movement, 256n12

history, social construction of, 22–23, 43–44

Hoerig, Karl: on portal market, 72, 74, 84, 263n21; on staged authenticity, 86

Horton, Sarah, 136, 181, 271n35

houses, Pueblo, 224–25

identity: assimilation and, 166–67; authenticity and, 232–33; co-constitution of cultural, 111; discussed in NRGNHA board meeting, 141; Española plaza project and, 113–14, 135; essentialist conceptions of, 219; and internalization of outsider expectations, 92–93; politics of authenticity and, 94–95; politics of recognition and, 9, 99–100, 138–39; of servicemen and veterans, 161–62; Spanish American, 136–39; tradition and, 89

imperialist nostalgia, 175

intentionality, 5, 24, 55

Jemez Pueblo, 79

Jesse Nusbaum Memorial Room. *See* Nusbaum Room

Jones, David, 194

La Jornada (Sabo and Rivera), 152–53

Joyce, Brian, 83

Kearny, Stephanie, 154

Kearny, Stephen, 154–55

Kirshenblatt-Gimblett, Barbara, 44

Kosek, Jake: on culture loss, 109; on Las Trampas migration, 181; on Los Alamos, 111; on mestizaje, 150; on New Mexico's forest politics, 277n7; shot at during fieldwork, 212, 280n25

La Jornada (Sabo and Rivera), 152–53

land dispossession, 109, 181

land grants, 109, 155, 159, 182–84, 206–8

language: death of, 225; in schools, 252n7

The Last Conquistador (Rivera), 147–49, 151

Las Trampas: antimodernism in, 184–85; author's fieldwork in, 211–14; boundary survey for, 208–11, 280n22; discursive construction of, 172–77; establishment of, 177–78; Hispanic New Deal and, 185–89; land grant, 182–84; as living history museum, 278n15; as living national monument, 200–203; modernization of, 189–91; and national heritage area model, 205–8; as National Historic Landmark, 192–95; overview of preservation in, 168–72; in regional community, 180–81; representation of, 214–16; representation of villagers in, 204–5; restoration of San José de Gracia and, 197–200; as timeless utopia, 178–80; villager reactions to preservation of, 195–97; widening of Highway 76 as threat to, 191–92

Las Trampas Foundation, 194, 195, 197–98

Las Trampas Lumber Company, 182–83

Lesotho (Africa), 174

Levine, Frances: on New Mexico History Museum, 57; on Palace of the Governors, 58, 254n6, 256n15; on portal market, 75–76

Linnekin, Jocelyn, 85–86, 88
Lippard, Lucy, 260n1
Livingston, Paul, 69–70, 261n11
Livingston, Sara, 69–70
Livingston v. Ewing (1978 and 1979), 69–71, 77, 82, 261n7
Loewen, James, 149
Lopez, Delfido, 192, 195
Los Alamos, 109–13, 267n14
Los Alamos National Laboratory (LANL), 109–10, 135, 159, 181, 274n50
Lotave, Carl, 29, 50
lowriding, 106, 107–8
Lucero, Richard: on Commemorative Spanish Colonization Center, 144–45; on Española culture, 267n16; on Española fiesta, 145; on Española plaza logo, 268n19; Española plaza project started by, 113; on history, 151; on hopes for Española plaza project, 114–16; on mercantile buildings, 133; on Misión-Convento, 124, 130; on NRGHNA and Española plaza project, 164; Pete Domenici and, 36; proposing reconstruction of church of San Miguel, 123; on regionalization, 269n27; Ross Chavez and, 270n28

MacCannell, Dean, 64–65, 66
Maestas, Joseph, 163
Main Street program, 133–34
Malinowski, Bronislaw, 215, 263n17
Markell, Patchen: on adoption of outmoded anthropological concepts, 280n1; on identity and recognition, 99; on politics of recognition, 282n10; on pursuit of sovereignty, 163
Martinez, Cameron, 79
Martínez, David, Jr., 182
Martinez, Eliu, 272n40
Martinez, Sarah, 73
Masco, Joseph, 159
McHugh, John, 194

Meem, John Gaw, 210–11, 276n6
mercantile buildings, demolition of, 133
metatourism, 51–55, 259n26
Mexican heritage, recognition or non-recognition of, 32, 37, 100, 159, 233, 240–41
migration, seasonal, 173, 180–81, 185–86, 189
military service, 161–62, 275n52
Misión-Convento: art in, 127–30; commemorative stamp and, 156–57; conception and construction of, 121–25; culture in, 269n26; as museum, 125–27; and objectification of heritage, 130–31, 223; religious significance of, 269n24; secularism and subversion in, 126–31
Mitchell, Timothy, 89–90, 262n13
modernity, construction of, 22–23
Montaño, Chuck, 110
Montoya, Harry, 107, 108
Morley, Sylvanus, 31
Mullin, Molly, 251n3, 265n2
multicultural domination, 11–13, 94
multiculturalism: colonialism and, 3–6, 13, 60–61, 94; in Española plaza project, 117–21, 145; hegemonic, 5, 25, 237; identity and, 100; Molly Mullin on shift toward, 251n3; prospects for new, 236–38
multicultural justice, 11–13, 230–36
multinationalism, 159–64
Museum of Indian Arts and Culture, 258n25
Museum of New Mexico: establishment of, 27; Evolution of the Palace exhibit in, 37–42; exhibits in, 36–37; historicity of, 45–49; Jesse Nusbaum Memorial Room in, 45–49; metatourism and, 51–55; as monument to Spanish past, 32–35; New Mexico History Museum and, 56–57; and objectification of heritage, 223; Palace of the Governors

as, 42–45; and progress of civilization, 254n7; renovation of, 27–30; Santa Fe–style architecture and, 30–32. *See also* Palace of the Governors; portal market

museum(s), in Santa Fe, 36, 255n9. *See also* Misión-Convento; Museum of New Mexico; New Mexico History Museum; Palace of the Governors

national heritage area(s): as commemorative designations, 2; defined, 8; Española plaza project and, 164–65; heritage development and, 6–7; Jayne Daly on, 223; Las Trampas as, 205–8; as new conservation model, 6–7, 205–6; popularity of, 14; as vehicle for cultural recognition, 8. *See also* Northern Rio Grande National Heritage Area

National Historic Preservation Act (1966), 194, 270n30

National Park Service: depoliticizing Spanish colonization, 235; and Highway 76 project, 192, 193–94; holding collaborative conservation workshop, 131–32; holding NRGNHA partners workshop, 188; introducing heritage area concept, 7; and Las Trampas as living national monument, 203; and Las Trampas as national heritage area, 205–6; Las Trampas boundary survey and, 208–10, 280n22; multicultural justice and, 234, 238; NRGNHA management plan and, 283n1; study by, 141–42; supporting NRGNHA, 10

Native American Artisans Program, 69. *See also* portal market

Native American Center, 121

Native Americans: and American colonization of New Mexico, 154–55; associated with past, 48–49; household traditions of, 83; and identity politics, 92–93; as living exhibits, 69–73; as

modern-day people, 232; political rights of, 12; at portal market, 68–69; represented in Española plaza project, 117–21; as servicemen and veterans, 161–62; Spanish mistreatment of, 142, 146. *See also* Pueblo Indians

Neckels, Jack, 278n14

Neumann, Mark, 260n3

New Deal. *See* Hispanic New Deal

New Mexican Hispanic Culture Preservation League, 137–38

New Mexico History Museum, 56–58, 233–34

"New-Old Santa Fe" exhibit, 31

normativity and politics of visibility, 60–61

Northern New Mexico Regional Art Center, 116–17

Northern Rio Grande National Heritage Area: as active organization, 239; "Alternative Concepts" report and, 144; anti-politics of culture and, 206–8; board meeting for, 17–18, 35–36, 55–56, 78–79, 140–41; brochure for, 8–9; development of, 7, 252n6; Española plaza project and, 164–67; establishment of, 1–3; grant program, 7, 239; land management and, 207–8; management plan for, 243, 283n1; multicultural justice and, 243–44; open house for, 239–43; partners workshop for, 188; purpose of, 7; Senate hearing on, 9–10; tour of, 131–32, 172

Northern Rio Grande National Heritage Area Act (2006), 3, 206, 245–50

nostalgia, imperialist, 175

Numbe Whageh (Naranjo-Morse), 152–53

Nusbaum, Jesse, 27–29, 30. *See also* Nusbaum Room

Nusbaum Room, 50–52, 56, 258n23, 258n24

objectification of heritage: authenticity and, 220–23; portal market and, 280n2; social and political contexts of, 223–27

O'Brien, Patrick, 208–9

Oñate, Juan de: colonization under, 102–3, 145–46; commemoration of, 145–50, 272n43, 272n44, 273n45; compared to George Washington, 163; demilitarization of, 145, 272n40

Oñate Monument and Visitors Center, 147–49, 150, 159

Orientalism, Edward Said's critique of, 173–74

Ortega, Ernest: author's relationship with, 35; on commemoration of colonization, 165–66; on heritage areas, 2, 79; on land management, 207; on losing cultural traits, 6; on NRGNHA, 56, 165

Ortiz-Junes, Elena, 275n53

Otero, Miguel, 26

out-migration, 173, 180–81, 189, 204

"overlapping citizenship," 162

Owings, Nathaniel: forming Las Trampas Foundation, 194; on Highway 76 project, 191; on Las Trampas, 178, 196, 201; on San José de Gracia, 193, 197, 198–200, 278n13

Paguin, Glenn, 72, 73

Palace of the Governors: and construction of history and modernity, 23; Evolution of the Palace exhibit in, 37–44; excavation of, 37–39, 48; exhibits in, 36–37, 58, 255n11; historicity of, 26, 45–49, 256n12, 257n17; as historic structure and history museum, 42–45; history of, 1, 21; Jesse Nusbaum Memorial Room in, 45–49; metatourism and, 51–55; as monument to Spanish past, 32–35; as museum, 21–27; New Mexico History Museum opened behind, 56–57; nor-

mativity and politics of visibility and, 60–61; and objectification of heritage, 223; and persistence of colonial power structure, 24–25; Prince Reception Room in, 256n13; renovation of, 27–30, 48, 255n10, 256n15, 257n20; Santa Fe–style architecture and, 30–32; as scientific institution, 33–34, 48–49; structure report on, 57–58; as symbol, 254n6. *See also* Museum of New Mexico; portal market

past, preoccupation with, 228 29, 282n8

Penitente rites, 211, 276n6

People's Department Store, 133

Percy, Walker, 65–66, 261n6, 264n24

period rooms, 37, 38, 51

Phillips, David, 71

Plan of 1912, 31

plaster, mud and cement, 198–99. *See also* adobe

Plaza de Española: as American project, 158–61; as commemoration of Spanish colonization, 144–45; logo for, 267n19; master plan for, *115*; Misión-Convento in, 121–25; names for, 271n39; NRGNHA and, 164–67; opposition to, 132–34; overview of, 113–17; and politics of visibility, 134–35; religion and, 125–27; secularism and subversion in, 127–31; triculturalism in, 117–21; use of, 114–17; zoning regulations for, 270n29

Poeh Center, 104

politics of authenticity: anti-politics of culture and, 177; culture loss and, 108–9; multicultural justice and, 231–33; NRGNHA and, 284n4; overview of, 12–13, 93–96; politics of visibility and, 233

politics of preservation: antimodernists and, 184–85; and discursive construction of Las Trampas, 172–77; establishment of Las Trampas and, 177–78; Hispanic New Deal and, 185–89; historicity of Palace of the Governors and, 256n12; Las Trampas and, 178–80, 192–97, 200–205; Las Trampas boundary survey and, 208–11; modernization and, 189–91; and national heritage area model, 205–8; overview of, 168–72; restoration of San José de Gracia and, 197–200; widening of Highway 76 and, 191–92

politics of recognition: and Americanness of New Mexico, 159–64; and commemoration of colonization, 149; costs of, 243–44; emphasis on accuracy in, 9; importance of, 13–14; and link between public image and psychological well-being, 138–39; New Mexico's colonial history and, 98; NRGNHA and, 8–9, 243–44; Patchen Markell on, 282n10; politics of authenticity and, 94; problems with liberal theories of, 98–99; suspicion toward, 244; tourism and, 264n24; and use of Spanish in schools, 252n7. *See also* recognition

politics of representation: author's writing and, 16–17, 211–12, 214–16, 226–27; Las Trampas and, 171, 204–5, 216; Palace of the Governors and, 254n6

politics of visibility: anthropology and, 16, 227; and Española plaza project, 134–35; multicultural justice and, 230, 233–34; Museum of New Mexico and, 24–25; and New Mexico's double colonial history, 153–56; and normativity, 60–61; overview of, 11–12; politics of authenticity and, 233

Po'pay, 150, 163, 275n53

portal market: authenticity in tourism and, 80; as commercial marketplace, 76–78; framing authenticity of,

81–84; function of, 73–76; history and operation of, 68–69; as living exhibit, 69–74; objectification of heritage and, 280n2; overview of, 62–64; regulations for, 74, 84–85; and search for really real, 87–90; self-regulation and private authenticity in, 90–93; and semiotics of tourism, 64–68; staged authenticity and, 86–87

postcolonialism, 5, 252n5

Povinelli, Elizabeth, 94, 95

preservation. *See* politics of preservation

Prince, Bradford, 256n13, 273n47

Prince Reception Room, 256n13

Pueblo Indians: colonialism's effects on, 142; Los Alamos National Laboratory's impact on, 274n50; as marked by heritage, 11–12; Museum of New Mexico and, 33–34; and objectification of heritage, 224–26; representation of, 79; Rina Swentzell's hopes for, 227–28; in San Gabriel, 102–4; Spanish colonial focus on, 251n1

Pueblo Revolt, 152

Puye Room, 29–30, 33, 50, 56

quadricentennial celebrations. *See* commemoration of colonization

race: Española plaza project and, 135; in Española valley, 97–98, 100, 101–13; essentialist conceptions of, 219

racial mixing, 150, 230–32

really real: deconstruction of authenticity and search for, 87–90; and staged authenticity, 79–81

recognition: cultural, 8–10, 67, 69–72; cultural geography of Española and, 101–13; Ernest Ortega on need for, 165–66; *Livingston v. Ewing* and, 69–72; Misión-Convento testing limits of, 127; Nancy Fraser on, 282n9; national heritage areas and, 8–9; politics of authenticity and, 94; problems of,

stamp, commemorative, 156–59, 273n49
stone facade of Palace of the Governors, 45–46
Strale, Sue Ellen, 106
stucco on Palace of the Governors, 45–47
Swentzell, Rina: on author's discussion of power, 226–27; on hopes for Pueblos, 227–28; on Indian images in Taos, 264n23; Jane Brown Gillette on, 281n4; on Misión-Convento, 125; and objectification of heritage, 224–27; on self-consciousness, 281n6; on tourist expectations, 262n15

Taylor, Charles, 138
Tewa Pueblos, 102–4, 224–25
Tierra Wools, 241–43
tourism: anthropology and, 218–19; authenticity and, 79–81, 84; heritage production and, 221, 222–23; Jayne Daly on, 223; Museum of New Mexico and promotion of, 31; and opposition to Española plaza, 132; Palace of the Governors and, 21; portal market and, 72–73, 75–76; preservation through, 190–91; pros and cons of heritage, 7; recognition in, 264n24; in Santa Fe, 254n4; semiotics of, 64–68; staged authenticity and, 86. *See also* metatourism
tourist gaze, 90–92
"Tourist Icons" exhibit, 258n25
tradition(al): in Aboriginal land claims, 94; art, 68, 83–84, 184, 284n4; construction of Misión-Convento, 125; debates in Española valley about, 107–9; deconstruction of, 86, 88–89, 92, 96; in development discourse, 174; heritage and, 6; Hispanic, 30, 117, 143, 167; Las Trampas as, 175, 178–79, 197, 199–200, 203–4; Los Alamos and, 111–12; modernity and, 12; money and, 78; Native American, 82, 117, 226, 266n10, 280n2; portal market

and, 70–71, 74, 76, 80–81, 83, 87–88; strategic essentialism and, 177, 183, 235
Treaty of Guadalupe Hidalgo, 154, 155, 159, 182
"Treaty of Santa Fe," 194–95
triculturalism, xvi, 11, 29, 117–21, 255n8, 267n19
Trujillo, Michael: on culture loss, 107, 108; on drug use, 107; on Española valley, 101, 102; on reconceptualization of Oñate, 272n40

Udall, Stewart, 193, 194
United States: and colonization of New Mexico, 3, 153–56; and commemoration of colonization, 165–66; Embudo watershed problems and, 190; New Mexico as part of, 159–64; as settler colony, 4–5; sovereignty of, 118, 163–64; Spanish colonialism's impact on, 143–44. *See also* federal government
Usner, Don, 111

Valdez, Connie, 162–63
de Vargas, Diego, 29, 32, 271n35
veterans, 161–62, 275n52
Veterans' Memorial Wall, 116, 161
Vigil, Loretta, 56
Villa, Clare, 128, 129–30, 269n25, 273n49
Villa, José, 10, 18, 56, 140–41
visibility, politics of. *See* politics of visibility

Weber, Michael, 37, 46
Whitten, Larry, 251n4
Wilson, Chris: on acknowledging cultural interaction, 231; on commemorative stamp, 157; on denial in New Mexican public history, 230; on Lotave murals, 29; on Misión-Convento, 124; on Oñate monument, 148; on Palace of the Governors renovation, 31, 32
women and restoration of San José de Gracia, 278n14

CPSIA information can be obtained at www.ICGtesting.com
Printed in the USA
LVOW11s1156020116

468759LV00002B/103/P

9 780803 249790